◆ HOW TO ◆

Rock Climb!

Second Edition

John Long

CHOCKSTONE PRESS
Evergreen, Colorado

COVER PHOTOS:

(front): Grant Murray climbing on the A.C.R.A. Wall at the Restaurant, E. Transvaal, South Africa; photo by Bill Hatcher

(back): John Long sitting on Glacier Point; photo by Bob Gaines

ISBN 0-934641-64-1

PUBLISHED AND DISTRIBUTED BY
Chockstone Press, Inc.
Post Office Box 3505
Evergreen, Colorado 80439

Acknowledgements

No one climber is the living authority on all the technical information and equipment covered in *Rock Climb!* Consequently, the manuscript passed through many expert hands to insure the facts were both up to date and as accurate as possible. In particular, I'd like to thank Bob Gaines, of Vertical Adventures, Charles Cole, of the Five Ten Company, and Russ Walling, of Fish Products, whose suggestions were invaluable. Thanks also to Mountain Miser, Neptune Mountaineering, The Boulder Mountaineer, Colorado Outdoor Sports, and Chouinard Equipment, who provided equipment for testing and photographing. The clean illustrations and line drawings were handled by Marj Leggitt and Annie Douden. Sharon Sadleir spent many chilly days posing for photos, and always looked hale doing so. After he excerpted text for his magazine, Climbing Magazine editor Michael Kennedy further obliged us by writing the foreword, probably the best endorsement we could ever get. Paul Edwards combed over the text, quickly pointing out where things weren't as clear as they should be.

To the many climbers who made suggestions for the second edition, I thank you. In particular, climber/engineer/guide Craig Luebben scoured the entire manual for some months, and his contributions were significant in revising and updating the text.

Foreword

When I started climbing twenty-five years ago, my friends and I learned our craft by trial and error, mostly from other climbers barely more experienced than we were. We made lots of mistakes, but were afraid enough (and conservative enough) to ensure our survival through these critical beginning years. And so we muddled along, gradually working up through the grades as our skills evolved, and having many wonderful epics (at least in retrospect) along the way.

The books we turned to were many: *Annapurna, The White Spider, Nanga Parbat Pilgrimage,* and the other great mountaineering classics inspired, but didn't say much about how our heroes learned the tricks of the trade. And one of the few instructional texts then available, *Mountaineering, Freedom of the Hills,* while offering a great overview of classic mountaincraft, was weak in its treatment of the arena which most inflamed our young hearts: technical rock climbing.

Then along came *Basic Rockcraft* and *Advanced Rockcraft.* Written by Royal Robbins, one of the top practioners of the day, these two slim volumes of wit and wisdom served to both inspire and instruct a whole generation of American rock climbers.

Now, over twenty years later, much has changed in the sport. New gear, a greater diversity in style, and a rapidly-expanding population of technical rock climbers has dated much of the information in the *Rockcraft* series. Yet there has been precious little to take its place, at least until now.

John Long is one of that generation of climbers inspired by Robbins' books, and many of today's climbers will find similar inspiration here. Long's broad experience as a pioneering free climber is evident on every page of *How to Rock Climb!* as, in clear, concise, and entertaining prose, he brings to life the vitality and intricacy of modern technical rock climbing in all its diverse forms.

And while this book may prevent a few epics of the sort I had while learning the ropes, it will help instill a sense of personal responsibility in the reader as well. After all, that's still a big part of what climbing is all about.

MICHAEL KENNEDY
Climbing Magazine

WARNING: CLIMBING IS A SPORT WHERE YOU MAY BE SERIOUSLY INJURED OR DIE

READ THIS BEFORE YOU USE THIS BOOK.

This is an instruction book to rock climbing, a sport which is inherently dangerous. You should not depend solely on information gleaned from this book for your personal safety. Your climbing safety depends on your own judgment based on competent instruction, experience, and a realistic assessment of your climbing ability.

There is no substitute for personal instruction in rock climbing and climbing instruction is widely available. You should engage an instructor or guide to learn climbing safety techniques. If you misinterpret a concept expressed in this book, you may be killed or seriously injured as a result of the misunderstanding. Therefore, the information provided in this book should be used only to supplement competent personal instruction from a climbing instructor or guide. Even after you are proficient in climbing safely, occasional use of a climbing guide is a safe way to raise your climbing standard and learn advanced techniques.

There are no warranties, either expressed or implied, that this instruction book contains accurate and reliable information. There are no warranties as to fitness for a particular purpose or that this book is merchantable. Your use of this book indicates your assumption of the risk of death or serious injury as a result of climbing's risks and is an acknowledgement of your own sole responsibility for your climbing safety.

Bob Gaines photo

C O N T E N T S

HOW
TO
ROCK
CLIMB!

JOHN LONG

CHAPTER 1

The Climbing Game

Old-timers might remember that Spencer Tracy movie where the plane crashes on a nether plateau and Spencer flakes out the rope and conducts a glorious rescue. I was about thirteen when I saw that movie and I really wanted to learn all those rope shenanigans, so I jogged to the library and checked out a book on climbing. That manual was a study for all its knots and puzzling rope constructs, august doggerel and narratives of horror and heroics on the cliffside. And I understood none of it. What I needed was a nuts and bolts, how-to book that assumed I knew nothing, and which broke it all down in plain English.

Since that first outing to the library, rock climbing has boomed. Along with the countless climbing schools, several outstanding instruction books have appeared; yet the changes in climbing have outpaced even the best of these. In the four short years since writing How to Rock Climb!, modern day sport climbing has not only replaced the quaint notions of Spencer Tracy taking on the mountain, it's been embraced as de rigueur by virtually the entire climbing world. Consequently, this second edition was undertaken to reflect the accelerated evolution of technology, techniques and trends in this, the "sport of kings."

As much as things have changed in the last four years, we'd have to hark back some two decades to perceive the extent to which the climbing game has truly evolved. For instance, when I first went to Yosemite as a teenager in 1971, my ultimate goal, like so many others', was to climb El Capitan. Back then, Yosemite was the sanctum sanctorum of the world rock climbing scene, from which came many modern techniques and by which every climbing area was measured. Many of us were still climbing in lug-soled shoes, and pitons were the preferred means of protection. Perhaps thirty (maybe as few as twenty) climbers in the entire country consistently climbed at an extreme level (5.10). This subject will be taken up in detail in the forthcoming Nutshell History of Climbing in this chapter. Suffice it now to say that a climber can hardly call him or herself an expert these days without a host of 5.12 routes under their harness. Of course, this is an easier prospect now than in years past, thanks to the "sports climbing" revolution, which places chief emphasis on explosive, athletic movement in comparatively

(page opposite)

John Juraschek liebacks up the razorcut dihedral on "Forest Lawn" (5.9), at Cochise's Stronghold, Arizona.

Bill Hatcher photo

safe, manageable conditions. This new preoccupation with safety, all the splashy magazines and coffee table books, documentaries and network sports specials on climbing, plus the slew of indoor climbing gyms popping up over the country may help you appreciate why active climbers in the United States alone number in the hundreds of thousands, if not in the millions.

Understand, however, that the cautious, athletic milieu of sport climbing has overshadowed, rather than replaced traditional "adventure" climbing. Many climbers are still out there climbing traditional, classic routes – extreme cracks, desert towers, big walls, alpine routes, frozen waterfalls and mixed rock and ice lines. As long as the spirit of adventure stirs in a few climbers, there will still be those pitting their own basic stuff against the wildest estate nature can offer. Here are the few not to be denied the orbit of fear and risk that has vitalized the climbing game since the first mountaineer scraped his way onto the first summit. For the vast majority of climbers, however, the principal desire is to have fun and to challenge themselves without compromising safety, for no sport is less forgiving if you do. More than anything, safety and fun are the focus of this book.

How to Rock Climb! is based on the Yosemite system – methods born out of the revolutionary climbs of the fifties and sixties in Yosemite Valley – supplemented with modern-day sport climbing techniques presently used the world over. The Yosemite "system" is in practice much more of a philosophy, stressing safety and simplicity. As with any complicated enterprise, the more fundamental you keep things, the more manageable they are.

One of the drawbacks of climbing's amazing popularity is the dumpsters of misinformation now out there. Much of it concerns "essential" gear and involved ways of doing very basic procedures. It's one thing to invent an easier and safer (therefore better) way to belay, say, as most of the newer devices have achieved. It's quite another thing to use a rappel device featuring more springs and widgets than a lunar module. Understand that many of the most technical big walls in the world were first ascended using pitons almost exclusively, with climbers belaying round the hip, and you'll know just how superfluous much of the new "essential" gear really is. There is specialized gear for specific situations, granted; but by trying to keep it simple, you'll invariably have more attention to pay to the actual climbing, which is the point after all. Just the same, there is much involved, and we have tried to frame the entire process with enough depth that the beginner – and even the advanced climber – can take something from the reading and safely discover how it applies to their own climbing.

Studying this book, or one like it, is the standard first step for all beginners. Next is to take a comprehensive climbing class, a thing no book can, or should, attempt to replace. Virtually everyone starts off this way, or is nursed or hauled

Against an alpine backdrop, Dana Houser clasps the arête on "Spank the Monkey" (5.12a), Smith Rock, Oregon. Many modern testpieces follow steep, outside corners, requiring hearty combinations of face and liebacking techniques.

Greg Epperson photo

up a host of climbs by a knowledgeable friend, which amounts to the same thing. The rare individual who learns the ropes completely on his own will later realize his learning curve was virtually a flat line for the first few months. It's easier, and far safer, to get the basics worked out from day one.

Modern rock climbing should never require do-or-die tactics. Such means are possible if a person chooses, but in no way do they represent what hundreds of thousands of climbers live to do. Statistically, rock climbing is the safest of all the so-called thrill sports because it employs over a century's worth of refined technique and solid technology to the normal end of having fun.

The basic system of technical rock climbing – how a rope and specialized techniques and equipment safeguard a climber – is so simple that anyone can manage the fundamentals in a few weekends. There is no mystery, and one need not be even a decent climber to have a working knowledge of rope management. The art of climbing rock is another affair, but even this tends to be more of a learned skill, requiring less natural ability than other sports. I've been astonished more than once by climbers who couldn't begin to dribble a basketball but were watch-and-weep wizards on the rock. Lastly, climbing is not a reaction sport (excepting the most extreme, gymnastic routes), so there is no reason a game climber cannot carry on at a top level until old age, as many do.

We can discuss equipment in definitive terms. Equipment is tangible, and its function, at least in theory, is pretty clear-cut, though involved. The most important element in safe climbing is not equipment, however, but familiarity with the vertical environment combined with good judgement. Any way you shake it, climbing prowess is your principal protection, as it precludes the necessity of relying on the gear to save you. The leader who relies on the equipment to safeguard his mistakes is far more likely to make them; and even when the backup system is perfectly arranged, one can still get hurt, even on an extremely "safe" sport climb. In parachuting, even a jump master carries a reserve chute. As a climber, your main chute is your climbing ability; your backup is the equipment. This said, the number of accidents due to defective gear is remarkably low. It's the climber who is safe or dicey, not the gear.

While equipment and its function within the whole system of climbing is fairly straightforward, the art of climbing rock is not. A lot of intangibles – judgement, instinct, and physical awareness to list a few – factor heavily in the process, making explanations pretty slippery affairs. The best we can hope for is to explain clearly and in some detail how things are done in a generic sense, leaving you to learn the how of it all through specific application. We've gone into exhaustive detail concerning climbing techniques, and in this respect, the book is "front loaded," meaning, a complete novice might find the explanations confusing on the first pass, but the more climbing he or she does, the more sense the book will make.

With any how-to book of this nature, there will always be the question of what is too much and what is too little. It is impossible to satisfy everyone on all counts, particularly since one could write ten volumes on rigging alone, and still have ten volumes of material to discuss. My emphasis throughout has been to stick with the most fundamental and practical concerns, and to serve up those things I would have liked to have been fluent in when I was just starting out. Also, in trying to keep things at a manageable length, I hope to convey the fact that only so much can be learned from any book, that time spent on the rock is the best teacher of all, and that if the fine points need a little more dialing in, a professional guide is the surest and quickest means to a safe and comprehensive understanding. It has been said that writing about wine is like dancing about architecture. If you really want to know about wine, you've got to pull the cork and drink up; and if you want to really know about climbing, you'll eventually have to tie in and cast off.

That climbing transcends mere sport is a conviction held by most anyone with a pair of rock boots, and everyone who has climbed a monolith like Yosemite's El Capitan. The airy exposed routes, the spectacle of ascent, the physical and mental demands – they all give a rush to your blood which continues running rich, regardless of experience. In a flash, mundane life is forgotten: your world is focused down to a scant toehold or saving "jug handle." Failure is a bitter pill, but as Montague noted, nowhere on earth is the taste of success so sweet as on the summit of some sheer granite spire that nearly drove you down in despair from the Herculean labor to achieve it. Basically, it is no more natural for man to dangle on the cliffside than it is for him to loft around the cosmos in the space shuttle. But when both astronauts and climbers gape at their world so very far underfoot, they understand how men have come to dream Gardens of Eden and Ages of Gold. And the dream never fades, the blood never cools, even in the face of chilling bivouacs and knuckle-shredding cracks. Climbing is not easy sport, and it has a lion's share of toil. But to thousands, even millions worldwide, the rewards are worth the struggle.

A NUTSHELL HISTORY OF CLIMBING

Early man was a climber. He climbed to escape predators and enemies, and to forage for food. Eons later, in the mid-seventeen hundreds, man began climbing again, out of desire, not necessity. Spread throughout the European Alps, villages big and small were nestled between spectacular mountains, and for a host of reasons, certain men aspired to climb the grandest peaks on the continent. The summit was the ultimate goal of these first mountaineers, and glaciers and snow slopes provided the most natural passage to the top. Following the first recorded alpine ascent, that of Mt. Aiguille, the rush was on and major peaks were climbed in succession. After the easier routes had been climbed, subsequent mountaineers found that some rock climbing skills were necessary to open up new mountains, and they discovered the lower cliffs and crags provided a perfect training ground to this end. To give some modicum of safety to the falling climber, ropes and rudimentary belaying techniques were introduced around the turn of the twentieth century. Climbing was effectively confined to the European continent, and (to a lesser degree) England. It was in Austria – circa 1910 – that rappelling was invented, along with heavy steel carabiners (snap links) and pitons, the latter to provide the aid and protection required on the modern, more difficult climbs. With the new equipment and techniques and the confidence they spawned, Austrian and German climbers established climbs far more difficult than previously thought possible.

Though isolated rock summits were occasionally bagged, the endeavor was considered of "lesser" worth than achieving the big summits of the Alps. In retrospect, some of the "training climbs" on these "practice" cliffs were remarkably difficult considering the gear. The leaders had little more than hemp ropes (which routinely broke), hemp-soled shoes, and boldness to see them through. Even today, in parts of Eastern Europe, particularly around Dresden, "summitless" crags are eschewed in favor of the spires which abound there; likewise, the method and style of ascent remained almost unchanged for fifty years.

Meanwhile, in pre-World War I England, rock climbing on the many backyard outcrops was being explored, albeit less aggressively than in Germany. The English discouraged the use of pitons, however, partly for ethical reasons, partly owing to the fragile nature of the "gritstone." Anyway, in the absence of big mountains, the English developed crag climbing as a sport in its own right. In the Americas, the sport's development followed the European lead, though with something of a time delay, with roped climbing only arriving in the late 1920s.

The 1930s heralded the golden age of alpine climbing, though the emphasis was still on climbing the major ridges and faces of the higher peaks. During this pre-war period, rock climbing standards rose steadily throughout the world. Although most of the glory was still in achieving mountainous summits – Alpine, American, and Asian peaks were conquered in succession – in many areas it was rock climbing standards that saw the most dramatic development.

Flat-footed in the Flatirons (outside Boulder, Colorado), turn-of-the-century "alpinists" grapple up the hemp rope.

World War II saw little climbing activity, but the war prompted technological developments which greatly impacted post-war climbing. Before, pitons and carabiners were expensive and rare; ropes were still fashioned from natural fibers, bulky and prone to snap during long falls. "The leader must not fall" was the incontrovertible dictum that all climbers observed if they wanted anything but a short career. World War II changed all this with the plentiful supply of surplus army pitons, lightweight aluminum carabiners, and most importantly, strong and light nylon ropes.

For the next twenty years, standards rose steadily in both England and the United States. English climbers maintained their anti-piton stance and developed anchoring techniques which used runners over natural rock spikes, plus the wedging of pebbles – and eventually machine nuts slung with slings – as chockstones in cracks. Not surprisingly, the English also pushed standards of boldness. They had little choice, for their protection was often dicey, at best.

A thousand feet up and ten feet out on a ring-angle peg, the late, great Willi Unsoeld (first American ascent of Mt. Everest) teeters up the "knobby wall" during the first ascent of El Capitan's East Buttress in 1953. This climb set the standard for the long, classic free climbs which remain the international draw of Yosemite Valley, California.

Allen Steck photo

European standards were consolidated but, with their continued emphasis on attaining Alpine summits, actual rock climbing standards advanced little outside some exploring of large boulders at Fountainbleu, outside Paris. European manufacturers did, however, develop new nylon ropes that were stronger and much easier to handle.

By the early 1960s, specialized rock climbing shoes appeared that were in appearance not totally different from the all-around shoes available today: the Varappe, essentially a high-top tennis shoe upper with a smooth rubber sole. These, in England and France, and the improved design of pitons in America, spurred standards in those respective areas. In the Americas and in England, rock climbing was pretty firmly established as a specialized sport, and routes that led, say, merely to a cliff feature or to rappel points in the middle of blank cliffs were commonly done and respected. Sparingly in America, but increasingly in England, climbers formulated strong aesthetic distinctions between using pitons and artificial aids to pull up on and using such anchors solely to protect the climbing of the cliff with hands and feet. This latter practice became known as free climbing. Styles and techniques remained largely provincial until the mid '60s, however; few climbers travelled widely to sample various climbing areas.

This changed dramatically by 1970, due in large part to the innovative development of rock climbing techniques born in California's Yosemite Valley (during the late '50s and through the '60s) which allowed the ascent of the spectacular cliffs there. To learn the piton aid techniques that enabled these ascents – and in splendid weather at that – climbers from around the world traveled to Yosemite. While they learned the American techniques, they also left as an heritage their own different approaches. By the early 1970s, American and English climbers completely dominated the

Spot marks the expert clawing up an indoor artificial wall during the Grand Prix d' Escalade '88 climbing competition in Europe, where leading climbers are media stars, amply sponsored by equipment manufacturers. American sponsorship consists of free T-shirts and "sponsored" slide shows for hamburger wages.

Beth Wald photo

development of the sport, and methods and equipment for climbing rock were becoming homogenized. Americans pitched the clunkier boots they had generally favored and adopted sensitive French and English smooth-soled shoes; in addition, the destructive and strenuous American pitoning techniques used in scaling the big cliffs were found to be less effective for free climbing than the gentler English nutting techniques. Moreover, innovative Americans started redesigning and commercially producing light and effective protection devices: first, aluminum nuts, then spring-loaded camming units. Simultaneously, rope manufacturers continued fine-tuning and improving the proper balance between strength, energy-absorbing stretch, and durability, which led to a much more relaxed attitude toward falling.

By 1980, many climbers were traveling the world over to explore different areas, and climbers from many countries were involved in pushing standards. While the best climbers now trained exclusively for climbing, and the techniques and equipment were common to all, a new, pure gymnastic approach was applied to the style of ascent, particularly by the French. Inspired by the technical difficulty of the free routes in Yosemite Valley, they returned to France to begin a quest for pure difficulty, linking long stretches of bouldering moves with convenient protection afforded by bolts. With easy protection they could concentrate on difficult, gymnastic movement in relative safety, and thus "sport climbing" was born. Today's best sport climbers often "climb" the hardest routes by first descending the cliff to prearrange their protection, inspect the route for available holds, and to clean away any loose holds and offensive effluvium. The subsequent ascent may take days, weeks, or even months of repeated falls, all to the goal of climbing the route – now an extremely complicated gymnastic routine – straight through without falls. This approach has further led to the development of a formal competitive circuit, where climbers compete against the clock and each other on man-made and often indoor artificial climbing walls.

European-style sport climbing began in the United States about a decade ago; it was accepted grudgingly at first, but is now the preferred form of climbing for many because of its safe and convenient nature. While the sport climbing movement did not change the way that all climbers climbed, it resulted in further fundamental shifts from the roots of rock climbing as simply one of a number of skills necessary to gain the top of alpine peaks.

Sport climbing itself has began to come full circle, as a few top sport climbers have applied their extreme free climbing skills to big rock walls and high altitude alpine walls around the world. As predicted by Yvon Chouinard in the 60s, the techniques and skills that were developed in Yosemite were exported to the most dramatic mountain ranges in the world. Huge alpine walls in Patagonia, Alaska, the Himalayas and other wild places were ascended using "the Yosemite system," further pushing the envelope of climbing and the influence of Yosemite.

To the average climber, however, climbing remains an exciting means to explore the natural world and enjoy the choreography of ascent – outside any arena.

RATING THE DIFFICULTY

Because the vast majority of your climbing will follow established routes already rated for difficulty and recorded in a guidebook, it is the following class system you will, with time, need to understand. It is your only yardstick as to how difficult a given climb is, and for this reason, it is both simple and comprehensive. The American rating system that follows is one of many in use around the world, as the chart on the next page explains.

Class

1. Walking.

2. Hiking. Mostly on established trails, or perhaps slogging along a stream bed.

3. Scrambling. Angle is steep enough where hands are used for balance. A handline is rarely used, even for inexperienced climbers.

4. Climbing risky enough that a fall could be fatal. Pulling with your arms required. A rope, some equipment, and protection techniques are used by most mountaineers.

5. Technical rock climbing, commonly called "free climbing." A rope, specialized equipment and techniques are always used to protect against a fall. Fifth class climbing is the subject of How to Rock Climb!

6. Rock so sheer or holdless that ascent by using hands and feet is impossible. The equipment is used directly to aid the ascent, hence the common usage names for class 6 climbing: artificial, direct aid, or simply, aid climbing. Recall the hoary image of the intrepid climber hammering his way up the rock, his weight suspended on a succession of creaky pins. Things have changed, but the old notion still best illustrates what aid climbing is all about.

It is commonly agreed that technical rock climbing starts at fifth class, and the bulk of this book will deal with fifth class climbing. Fifth class climbing varies from low-angle slabs, where only the beginner will relish a rope, to 125-degree face climbs so extreme that world-class climbers might fall fifty times before they work out the entire sequence, if indeed they ever do. In the early 1950s, fifth class climbing was designated as "easy," "moderate," and "advanced." As climbers got better and the climbs harder, a decimal system was adopted to more accurately rate the levels of difficulty within the class.

Devised in the early 1930s by the Rock Climbing Section of the Sierra Club, this system is principally used as an index of difficulty. The original scale, 5.0 through 5.9, was intended at the time of its adoption to cover the whole range of humanly possible rock climbs, anything above 5.9 being regarded as impossible. Standards are made to fall, of course, and shortly that one did.

WORLD RATING SYSTEMS

West German (UIAA)	American (Decimal)	British	Australian	East German (GDR)	French
	5.5	4a — vs			
	5.6	vs			
5+	5.7	4b		VIIa	5a
6-	5.8	4c — hvs	16	VIIb	5b
6	5.9	5a	17		5c
6+	5.10a	E1	18	VIIc	6a
7-	5.10b	5b	19	VIIIa	
7	5.10c	E2	20	VIIIb	6b
	5.10d	5c	21	VIIIc	
7+	5.11a		22	IXa	6c
	5.11b	E3	23	IXb	
8-	5.11c	6a	24		7a
8	5.11d	E4	25	IXc	
8+	5.12a	6b E5	26	Xa	7b
	5.12b		27	Xb	
9-	5.12c				7c
9	5.12d	E6	28	Xc	
9+	5.13a	6c	29		8a
10-	5.13b	E7	30		
10	5.13c	7a			8b
	5.13d		31		
10+	5.14a	E8	32		8c
11-	5.14b	7b			
11	5.14c	E9	33		
	5.14d	7c			9a

Though ratings vary from one area to the next, the fifth class decimal system is pretty uniform throughout the U.S.: a 5.8 in Yosemite would most likely be rated 5.8 at Tahquitz Rock as well. Climbers rely on the rating system being consistent, lest they are misled by guidebooks and end up on climbs either too hard or too easy for their fancy. Once a climber travels to a foreign area, however, he must become fluent in another rating system, for every country has an individual method of rating the difficulty of rock climbs. The attending graph plots comparative difficulties relative to various national rating systems. It is reasonably accurate, but not unequivocal. All rating systems are open-ended, but the differences in difficulty between various number or letter ratings vary from country to country. There are other differences also: the British system factors a seriousness appraisal into the rating which preceeds the standard technical rating. (E5 6a) Note that the seriousness ratings overlap each other considerably in relation to the difficulty rating, as represented in the chart by the dashed lines.

The decimal system ceased to be purely "decimal" when aggressive pioneer climbers sought to rate climbs harder than established 5.9s. Like other rating systems used throughout the world, the decimal system has evolved into an open-ended system that now includes climbs from 5.0, the easiest, to 5.14+, to date, the most difficult leads achieved. Climbs of 5.10 through 5.14 are in the realm of the advanced or expert climber; to better shade the nuances of these advanced levels, the letters a, b, c, and d were tacked onto the rating. For example, 5.12d represents the extreme end of the 5.12 standard, whereas a 5.12a or 5.12b is "easier," low-end 5.12.

Modern routes tend to be rated somewhat softer than older routes, meaning you can almost count on an old 5.10 to be more exacting than a new one. Convenient bolt protection, the earmark of the sports climb, at once removes the psychological factor while reducing the physical strain of hanging by fingertips and frantically trying to place gear in the rock. Because most sports climbs are first and foremost physical challenges, they likely will seem "easier" than older climbs of the same grade that feature psychological trials as well.

A related point worth mentioning is that in years past, you would only call yourself a 5.10 leader if you could consistently lead any 5.10 route, including thin faces, roofs, finger cracks, off-widths, et al. Today, many climbers who have hangdogged up a 5.12 sport climb tend to consider themselves 5.12 climbers. Put them on a 5.9 adventure climb, where the runouts are stiff and the required techniques manifold, and they might back off at the first difficulties. The point is: since the rating system was first devised, climbers have been preoccupied with bandying about high numbers in the most offhand manner. Don't be swayed by such talk. And wait until you get out on the rock to form your opinions about potential climbing partners. Many sport climbers are remarkably inexperienced, and can perform only under very circumscribed conditions. The danger here is that many of them don't realize this themselves, and they subsequently can make very dicey partners outside a climbing gym or practice area. The difference between top-roping a difficult climb in an indoor climbing gym and leading a complex route in the mountains is significant indeed.

Sixth class, direct aid climbing is divided into five rating classes: A1 through A5, depending on the difficulty of placing protection anchors and their precariousness when placed. Put figuratively, this means you can hang your van from an

Featuring...

Arête: an outside edge or corner of rock, perhaps as large as a mountain ridge.

Buttress: much broader than an arête, a buttress is definitely mountain-size.

Chickenhead: a bulbous knob of rock.

Chimney: a crack of sufficient size to accept an entire body.

Dihedral: an inside corner, formed by two planes of rock.

Headwall: a much steeper section of a cliff, residing towards the top.

Horn: a flake-like projection of rock, generally of small size.

Line: the path of the route, usually the line of least resistance between other major features of the rock.

Rib: a narrow buttress, not so sharp as an arête.

Roof or Ceiling: a section of rock that extends out above your head like a roof or ceiling.

Slab: a section of rock of gentle angle, sometimes a relative reference when it's a part of a vertical wall.

Al placement, but falling on a tenuous A5 thread of bashies will surely result in a harrowing hundred-foot zipper.

Grade

The decimal system tells us how difficult a climb is. The attending grade rating tells us how much time an experienced climber will take to complete a given route:

I. One to three hours
II. Three to four hours
III. Four to six hours – a strong half day
IV. Full day – emphasis on full
V. One to two days – bivouac is usually unavoidable
VI. Two or more days on the wall

The decimal rating is a relatively objective appraisal of difficulties, usually arrived at through consensus. The grade rating is posited as objective, but it uses the theoretical "experienced climber" as the example of how long a given route should take. Compare the grade rating with the par rating on a golf course. A par five means a honed golfer can probably hole the ball in five shots, rarely less, but a hacker will smile at a bogey six. Likewise, a couple of good climbers can usually crank a grade V in one day, whereas the intermediate climber had best come prepared to spend the night. World-class climbers can sometimes knock off a grade VI in an inspired day, depending on the the amount of difficult direct aid on the route. The more hard aid, the less likely that any team can "dust" a grade VI route in a day.

FREE CLIMBING

There are two types of individuals who climb without a rope: the world-class climber whose experience is extensive and who knows his capabilities and limits perfectly, and the sorry fool who doesn't know any better and is courting disaster. More will be said on this topic in Chapter 5: *The Art of Leading*, but let it be clear that, with rare exceptions, a rope and equipment are always employed in modern fifth class climbing. Accordingly, the layman often assumes that equipment directly assists a climber's ascent. It does, in the advanced realms of aid climbing, but not in the form known universally as free climbing.

Free climbing is the basis of all sport climbing, and can be loosely defined as upward progress gained by a climber's own efforts – using hands and feet on available features – unaided, or "free" of the attending ropes, nuts, bolts and pitons, which are employed only as backup in case of a fall. These "features," the irregularities on the rock – cracks, edges, arêtes, dihedrals, flakes – provide the climber his means for ascent. The variety is endless, and even uniform cracks of the same width have many subtle differences. It is precisely this fantastic diversity that gives climbing its singular challenge, where each "route" up the rock is a mental and physical problem-solving design whose sequence and solution are unique. Every climb is different, so discovering what works, for what climb and for what person, is the process that keeps the choreography of ascent fresh and exciting.

But it's not all ad-lib. There are numerous fundamental principles that apply to all climbing: the smooth coordination of hands and feet allows fluid movement; balance, agility, and flexibility are often better weapons against gravity than brute strength; endurance is generally more important than raw power; preservation of strength is accomplished by keeping your weight over your feet, rather than hanging from your arms; and the best execution of any climb is that which requires the least effort. Finally, staying relaxed is half the battle. Much of climbing is intuitive, and the moves come naturally to the relaxed mind. However, climbing requires certain techniques that are not obvious and must be learned and practiced before you can hope to master them. Climbing is one of the most primal activities a person can undertake but, unlike Java Man, the modern climber usually wears shoes.

Rock Shoes

For your first couple of outings, snug-fitting tennis shoes will suffice, but try to rent a pair of rock shoes if at all possible. Many mountain shops and guide schools have rental gear. Climbing shoes make the experience much more enjoyable and considerably easier for a beginner. Should you choose to pursue climbing, your first purchase should be a pair of shoes. Entry level shoes go for about $100, while top-end shoes can run upwards of $160. Climbing shoes can be resoled as they wear out, perhaps after 75 days of climbing.

Rock shoes have steadily evolved from the days of clunky, lug-soled boots, to the advent of "sticky rubber" soles in 1982. These shoes were so effective that many old-timers claimed it was "cheating" to use them. The old-timers should know, since they were the first to buy them. Built on orthopedically perfect lasts, with a glovelike yet bearable fit, they are a remarkable innovation. Since there are at least twenty brands currently available – with a host of particular features – choice for the beginner is mainly a matter of price and fit. For the expert, the choice is usually an attempt to match a specialized shoe to a particular kind of rock or a specific technique. Some shoes are stiffer, good for standing on minuscule footholds, but poor for pure friction. There are shoes for cracks, for limestone "pocket" climbing, and shoes designed to fit inside insulated high-altitude boots. In short, an expert will often have a whole quiver of boots for various applications, much as a champion skier will have various skis for different conditions and uses.

A beginner can get confused, but each manufacturer has a generic, all-around rock climbing shoe best suited for the novice. Since a beginner's footwork is generally poor, he will trash his shoes much faster than an experienced climber, so consider buying the cheapest pair you can find, at least for that first pair. Most manufacturers are continually redesigning their shoes, and if you shop around, you can often buy last year's models at considerable savings.

While a "general use" shoe is probably the novice's most practical choice, you will eventually want the shoe best suited to the type of climbing you prefer. For lower-angle face climbing, a soft sole and a supple upper is best. For steep wall or pocket climbing, you'll want a tight-fitting shoe

Typical rock shoes, with high-friction soles, outside rand, and snug fit. A laceless slipper is pictured at top left.

with good lateral support, a pointy toe, and a low-cut upper for ankle flexibility. Climbing magazines routinely have an equipment review that rate the relative merits of each brand's wares. These are usually reasonable guides in a sweeping kind of way, though many assessments are shamelessly tainted by the individual preferences of the reviewer and his considerations to particular manufacturers. Rock shoe manufacturers are big advertisers in climbing magazines, and the rags are becoming extremely reluctant to publish critical reviews even if certain shoes are so shoddy you could barely make it across the street in them without falling on your ass. Whatever, remember that despite significant advances in both rubber and shoe construction, there's no magic in shoes: the key is knowing how to use them.

Climbers have traditionally worn boots which are painfully snug because the boots rarely fit correctly, and you compensated by forcing your foot to fit the boot. If you didn't, your foot would rotate inside the boot when standing on small holds. Also, even climbing shoes have a tendency to stretch with time (although they have stitched/glued-in liners meant to remedy this), so the perfectly-fitting shoe may be quite snug when new. As mentioned, modern climbing shoes are constructed on anatomically correct lasts, contoured to fit your foot, thus eliminating the cruel fit of undersized boots. Some brands may favor a wider or narrower last, so try on an assortment of different shoes until you find the perfect fit. It is probably more important to your climbing to have a good fitting shoe than one that is specifically designed for the type of climbing you intend to do.

The foot should not rotate in the shoe; neither should the toes be painfully curled in the toe box – unless you're climbing at a very high standard. Climbers wear their shoes with and without socks – sans socks for a better fit and increased sensitivity (though after a time their shoes tend to take on a grievous bouquet). Others prefer to wear thin socks, citing better comfort. Try it both ways. A floppy pair of shoes is frustrating to climb in, and you don't want to spend to the tune of $150 and waste all the technology on a sloppy fit. Most climbing shops have rentals, so you can feel how the shoes perform before plopping down your greenbacks.

An alternative to proper shoes are "slippers," which resemble snug bedroom slippers with a sticky sole. For the veteran whose feet are chronically sore after a decade of cramming them into undersized boots, these slippers are a boon, for they work surprisingly well and most are very comfortable. They do require strong feet, but make for a sensitivity on rock not found in regular shoes. Slippers are excellent for bouldering, steep sport routes and indoor climbing. However, on traditional climbs slippers definitely underperform a proper shoe, so beginners, who need every advantage available, might do well to stick with a normal rock shoe – for that first season, anyway.

Dirt, grime, oil, tree sap, and such can dramatically effect a sole's performance, so always keep your shoes clean, and limit walking around in them to a minimum. Most climbing soles are not rubber at all, but TDR – Thermo Dynamic Rubber – a petroleum-based synthetic. Regardless, the TDR oxidizes and hardens just like rubber, and though this is only a surface condition, it can affect performance on all but the so-called "Stealth" rubbers. An occasional wire brushing is the solution for both grime and hardening. Hot car trunks loosen the glue bonds of the rands and soles. Super Glue can fix this, but it's better to avoid excessive heat. Foot powder helps avoid stitch rot from sweaty feet.

Chalk

The use of carbonate of magnesium – or gymnastic chalk – to soak up finger and hand sweat, is one of climbing's ethical issues, and arguments pro and con are continually waged, as they should be. The advantage is that chalk increases your grip, especially if your hands tend to sweat. On coarse sandstone, in forty-degree shade, the advantages are minimal, if any. But stick a climber on a greasy, glacier-polished Yosemite crack in mid-summer swelter and his hands will sweat like he's going to the electric chair – and chalk can make a huge difference. The arguments against chalk are many, almost all true. The golden rule for all climbers is respect for the environment: you leave the place as you found it. Though not permanent, excessive chalk buildup is not only an eyesore, it telegraphs the sequence of holds to subsequent teams, diminishing the factor of discovery so vital to the climber's experience. Also, too much chalk on the holds can make the grip worse than no chalk at all, a common condition that has caused many climbers to carry a toothbrush to uncake chalky holds. Knowing that an afternoon thundershower usually returns the rock to pristine status, and in light of the real advantage chalk affords, chalk has generally become an accepted evil the world over. But there are exceptions. On cliffs so steep rain never touches them, any chalk will be there until Jesus comes home. For this and other reasons, a very few areas have, through consensus, decided chalk will not be tolerated, and visiting climbers should respect the local custom.

Several manufacturers began making chalk in colors, intending to match the color of local rock, but this chalk tends to have a slimy feel, and on the wrong rock looks even worse than white chalk; so it has never fallen into widespread favor, except in a few isolated places where its use is mandated. A new, environmentally unobtrusive product called X-Factor has been introduced to replace chalk, but those with sweaty hands will continue to prefer chalk. Perhaps in time the right chemistry will be found, and the cliffsides will not be peppered in white paw marks. In the meantime, climbers will continue to use white chalk.

Helmets

In pure rock climbing areas like Yosemite, Colorado's Eldorado Canyon, Tahquitz rock in California, or the Gunks of upstate New York, you can climb for years and rarely see anyone wearing a helmet. The reason is that in these areas, rockfall is rare, and while it is possible to injure your head in a fall, for some reason serious accidents rarely happen. Climbers have accordingly avoided wearing helmets because they feel awkward; others consider them unstylish and gauche. A number of head injuries do occur each year in rock climbing that could be avoided through the use of helmets, however (primarily from rock fall and leader falls). Understand that wearing a helmet does not make you a doddering old sap, nor does it make you a "safe" climber. In the mountains, where the terrain is often anything but glacier-polished granite or dense sandstone, it's only the certified madman who doesn't wear a helmet. It's your choice. If you feel better wearing a helmet, do so.

On the edge, Angus MacGuillicuddy lofts up "Who'd rather be sailing?" (5.8), Blue Mountains, Australia. Often, sensational climbing and bracing locations are found on arêtes and sharp, outside corners.

John Sherman photo

Face Climbing Skills

Picture a climber on a steep wall of orange sandstone. Above her, the rock sweeps up like a cresting wave, without a single crack to lodge her hands or feet in. From our point of view, there appear to be no holds at all, just a polished wall; yet she moves steadily up – hig- stepping, counterbalancing, reaching, ever fluid and graceful. She's face climbing, and to the beginner it looks harrowing. But you'll soon learn that face climbing is the most natural form in all the climbing game. It varies from low angle slabs, where balance and the friction of good shoes are all that's required, to 120-degree overhanging test pieces where simian strength and flawless technique are essential to even get off the ground.

The fundamental rule in face climbing is to keep your weight over your feet. We live much of our lives on our feet, which are better suited for load-bearing than the arms, which tire quickly regardless of their strength. Keeping your weight over your feet is the result of *correct body position.* On face climbs less than 90 degrees (or dead vertical), the body should remain in the same upright posture as when you're walking on level ground, with your center of gravity directly over your feet. The reasons are these: first, the vertical posture is the only one that is naturally balanced. If you've ever balanced a stick on your finger, you'll remember it is only possible when the stick is vertical. Second, when your body is vertical, gravity forces your weight straight down onto your shoes, which is best for maximum friction and purchase. A beginner's initial reflex – to hug the rock – may feel more secure, but this actually throws the whole body out of balance; and when all the unbalanced weight is transferred to the feet, the shoes tend to skate off. Lastly, when the body is vertical, the climber's face is not plastered against the rock and his field of vision is open to see how and where to proceed. So stand up straight,

Correct body position is standing with weight over the feet.

---

stay in balance, and keep your weight over your feet. These are easy concepts to understand, but until you can consistently perform them on the rock, you will never advance beyond beginner's status.

FOOTWORK

Good footwork is one of a climber's most important assets. Excepting overhanging rock, you will climb basically on your feet, the arms acting only as a support mechanism to maintain balance as you step up from one foothold to the next. It is almost magical how well the sticky shoes adhere, but even so, a beginner will take some time before learning to trust his feet. Once you realize that the shoes do indeed stick, you can begin exploring the various ways to stand on holds. With practice you'll find that even the tiniest footholds can provide some support.

The variety of different footholds encountered is virtually infinite, but aside from pure friction, where you simply paste the sole of the shoe flush to the rock, there are basically two different ways to stand on face holds: by smearing and by edging.

Smearing

The name derives from the action of "smearing" that part of the sole (generally, but not always, beneath the big toe) onto a slightly rounded hold. You will generally want to smear as much of the sole over as much surface area as

possible, thus maximizing the friction. Beginners may have to consciously think about pushing down with the toes to hold the smear. Much of the art comes from one's ability to choose just the right place to step, having a keen eye for any irregularities, rough spots, or indentations. Even the most flawless face usually has slight ripples, and above these ripples is a lower-angled spot – if only a single degree less than the mean angle. The experienced climber scours the face for these. In smaller dishes and scoops, the heel is kept rather high when pure frictioning, for this increases the frontal pressure on the sole. On more uniform slopes, a lowered heel puts the relatively wide rubber under the ball of the foot to the rock while putting the calf muscle in a more relaxed position. Try it both ways. Smearing places a greater strain on the feet and calves than edging does.

Smearing

Perhaps more than in any other type of climbing, keeping your weight correctly balanced over your feet is absolutely essential when smearing. A good exercise is to get on a slab and, starting from the upright posture, slowly lower your torso closer to the rock.

You will immediately feel that the closer you get to the rock, the less your shoes will stick. Different rock has different friction properties. Polished limestone is desperate even at 45 degrees; but the coarse quartz monzonite at Joshua Tree allows pure friction well into the 70-degree realm; and given some supporting handholds, smearing can be useful even on overhanging rock. If the foot slips, try to push into the rock more by moving your center of gravity out, away from the rock, or by pulling out slightly on the handholds.

Discovering just how steep an angle you can smear on and picking the optimum foot placements is a function of experience, but as with all face climbing, smearing is natural and readily learned however insecure it may at first seem. In the era of the hard-soled rock shoes, particularly when many rock shoes had cleated soles, smearing was a risky practice, rarely done. With today's sticky rubber soles, smearing has become the favored means of using ill-defined footholds.

Edging

The practice of placing the very edge of the shoe on any hold which is clear-cut – the serrated edge of a flake, a cluster of crystals, a pronounced wrinkle – is called edging. "Edge" applies not only to the shoe's running edge, but also to the "edge" which forms the top of the hold. You usually edge when the hold is sharp. The edge of the shoe is placed directly on the best part of the hold and the sole finds purchase by conforming and biting onto the edge once the shoe has been weighted. On vertical and overhanging terrain, edging allows the climber to get his or her lower body closer to the wall to distribute more weight onto the feet, reducing the strain on the arms. Edging is the most basic method of standing on holds, but it takes a lot of practice to become proficient.

We generally edge with the inside of the shoe, near the outside of the big toe. Both your foot and most modern shoes are designed to stand most easily on this section of the shoe. Also, when edging on dime-sized holds – and you will – it is necessary to feel just how good or bad the shoe is holding, and the area around the big toe is the most sensitive and best suited for this. However, it is not unheard of for people to prefer edging off the ball of the foot, which requires less foot strength; and many times it is necessary to edge with the shoe pointing straight on the hold (called "toeing-in"). Toeing-in requires strong toes, and is especially useful in the small pockets so common on limestone and volcanic crags. While we normally climb directly facing the rock, many times you will find it necessary to step one leg inside the other, particularly when traversing. Knowing how to edge with the outside of the shoe is essential here.

Edging, using the outside of the right foot and the normal edging area of the left.

Back-stepping, a technique particular to steep rock, also makes use of the outside edge to increase your reach and force your hips in. (See picture.) Outside edging is almost always done just back from the origin of the small toe. The foot's bone structure makes that section of the foot fairly rigid as opposed to the rest of the outside part of the foot, which is fleshy and flexible, and which gives the shoe edge every reason to "butter off" the hold.

Craig Smith back-stepping on "Darkness at Noon" (5.13a), Smith Rock.

Beth Wald photo

Edging is an exercise in precision. Many edges are so small they can't be seen until you're at them. Careful placement of the foot is essential, and once the shoe is weighted, it is likewise essential not to change the attitude of the shoe lest you pop off. Thus, one key to proficient face climbing lies in learning to isolate the movements of your legs and upper body from the rigidity of your foot placement – in short, knowing how to keep your foot perfectly still on the edge while the rest of your body carries on. This is especially key when extending the leg, or "pressing out" the hold.

Contrary to common sense, a razor-sharp shoe edge is not ideal for standing on small holds. Because rubber stretches once weighted, a slightly rounded edge is less likely to "buttress" or fold off of smaller footholds. Most shoes feature a sole that is beveled back underfoot, resulting in more stable edging and less "buttressing."

Edge holds will appear at all kinds of different angles, and it is not the norm that an edge is formed perfectly for a foothold. Here, the edge of the shoe must be applied to the foothold at the angle of the hold, which requires ankle flexibility; and again, that foot attitude must be maintained while your weight is on it. In the case of extreme edging, when the holds are very small indeed, many of the edges are "time-bomb" in nature, meaning the climber cannot "camp" on them too long without the shoe "blowing off" from either toe fatigue or the fact that even the best shoe cannot stick to marginal holds indefinitely. More will be discussed about this in the Chapter 5: *The Art of Leading.*

It is sometimes best to smear an edge ("smedging"), particularly if the edges are small or the moves dynamic. Remember, you can smear an edge, but you can't edge a smear.

Rest Step

Often on sustained face climbs your calves will become exceptionally fatigued, which can lead to "sewing machine leg," where the tired limb will shake as though you have the palsy. To rest your calves, try the rest step: find a good edge and stand on the heel of the foot, with the leg straight, the center of gravity directly over the heel, and most of your weight on that foot. If possible, use the rest step whenever you have to stop to place protection, or when you need a rest. Imaginative resting is one of the keys to efficient climbing.

Tricks and General Technique

The technique of footwork is one of subtle precision and is tough to explain, let alone illustrate; but if you understand the principles, practice will bring to light what good technique can do for you. In general terms, the primary steps to good footwork are:

1) Scan the rock to find the best possible foothold. Don't move your foot until you know where you're going to put it. The size and location of the foothold determine its utility. When possible, place your feet directly beneath your hands to minimize the strain on your upper body.

2) Place the foot precisely on the best part of the foothold. "Zero in" on the foothold like an archer to a bull's eye. Concentrate on the foothold as you bring your foot to it.

Heel hooked overhead, Paul Piana cranks out a bleak line of overhanging holds on "Desdichado" (5.13c), Eldorado Canyon, Colorado. In the absence of footholds, the heel hook can act as a third arm, easing the strain on beleagured fingers.

Beth Wald photo

3) Fluidly transfer weight to the new foot placement.

4) Hold the foot absolutely still as you stand/move on it. Use the ankle as a hinge to cancel upper body movement. Foot movement can cause the foot to slip off its hold. Focus on keeping the feet still, and maintaining fluid movement and weight transference between holds. With experience this will become second nature.

The problem with most novice climbers is that they rush things. They hug the rock, their feet are kicked towards, not placed on, the holds, and because they don't trust their shoes, their limbs quake and their shoes are often skedaddling all over. You've got to settle in and relax. The frantic climber is the first to make a mistake, to miss a key hold. You must choose your holds carefully and always follow the line of least resistance. This sometimes means passing a good hold that is off to the side and would require awkward, more difficult moves to get to. Maintaining balance often means using smaller steps and smaller holds rather than awkward, off-balance strides between larger holds. The climber must move methodically and with precision, placing his feet carefully, staying balanced, and easing up onto doubtful holds, rather than jumping upon them. The aim is to climb smoothly and gracefully, and to use as little energy as possible. A good rule is whenever you reach a good hold, pause and compose yourself. Use the rest step when the chance arises. This takes the strain off the calves and puts it onto the skeletal system, which never tires.

Sloppy footwork is generally the result of impatience and fear. If fluid footwork seems impossible, if your shoes simply keep skating off even large holds, practice on slabs low to the ground. Get used to standing on marginal holds, keeping your weight over your feet. Experiment and learn. Traverse along the base of the cliff, where a fall means slipping four inches to the ground, and where you can try even the most improbable sequences. Practice walking over little slabs with no hands. Always aim to climb precisely, fluidly and relaxed. Striving to meet goals of control, rather than for success at all costs, will help build good technique. And always fight the initial instinct to only look up for holds. Many times the beginner will look down only to gauge the distance he is above the ground. You must pay attention to the climbing at hand. If you watch an experienced climber, you'll quickly see at least half the time he is looking down at his feet, scanning for holds, and placing them with keen eyes.

Heel Hooking

Heel hooking is the attempt to use the foot as a hand and is rarely used on climbs less than vertical. Basically, you hook the heel of your shoe over or behind a flake, knob, corner, or any feature that will accommodate such a move. Most often, the foot is actually kicked over the head and hooked over a shelf or ledge. You then pull with the foot, folding the chest in and up until you can reach the hooked hold. A heel hook is often a way to avoid throwing a strenuous and risky dynamic move; and in isolated cases, a climb is impossible without using this technique. Though it is sometimes possible, even necessary to hook something other than the heel (the toe, perhaps), try not to hook anything above the shoe's rand (the strip of rubber that circles the shoe above the sole). The rand is usually made from the same compound as the sole and grabs the rock well, whereas the leather upper is prone to shoot off even a jagged flake.

When lateral movement is required on steep climbs, the body will often feel like it's set to hinge out and away from the face. Climbers often look for a side hold or flake at or below waist level to hook a heel on, thus holding the body in place while the hands are arranged on other holds. Heel hooking requires good flexibility and moxie. The applications and variations are many, but it's normally a technique to employ a "third arm," or to stay in balance where otherwise it would be impossible. Words can take us only so far. Experiment and learn.

Torque between the toe and heel placed in a hole or horizontal crack below an overhang can keep the body from swinging out and provide stability and reach.

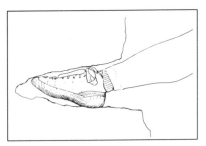

HANDHOLDS

There seem to be as many different kinds of holds as there are ways to grab them, but there remain five basic techniques: the open grip; the cling grip, or "crimp"; the vertical grip; the pocket grip; and the pinch grip. Again, as with footwork, a calm and deliberate manner, coupled with feeling different ways of using the hold, will result in added confidence that you are getting maximum performance from the hold.

The open grip is the way you latch either a big hold or a rounded hold. Your fingers conform to the natural curvature of the hold and you pull. The notion is to grab the best section of the hold, and the climber should feel around for the most secure position rather than just pulling straightaway the moment the hand is placed. With big holds, this is not so important; but when a hold is both small and rounded, the slightest shift in hand and finger position can make a huge difference.

With the open grip, the hand functions like a claw. The forearm muscles fight the tendency of the fingers to straighten out, but if the hold isn't incut the friction of the finger pads supplies the actual purchase on the hold. Accordingly, you try to cover the most surface area possible, increasing the friction at the power point. As with any handhold, if the hold is too small to accommodate all your fingers, give priority to the strongest digits, starting with the middle finger, on down to the pinky.

Experts in biomechanics insist that the open grip is least stressful on both joints and tendons and should be used whenever possible, especially when training on fingerboards. The one drawback with the open grip is that on severely rounded holds, the forearm muscles work overtime to keep the fingers from straightening out, and if the climber hangs too long, the forearms are sure to get "torched."

The cling grip (aka crimping) is one of the most useful handholds, and is used most commonly on flat-topped holds, be they minute edges, or inch wide shelves. The fingers are bent at the second knuckle and the thumb is wrapped over the index finger if possible. Sometimes the thumb is braced against the side of the index finger, but whatever position the thumb ends up in, it's your best friend, as it's considerably stronger than any of your fingers. Remember that the thumb lies close to the rock, negating any leverage effects, while the fingers often project one or two inches away from the edge, which forces them to work against their own leverage. Crimping works much like a shoe does when edging. Once weighted, the fingers dig into the rough contours of the hold.

As a result, and because the second knuckle is locked off while your fingers are reinforced by your thumb, you can apply remarkable amounts of torque to a hold using the cling grip. You can also shred your fingertips on sharp edges, and the overly ambitious climber can incur finger injuries owing

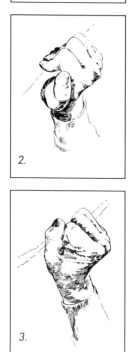

1. The Open Grip
2. The Cling Grip
3. The Ring Grip, with the use of a thumb to reinforce the fingers.

to the sharp angle the tendons make and the stress the knuckles absorb. Regardless, the cling grip is far and away the chosen technique when clasping sharp holds.

Some experts claim the cling grip is a natural posture, but most beginners find it otherwise. It's a foreign configuration, and it takes time for the knuckles to get accustomed to the stress. Because you don't want the fingers to rip off the rock, you'll feel around for the best part of the hold, which might also be the most painful. Only practice can reveal exactly how this all works, but you've got the basic notion.

The vertical grip involves bending the first and second knuckle and pulling straight down on the hold, oftentimes with one's fingernails behind the tiniest of edges. This grip is used exclusively on micro-flakes found on steep slab climbs, is painful, and has been said to be the climbing equivalent of "en pointe" in ballet. At 210 pounds, I can't say I've ever really fancied the vertical grip. Perhaps if you're skinny as a broom straw, your fingernails can take the strain. Mine never could.

The pocket grip is most often used on limestone and volcanic rock, which is typically pocked with small holes. The ultimate form of the pocket grip is one finger stuck into a hole. Because it is rare that a pocket will accommodate all of one's fingers, the first choice is the strong middle finger, next the ring finger, then the index finger, and so on. Using the middle and ring finger in a two-finger pocket better balances the load on your hand. It is sometimes possible to stack the fingers on top of each other for increased torque. Feel the pocket for any jagged edges, which can cut into the finger. Also, keep the pull in line with the axis of the finger, not pulling side to side, which is like bending a hinge – your knuckle – the wrong way. This is advice you will invariably have to shun should you someday tackle the really grim sport routes. Just be prepared for some sore joints and a few layoffs when a tendon goes.

The pinch grip is the action a lobster does with its pincers, and what a climber does when pinching a knob, flute, rib, or other protuberance. Though self-explanatory, a climber will often feel around quite a bit to find just where his thumb and fingers fit best. On small knobs, the most effective pinch combines the thumb with the side of the index finger. Few people outside the ranks of brick layers have much natural pinching strength. For the most part, it has to be developed.

In addition to these five different grips, there are two other basic techniques which are often called upon in face climbing: mantling, and the undercling.

Mantling

A mantleshelf is a rock feature, typically a ledge (small or large) with scant holds directly above. The act of surmounting it is called mantling. Picture a youngster heaving himself up and onto the top of a wall, then standing

4.

5.

6.

4. The Vertical Grip
5. The Pocket Grip
6. The Pinch Grip

THE MANTLE:
1. Select the best hold.
2. Walk the feet up as high as possible and cock an arm.
3. Press out the mantle.
4. Step up, rock your weight over your foot, and balance up, perhaps with the help of a higher handhold.

upon it. This is the basic form. Mantling is often performed on large features such as shelves or knobs, but when the face offers only one hold, you might find yourself mantling – albeit gently – a mere pencil-width crease. The technique has four components. After placing both hands on the mantleshelf, inspect the shelf or hold for the best place to mantle on, usually the biggest, flattest spot. If the spot is left of your face, you'll mantle with your left hand, and if it's to your right, then you mantle with your right. The second step involves hoisting the body up high enough to enable cocking one or the other arm on the mantleshelf. To get this upward impetus, use available footholds to ease the requisite arm power. On steep mantles, it is important to get the torso as high as possible before cocking the arm. If the arm is cocked low, with your weight checked only by skeletal tension, it is very strenuous for the triceps to initiate upward thrust from this "bottomed out" position. The third part, the press, can be very strenuous, and often depends on the free hand pulling, plus a certain body English to get started. The concern is to make sure the palm doesn't skate off the shelf, a real possibility on a rounded or slick surface. Most climbers find the bottom, or "heel" of the palm is best suited for mantling. Once you have "pressed out" the mantle, try to find a handhold above for the free hand. This makes it much easier to execute the last phase: the step up and leg press into the standing position. For balance, you'll want the foot close to the supporting hand. Often the hand must be moved to free up space for the foot. Using the knee is tempting here but only makes it more difficult to get into the standing position. Rock your weight from your mantling hand to over your raised foot and try to stand up smoothly, without jerking motions which can dislodge the foot.

In extreme cases, you must mantle using only your fingertips in the cling position, or perhaps with the thumb in a small divot. Many times you will step onto a hold different than the one you have "pressed out." Regardless, the basics remain the same: staying balanced, utilizing footholds, not getting stuck in the "bottomed out" position, avoiding use of the knee, finding a handhold above for the free hand, and a smooth step up are key functions with any mantle.

One element of mantling often used as a stabilizing influence on slabs and in corners is called "palming." In its usual form, you lean off a straight arm and palm that has been placed below and to the side of the torso. The palmed hold can often bear enough weight to allow you to reach up and above, or to shuffle your feet up onto higher holds, or both. Generally you'll want to avoid mantling if at all possible. Tough mantles are almost impossible to reverse, and it's common to get "mantled out" with no place to go. So try to face climb around a mantle whenever possible.

The Undercling

Anytime you grab a hold with your palm up, whether you have your fingers behind a flake, or you're grabbing the underside of a small roof or step in the rock, you are underclinging. The technique is often used as a balancing tactic until a free hand can reach above to a better hold. In its pure form, it functions through the opposing pressures of the

THE UNDERCLING:
1. Reach up to the hold.
2-3. Step up while exerting outward force on the undercling hold.
4. Make the reach above to other holds.

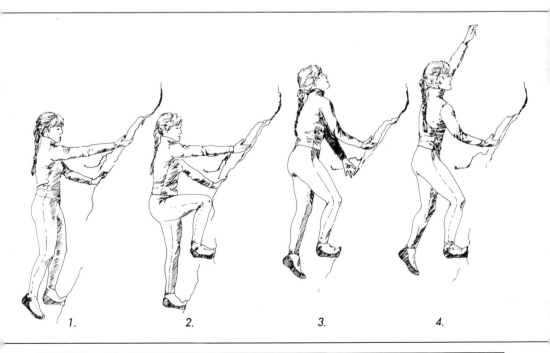

1.　　　2.　　　3.　　　4.

hand or hands pulling out from the hold under which you are clinging, and the force which is directed onto your feet. Counter-pressure, in simple terms. The technique is absolutely intuitive and self-explanatory, but the following points are often helpful.

On a full-blown undercling, where you must traverse under a long flake, try to keep the arms straight, as this transfers some of the load off your biceps and deltoids and onto your bones. Utilize footholds as much as possible to ease the load on your arms. Rather than undercling off the very tips of your fingers, try to get as much of your hand as possible behind the hold. Difficult underclings can involve lots of shuffling and crossovers of both hands and feet. Only experience can show you the how and why of it all.

Sidepulls

When a handhold is oriented vertically, or near-vertically, it's very difficult to pull straight down upon, so you'll most likely use it as a sidepull. The idea is to lean away from the hold, with your hands and feet working in opposition, similar to laybacking a crack. If the sidepull faces right, you'll want your body to be left of the hold, so you can lean against it. Ideally you'll find some left-facing footholds below and slightly right of the sidepull to provide the opposition. You can often make a longer reach from a sidepull than you could from a horizontal handhold.

A sidepull is similar to the crack technique of laybacking, with your hands and feet working in oppostion.

MOVEMENT: THE UPWARD FLOW

While we have discussed hands and feet separately, the aim of all climbing is to choreograph the different moves into fluid upward movement. To look closely at different types of face climbing is the best way to understand the dynamics of this upward flow. Three basic ways exist for using your legs to propel your mass upward against gravity:

The Static Step

The static step is generally the most strenuous and therefore least efficient way to move. The static step involves statically pressing your weight up on one leg while simultaneously bringing your other foot up to the next hold. On difficult slab and friction routes, where the weight transfer must be extremely smooth, the static step is almost always used.

The Spring Step

The spring step takes advantage of dynamic movement to efficiently move the climber's weight. The technique really comes into its own on vertical to overhanging rock. At the moment just before bringing a foot up, "bounce" off that foot to dynamically propel your weight upward. The bounce may be subtle or exaggerated, depending on the move, the individual climber's style, and the relative security of the hold. Many times it's no more than a little juke with the calf muscle. Depending on the terrain, this move should be used most of the time for efficient upward movement. If you watch experts use the spring step, you'll note it gives them the appearance of being light on their feet. It takes some practice to do this move smoothly and controlled enough that you don't either shock-load the foothold and blow off it, or change the attitude of the shoe on the hold and fall off that way. Lest you get the wrong idea, the spring step is rarely if ever an explosive movement, as though the climber were literally jumping off the foothold to slam dunk a basketball. Also, it's an all but worthless technique when delicate weight shifts are required between small or marginal weight-bearing holds.

The Frog Step

The frog step entails bringing one foot up, then the other, while the torso stays at the same level. After the second foot comes up the climber is essentially in a crouched, or "bullfrog" position. At this point both legs can work together to push the weight up.

Slab Climbing

Slab climbing refers to smooth rock "slabs," usually ranging from fifty to seventy degrees. Beginning climbers are always startled to see a honed slab climber move over seemingly holdless rock. Slab climbing requires the application of every face climbing technique: smearing here, palming there, edging, mantling. The ace slab climber is fluid and rarely stops, lest he interrupt the rhythm of ascent. The body is kept well away from the rock, eyes ever scanning the rock for usable features, stopping when a good hold allows. A baseball player watches the ball all the way to where it meets the bat. Likewise, once a climber has chosen a hold, he watches the hold until he gains purchase with his hand or foot. Because you can only watch one hold at a time, you only move one limb at a time. Keep this in mind and you will naturally assume the "tripod" position, maintaining at least three points of contact with the rock while shifting your weight accordingly as you move each limb. Your feet will mostly be smearing on slabs. A series of small steps is generally most efficient for movement up a slab, but occasionally the footholds will be far apart and you'll be forced to high step.

Because slabs are relatively low-angle, climbing them is much more a process of balance and friction than of the brute strength required on steeper climbs. Consequently, slabs are far and away the best place for a beginner to get accustomed to the nuances of footwork, body position, handholds, and general movement.

While slab climbing is usually thought to be more fun

than toil, there are exceptions. Extreme slab climbing occurs when the angle is too steep to just friction, yet the rock is devoid of holds – the classic "bald face." On these, balance, precision, unwavering concentration, and a dash of magic are most often your ticket to ride. "Micro-edging," often painful and always nerve-wracking, is surely one of the most absorbing forms of climbing, for even the experienced expert is astonished just how small a hold it is possible to stand on. Unlike other forms of climbing, intricate sequences of movement are rarely necessary to ascend slab and friction climbs. There are usually several ways to make upward progress, and this characteristic has led some climbers to label all slabs "boring." Slab climbing has fallen out of favor with many top climbers, who are ever becoming more specialized and seeking steeper and steeper rock.

However, for the beginner, there is no quicker way to hasten climbing prowess than to spend an initial few weeks working on the slabs. Assuming the upright posture, keeping the weight over the feet, learning the various holds and grips and how to move precisely while relaxed are all essential things which are learned much faster on the less strenuous arena of slabs. Trying to break in on steep rock is a bad practice, and tends to foster bad habits. This has been proven time and time again by my good friend, "Brother" Bob Gaines, who runs a very successful climbing school in southern California. During his longer seminars, Bob has found that spending an initial two days honing up on slabs helps students transition to the steeper climbs considerably faster than if he straightaway threw the same folks onto vertical terrain. He's tried it both ways, and without exception, starting on slabs has proven the way to go.

Steep Face Climbing

Many of the recent strides in technical expertise are due to climbers venturing more and more onto the steep faces which past generations wrote off as either impossible or too contrived. Before the mid-seventies, a climbing route normally followed a prominent weakness or "line" up the cliff – a crack system, or an obvious dike or intrusion. As most of these natural lines were climbed, later generations, wanting the same notoriety and thrill of exploration that past climbers enjoyed, turned to the steep and often hold-bereft faces. No longer did climbers only seek out natural lines, but often chose the blankest, most difficult way up a cliff in their quest for the limits of technical difficulty.

But steep face climbs need not be extreme. Many are rife with big holds and ledges, and are technically easier than difficult slabs. It's not simply the angle but also the architecture and size of the holds that determines difficulty. However, steep face climbs, even if they have bulbous holds from bottom to top, are invariably more strenuous than lower-angled climbs. They require much more from the arms, and in their most extreme expression, can involve

(page opposite)

Like gnats on a windowpane, three separate teams savor the fine slab climbing on the "Weeping Wall," Suicide Rock, California. Popular climbing areas like Suicide will find a host of climbers enjoying themselves on a given weekend. Because the routes take separate lines, the proximity may be close, the dangling banter as amusing as the climbing, but crossing paths is not a problem.

Bob Gaines photo

hoisting the body up off one finger stuffed in a shallow, rounded pocket.

The overall strategy of climbing long and sustained steep faces will be discussed in greater detail in Chapter 5: *The Art of Leading*. For now, understand these basic principles: unlike slab climbing, you will often see the steep face climber sucking his hips and chest into the wall, trying to get the weight over his feet. Keeping the weight off the arms is essential to climbing steep faces efficiently, for you are often called on to make a strenuous upper body move, and if you've been needlessly hanging off your fingers, the strength might not be there when you most need it. The steeper the angle, the more the arms come into play; but try not to overpull, try to only hang on, and rely on the legs for upward thrust. It's often better to make two small moves than one long one. Try to avoid getting your body too stretched out, for this negates all your balance and decreases the efficiency of your muscles, making the moves more strenuous. Avoid body positions that require yogi-like contortions; if you have to execute them, get into a more natural position quickly. And never pass up a good rest hold.

If you cannot find a decent foothold to snatch a breather, at least stop at the best handhold and alternately drop each hand and shake the blood back into them. As much as anything, the good steep face climber is the one who exerts the least energy, who figures out the most natural and easiest way to the top.

A beginner can benefit greatly by watching an expert climb, but in the case of steep face climbing, this can be misleading. The expert may appear to be, and may well be, simply hauling himself up on his arms. What you might not know is that the expert climbs 300 days a year, has done so for a dozen years, has developed fantastic endurance and cardiovascular strength, and at the moment he can't be bothered to fiddle with footholds. But put the same climber on a route at the very limit of his ability and you can bet your bottom dollar that he'll be observing the basic principles we've mentioned above. The reason is simple: the climber has not been born – nor will he be – who can hang indefinitely on his guns. Given enough stress, even the mightiest arms will flame out.

Overhanging Face Climbing

Owing to the development of areas like American Forks, Rifle, and Hueco Tanks, radically overhanging climbing has become all the rage among the elite climbing set. While the realm of sustained, overhanging climbing is strictly the expert's turf, most climbing areas have moderate routes which feature an overhang, or a short overhanging section. In the Shawangunks in upstate New York there are numerous, moderate overhanging routes, moderate only because the holds are terrific, and the climb resembles swinging around on a big jungle gym. The technique does

(page opposite)

The route spangled with tell-tale chalk marks, Ron Kauk works out the moves on "To Bolt or Not to Be" (5.14b), Smith Rock, Oregon. Typical of today's harder face climbs, success here dictates a long series of finger and toetip moves, as shallow pockets and slanting rugosities are the only features on this steep, volcanic testpiece.

Mark Chapman photo

not differ radically from that required on steep faces, save that everything is more strenuous. Most all overhanging climbs go from one good hold to another. However, "good" here might only mean "not as bad" as the "bad" holds.

Climb the difficult stretches aggressively but not so fast that you feel rushed. While you cannot get your weight directly over your feet, footwork on overhanging rock is probably more important than any other factor, for even the poorest foothold takes more weight off the arms than common sense would tell you. Try to keep your arms straight; when bent, the arms tire much faster. Ideally, the hands would act only as a hinge, holding your body to the wall as your legs push you upward. This is rarely possible, however. Try to avoid extremely long reaches, for this requires the other arm to be locked off, and the locked-off position, on overhanging ground, is probably the most strenuous position in all of climbing. When you must lock off a hold, try to keep the hand close to the shoulder and the elbow close to your side. This is easily confirmed on a pull-up bar. Try letting go with one hand and keeping your chin above the bar. You'll quickly realize your only chance is to assume the lock-off position just described. The geometry of the body makes it so. In rare instances on exceptionally arduous climbs, you might see a climber briefly locking off a hold well to one side of his body, and reaching up quickly to a hold on the other side. Be consoled that such a maneuver is limited to the very best and requires a degree of strength unusual in even world-class climbers.

Back-stepping often beats locking-off when you must make a long reach on steep rock. A classic back-step move reaching left, say, would have the outside edge of the left foot on the rock, opposing the right hand which is ideally side pulling. The right foot is splayed out right, and propels the body as the left hand reaches for the faraway hold. We will take up this topic in greater detail in Chapter 3: *Crack Climbing Skills*.

Dynamic Climbing

A dynamic move is another way to describe a lunge, where a climber vaults off a hold and is propelled to another. Dynamic moves range from six-inch slaps to all-out jumps, where a climber is completely clear of the rock, before quickly clasping holds above, at the apex of his leap. Only a decade ago, dynamic moves were virtually unheard of on all but practice rocks. As climbs got more and more difficult, dynamics ("dynamos," or simply " 'mos") became a requirement on many of the harder test pieces. Properly performed, dynamics are climbing's most athletic expression, requiring perfect coordination, raw power, and precise timing.

Usually, dynamic moves are "thrown" on overhanging rock to span long stretches between good holds. But not always. Sometimes dynamics are thrown from a poor hold to

a pathetic hold. While it is very occasionally necessary to generate the thrust solely with the arms, with the feet dangling in space, dynamics are usually performed by an explosive pull from the arms, aided by propulsion from the feet as they kick off footholds.

Start by hanging straight down from your arms, with your legs crouched and ready to spring. Don't pump up and down on your arms setting up for the lunge; that simply wastes energy. Rather, eye the hold you're going for, see yourself grabbing it, then launch single-mindedly for the hold like a cat. Once the lunge is underway, one hand shoots up and slaps onto the hold for which you're lunging. Ideally, the climber takes advantage of the brief moment of weightlessness that occurs at the apex of the leap – the dead

In flight! All limbs dislocated from the holds, Mike Paul slaps for the sloping top on "Saturday Night Live," a difficult dynamic boulder problem at Joshua Tree, California. Having generated momentum off lower holds, Mike must fly upward and stick a one-hand latch, not letting his lower body swing him off the top.

Gregg Epperson photo

point – to grab the hold with accuracy. But remember, the hold you're going to may not be what it appears.

Sometimes a hold is too greasy or rounded to lock off and reach above, but while hanging below, it is possible to generate enough momentum to literally fly to that upper hold. This phenomenon is difficult to explain, but is obvious when you encounter it. Rounded holds, even on very overhanging rock, are often fairly secure when your arms are extended and your bulk is hanging directly below them. But the higher you pull up, the worse they become because your body position forces you to pull increasingly out, rather than down on the hold. For this reason, big dynamic moves are usually initiated with the arms fully extended.

This is the basic form of the intentional dynamic. Much more common is the dynamic thrown out of desperation, where a climber has worked himself into a compromising position, and just before peeling off, he slaps for a hold. Another situation is: you pull up statically to a certain height; there is a hold right above your face, but if you let go, you'll fall off. You let go with one hand and hope you can slap the hold faster than gravity takes you down.

There are many more examples of dynamics which one can discover for oneself. Be certain to understand that, except on upper level routes, only one climb in a hundred requires any dynamic climbing, and that the place to practice dynamics is not on a long climb, but inches off the ground, or on a steep sport route with a bolt not too far below.

Crack Climbing Skills

The most visible and tangible weakness up a cliff is a large crack that runs from bottom to top. When you walk to the base of the rock and your partner asks where the climb is, there's no mystery to it. A climbing route is often referred to as a "line," a term derived from the line the crack forms on the cliff, but a "good line" doesn't necessarily follow a crack. It may pass over steep, otherwise featureless rock, be clean, offering exciting locations, great exposure, and a straight, or "plumb line" topography. A "poor line" might wander all over a rubbly cliff, through vegetation, up dark and dripping recesses. But good or bad, a line is a route waiting to be climbed, if it hasn't already been climbed. A prominent crack system is nature's way of telling us where to climb and when expeditions are mounted to big, faraway cliffs, or when a beginner studies a crag for the first time, eyes naturally home in on any crack system the cliff affords.

While face climbing might be a natural movement, few face climbs follow natural lines, and while cracks are natural lines, crack climbing is a very unnatural enterprise. Crack climbing requires subtle and strenuous techniques where the only hope of mastery lies in experience. All crack climbing involves either jamming or torquing the limbs or body inside the crack. Just as in face climbing, the idea is to keep your center of gravity over the feet as much as possible. On low-angle climbs, the hips and torso should remain back away from the rock; as the angle steepens, the hips move closer to the rock.

There are two types of "jamming." With the classic "hand jam," the hand is placed in an appropriately-sized crack, and the muscles expand the hand inside the crack. The various counter-pressures result in a locked, or "jammed" hand, which can be very secure when properly placed. The second method involves torquing and camming the appendage in a bottleneck or constriction in the crack. In wide cracks, the limbs are often twisted or stacked; and in very wide cracks you'll find that wedging and cross-pressures are the only way up. No two climbers are exactly the same size, however, and where one climber might pull fist jams, another might get hand jams, and so on. Anyone with aspirations towards big, classic climbs will soon discover such routes predominantly follow crack systems.

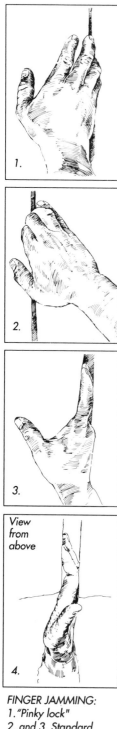

The names and different techniques do not correspond to any standard crack dimension (though a "handcrack" does generically refer to a 2-inch crack), but refer to the method you must use based on how your fingers or hands fit a given crack. Climbers with extremely thin hands enjoy advantages on thin finger and hand cracks, but work at a disadvantage on most wider cracks. Regardless of crack size, a smooth rhythm is desired – hand, hand, foot, foot, repeat. In its purest form, crack climbing is a very mechanical endeavor, with the climber repeating essentially the same move over and over, ad exhaustion.

Finger Cracks

Finger cracks vary in width from shallow seams into which you can only get the tip of your pinky, to a crack which swallows your fingers up to the third knuckle. Halfway between pure crack climbing and pure face climbing, thin cracks require techniques from both forms. Consequently, finger cracks are often technically demanding.

Except in the Windgate sandstone of the Canyonlands, it is a very rare crack that is absolutely parallel-sided. Most cracks, thin and otherwise, vary in size, if only barely; and it's these constrictions that you look for. The knuckles are the thickest part of the finger, particularly the second knuckle. It is possible to jam the knuckles above constrictions in the crack, and when the wrist is bent and the arm pulls down, the knuckle becomes locked like a chock in a crack – the standard "finger lock." This practice may be as painful as it sounds, and it's crucial to first wiggle the fingers around to attain the best fit before you weight them. The fingers are usually inserted so that the thumb is down, but this can be varied depending on the situation.

Many times it is better to jam the shank of the finger – the fleshy section between knuckles. Find the appropriate slot, insert as many fingers as possible (hand in the thumb-down position), then rotate the wrist downward. This will naturally create a camming torque on the stacked fingers, so the fingers will stick even if the crack is nearly parallel. Remember that the thumb is stronger than the fingers, so always try to brace it against the index finger in whatever position feels best. This reinforces the jam to prevent it from rotating out.

For ultra-thin, less-than-first-knuckle cracks, you assume the thumbs-up position to utilize the thinnest digit – the pinky – and any other parts of your fingers that you can snake into the crack. "Pinky locks" are marginal jams at best, and function well only if the pull is straight down. Oftentimes a straight-in crack (a crack splitting a uniform face) requires a combination of thumbs-up and thumbs-down jamming. When liebacking, the upper hand is usually "thumb-down" and the lower hand is "thumb-up." (See pages 55 to 58 for a full discussion of liebacking.)

1.

2.

3.

View
from
above

4.

FINGER JAMMING:
1. "Pinky lock"
2. and 3. Standard
   finger locks.
4. Off-size fingers

No buccaneer, svelte Lynn Hill, one of the world's great free climbers, smears, edges, liebacks, and clings up the "Pirate" (5.12), Suicide Rock, California. Too thin to jam, too bald to face climb, the climb requires creative face and crack combinations to succeed. On such difficult routes, confusing postures and withering fatigue may so vex the leader that performing the winning sequence may come only after dozens of falls and days of effort, if at all.

Greg Epperson photo

When the constrictions are slight and the jams are loose or marginal, leaning to one side or the other will often add a degree of stability to the adventure. If the crack is offset, where one side of the crack is raised above the other, the thumb can apply opposite pressure against the offset edge.

Such are the basic positions for vertical cracks. But many thin cracks slant one way or another, and just as many snake around in the course of even a short climb. As the crack leans, your body will inevitably be below the crack, and this pretty well dictates that the upper hand will have to be kept in the thumb-down position, your lower hand in a thumb-up position. With leaning thin cracks, it is sometimes possible, even desirable, for the lower hand to be thumb-down. But to place the upper hand thumb-up means to crank against the knuckles the wrong way, since slanting thin cracks are usually a combination of jamming, and pulling down on the lower edge of the crack. Extended sections of finger-jamming, especially if the rock is sharp, can gnarl your knuckles, so you may want to run a couple wraps of ½-inch wide tape around the joints. The torquing action of extreme finger-jamming can result in tendon damage, so lay off if you feel your fingers getting "creaky."

No one can climb a thin crack without feet. Even the best jams pump the arms quickly, and without good footwork, you're lost. Like face climbing, thin cracks are usually a matter of finding the hand positions which best support the upper body, while your legs supply the upward thrust. Thin cracks get progressively more difficult as the footholds disappear. Always scan the face for footholds. Thin cracks are strenuous, so never pass a rest spot, even if you're not tired. Leaning off the jams puts the climber to one side of the crack. If there's a foothold on that side, use the outside edge of the upper foot on that hold, for it keeps you more balanced, in a far less twisted attitude. Thin cracks occasionally open up and allow a flared "toe-jam." Most rock shoes feature low-profile toes tapered particularly for this. Twist the ankle and get the sole of the shoe vertical, then jam the toe in above the constriction; and try not to move it once weighted. When there are no footholds and no pockets for toe-jams, climbers will sometimes stick the outside edge of the shoe vertically in the crack. Though this is marginal, it works surprisingly well, for it creates a foothold, and invariably takes some weight off the arms. The last choice is to simply use friction, with the sole flat against the rock, the foot pushing in somewhat to gain purchase.

Save for a substantial shelf to stand on, "stem" holds are a thin crack climber's best friend. These are holds, one on each side of the crack, which slant in, and on which the climber can "stem," or bridge his feet. A good stem provides a solid base for the lower torso and often allows the climber to shake out a tired hand, sometimes both hands. On a steep thin crack, you hope for two good finger locks within reach. Keeping the arm extended (remember, a bent arm tires quickly), suck the chest in and get your weight over your feet. Shake out one arm at a time until you've recovered enough to carry on.

When climbing thin cracks in corners, it is often possible to stem between the two walls using pure friction. If you find a stem hold, look to paste one foot in the corner, and "back-step" the outside foot onto the stem hold.

All these descriptions may sound straightforward, but climbing a thin crack rarely is. The best solution is usually a subtle blend of all these techniques. The correct sequence is rarely obvious, requiring patience and a certain amount of feeling about to discover what best works for you. Hasty moves can result in painful abrasions, so climb fluidly. We have effectively broken down the variety of individual moves likely to be encountered on thin cracks. Putting these moves together, with tips on strategy and approach for all crack climbing, will be taken up in Chapter 5: *The Art of Leading*.

Off-Finger Cracks

An off-finger crack is too big for the fingers and too small for the hand, where the third knuckle butts into the crack and the fingers rattle around inside. Cracks this size rarely allow good toe jamming – just a tad too thin – so you're doubly cursed. This is the hardest size of crack for most climbers, save for the notorious off-widths. Everything's wrong about this size, and there are no easy solutions. One way to approach the problem is to keep the fingers straight and together and stuff them in to the hilt, thumb-up. You lever the fingertips off one side of the crack and the back of the fingers – or knuckles – off the other side – sort of a crowbar effect. This "bridge" jam is terrifically strenuous, difficult, and worthless most of the time. Another way is to insert the hand thumb-down, overlap the middle finger over the index, overcrank with your wrist, and pray that it doesn't rip out. Far and away the best method is the "thumb-stack" – or "butterfly" jam. Place the thumb near the outside of the crack, the first knuckle against one side, the thumb pad against the other. (For this to work effectively, the crack must be thinner than the link of jammed thumb. The thumb is inserted at an angle, the pad higher than the knuckle.) Curl the fingers over the thumbnail and pull down, effectively wedging, through downward pressure, the thumb between the two walls. At first this technique feels strange and impossible, but with practice it's really the only viable technique.

Because off-finger jams are always cammed or wedged, they're invariably less secure, and more strenuous than a good finger lock. Hence, footwork is key. It will help to wear tiny (i.e. painful) slippers with a thin toe profile. The drawback is that while these might be perfect for a short pitch, they certainly won't cut the gravy on a longer route. With luck, the crack will open up enough to allow at least marginal toe jams. If not, you're essentially face climbing with your feet. If there are no face holds, your world is a pretty bleak place.

Hand Cracks

Most climbers think hand cracks are the last word in crack climbing. The crack is perfectly suited for both hands and feet, the technique is readily learned and very secure, and vertical, even overhanging hand cracks are often reasonable. An added boon is that (for reasons only a geologist can guess) hand cracks often bisect spectacular sections of rock, and many of the world's classic climbs involve extensive hand jamming.

Hand jamming is usually done with straight fingers, bent at the palm, or third knuckle. The thumb-up hand jam is a tripod configuration, with the fingertips and heel of the palm on one side of the crack, pushing against the back of the hand and knuckles on the other. In a tight hand jam, increase the outward pressure by bridging the thumb off the

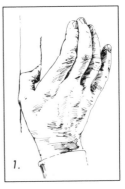

View from above

OFF-FINGER CRACKS
The thumb stack:

1. Place thumb.

2. (From above) Curl fingers over and pull down.

3. Step 2 seen from front.

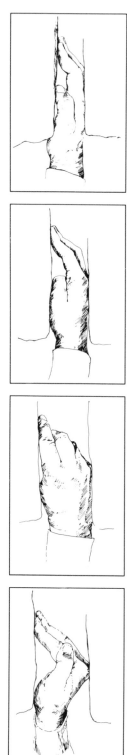

index finger. If the crack is large enough, wedge the thumb into the palm to create additional outward pressure. The importance of squeezing the thumb, though neglected in most climbing manuals, cannot be overstated. It's the expanding action of the hand and the wedging of the thumb that creates the actual hand jam, which when properly performed, is the most powerful jam of all. Once mastered, an experienced climber will often prefer to hang off a "bomber" hand jam than off an equally good shelf – though most uninitiated sport climbers would prefer the shelf.

When climbing straight-in "splitter" hand cracks, most climbers prefer the thumb-up position, though in some situations the thumb-down jam works better. When the crack jags, or is a little slim, the thumb-down jam is normally – but not always – employed. With the thumb-up jam, the wrist is straight. The wrist twists with the thumb-down jam, and the result is a torquing action that can sometimes add power to a thin or bottoming jam. As you move up, try keeping the arms straight and penduluming from jam to jam, leap-frogging each hand jam above the previous one to increase speed and efficiency.

With slanting hand cracks, or in corners, you will generally jam the upper hand thumb-down and the lower hand thumb-up. When you find it necessary to lean off the crack, the top hand is invariably thumb-down, the bottom hand thumb-up. There are exceptions to these examples, and climbing even the most peerless, straight-in hand crack may require all these techniques, if only to vary the stress and to use other muscles. A hand jam is often tight, and the back of the hand is frequently set against coarse rock. Hateful abrasions can result from hasty jamming, or rotating the hand in the crack – which is a common mistake as you pull up and past a poor or insecure jam. To avoid this, place the jam so the fingers are pointing straight into the crack. As you pull up, rotate your wrist – not your hand – keeping the jam locked tight. Even with good technique, extended sections of hand jamming can seriously trash your hands if you don't protect them with tape. Tape also adds confidence by allowing you to jam a little harder without feeling excruciating pain. Check the end of this chapter for details.

With hand cracks, which readily accept feet, turn your foot on its side so your inside ankle faces up. Slot the foot in the crack, then pivot the foot toward the horizontal. As you weight it, keep trying to rotate it tighter in the crack. Properly set, such foot jams easily support the bulk of your weight. It's a mistake to think the foot jam improves the deeper you set your shoe, however. Keeping the foot as far out of the crack as can be easily secured allows easy removal and keeps your center of gravity away from the rock and a bit of your weight off your arms. You rarely have to stick the shoe in past the ball of the foot. Any constrictions make foot jams that much more secure. Always try to keep the feet relatively low, and the legs somewhat straight. The higher the feet, the more your rump hangs out and the more you hang on your arms.

Cupped or Cammed Hands

As the crack opens up too wide for tight hand jams, the security of the jams begin to diminish, peaking at the point just before a fist jam fits in the crack. For these wide hand jams, try "cupping" the hand by pushing the fingers forward into the crack, and stuffing the thumb into the palm, or "camming" the hand by rotating the hand sideways until good purchase is made on both sides of the crack. For cammed hands, it is necessary to keep the hand torqued to maintain the stability of the jam.

Fist Jamming

Even experienced climbers find fist jamming a precarious technique, in part because it's seldom used, but mostly because the fist jam rarely feels quite right. The jam is set by clinching the fist, which enlarges the small fleshy muscles on the outside of the hand; and since these expand very little, the best fist jam is usually a matter of matching fist size with crack size. When the fit is snug, the fist jam is very secure.

Look for a constriction to jam above. If the crack is parallel-sided, choose the spot where your fist fits snugly. Sometimes you will slot the fist straight in, like a boxer throwing a slow-motion jab. The fist is then flexed as the hand is rotated into the vertical position. Other times the fist is simply placed vertically and the hand flexed. Depending on the crack, the fist, once slotted, can assume several basic forms. With an exact fit, the thumb is wrapped across the index and middle finger. The thumb may be tucked across the palm on a tight fit. On an ultra-thin fist jam, let the middle and third finger float above the index finger and the pinky, which narrows the profile of the fist. This "ball-jam" can be expanded very little, and is only "bomber" above a constriction. (A wide hand jam is usually preferable over the "ball-jam.") An even less reliable position is sometimes (though very rarely) used when the crack is too wide. Keep the thumb on the outside of the fist, braced over, or against the index finger. This is a painful, and most often makeshift jam, which will rarely bear much weight. Sometimes the flex of a forearm inserted into the crack will add security to a loose jam.

FIST JAMS

On straight-in fist cracks it is often possible to jam the entire crack with the back of the hands facing out. However, many climbers prefer to jam the lower fist palm out, finding the strain is distributed over a greater range of muscles. Picture yourself picking up a big barrel, then tilting the barrel horizontally. Your arms would form a circle, with the lower hand palm up, supporting the barrel. If your lower hand was palm down, the barrel would be resting, no doubt precariously, on the back of the hand. Turn your hand over, and you kick in the full power of your shoulder, back, and biceps. With extreme fist cracks, by jamming the lower fist palm-up, you form a sort of ring of power; and using this configuration, many of the hardest fist cracks have been climbed.

(page opposite)
HAND JAMS

Fists torqued tight, Nic Taylor punches through "Twilight Zone" (5.10d), Yosemite Valley

George Meyers photo

When the crack leans, you will invariably use this technique. Also, unlike jamming thinner cracks, you will seldom reach above the upper fist with the lower one, for this is most often too awkward. Better to shuffle the fists up the crack, locking off the lower jam, and reaching above for the next one.

If the fist jam is just a bit too large, try the "teacup" fist jam, with the thumb placed along the side of the hand to widen the fist. Better yet, try the "bridging" hand, with the tips of the fingers bridged against one side of the crack and the back of the hand against the other side. Both of these are dicey.

Fist cracks are often very strenuous; and even world-class climbers are prone to rotate their jams. Again, dreadful abrasions can result, so many climbers opt to tape their hands for even moderate fist cracks.

Since the breadth of your hand and foot is roughly the same, if your fist fits, so will your feet. Look for a constriction. Otherwise, the foot goes straight in. If it's loose, torque it laterally for stability. As with all jamming, try to keep the feet low and the weight over them. Resist the temptation of kicking the shoe into the crack or jamming it too deeply. The shoe can get stuck, and it's no fun trying to extract it.

Off-width Cracks

Off-width, or off-sized cracks are too wide for fist jamming and too narrow for anything but the knee, if that. The extreme off-width crack is far and away the most feared prospect in all of climbing. There is simply no easy means to climb them, and success often involves more grunting and cursing than finesse and elegance because very few climbers have taken time to master this, the most awkward technique of all. The reasons are several. Very few climbing areas have many off-width cracks, and if you can't practice, you'll never master them. The technique is more battle than dance, and in an era of spandex leggings and hot pink shoes, off-width cracks are about as popular as walking barefoot in the snow. History also plays a part in the disdain climbers have for off-width stuff. In the early sixties, America's greatest climbs were in Yosemite Valley, and most featured off-width climbing. When up-and-coming climbers wanted to bag the big-name routes, they had no choice but to tackle these off-width test pieces. The first few encounters were desperate, thrashing, villainous affairs; but they stuck to it, and one season was usually enough to master the technique. As the newer generations turned towards thinner cracks, the nasty off-widths were gratefully overlooked, and today, most climbers simply avoid the technique because they lack the requisite experience for the climb to be anything but a pitched battle. If one of the international climbing com-

OFF-WIDTH TECHNIQUE

Set the feet, one leg torqued high in the crack, perhaps heel-toeing, the other on the outside of the crack in a heel-toe. The arms, set in arm bars or locks, provide the stability for the feet to step the body up the crack.

petitions were staged on an overhanging, 5.13 off-width, we'd probably see contestants trying to paw up the bald face on either side of the crack.

The most arduous off-widths are about four inches wide, where you cannot get your knee in. Upward progress involves locking off the upper body, moving the legs up, locking them off, then jack-knifing the upper body back up. Repeated ad nauseam, this sequence makes the Eight Labors of Hercules seem like light housework.

You must first decide whether to climb left or right-side in. In a vertical crack, if the crack is offset, you will probably climb with your back against the raised edge, which may provide a little extra leverage, allowing you to stem outside of the crack. If the crack edges are uniform, or flush, you find what side of the crack has the best edge and/or footholds. While the outside arm grips the outside edge, the inside arm is locked inside the crack. In thin off-size (normally 4-inch and 5-inch), the back of the upper arm is held in place by pushing the palm against the opposite side – the classic "arm-bar." The outside arm can add torque by pulling out on the crack's edge. For optimum leverage, place the arm bar diagonally down and away from the shoulder. This kicks in the front deltoid and upper chest muscles, and adds to the fulcrum effect of the arm bar. If you cannot get your knee inside the crack, you must jam your inside foot (and sometimes your calf), usually by torquing it horizontally. If the crack is slightly larger than the width of the foot, torque the foot diagonally across the crack so the toe jams against one side of the crack and the heel wedges against the other side to create opposition across the crack.

Usually it's best to use the outer foot to propel your body upward, while the inside leg and arms stabilize the body. Make sure to use any edges or stem holds for the outside leg. Once the feet are set, the outside hand moves up and pulls hard against the lip of the crack, then the arm bar is quickly shuffled up and locked off, usually level with, or just beneath the outside hand. Then the process is repeated. If the crack is overhanging and you can't get the knee in, the hardest part is moving the arm bar up. Sometimes this is only possible with little dynamic hops, shuffling the arm bar up and quickly locking it before you fall out backwards.

Once the crack opens up enough to get a knee inside, the technique is much more manageable. While the jackknife motion may still be necessary to move up, your lower body can now be securely jammed. The inside leg is in a vertical version of the arm-bar, with hip, thigh, knee, heel, and toe all torqued and counter-pressuring. Both the outside and inside foot should be in a heel-toe jam. Keep the toes lower than the heel, which allows the toes to be smeared for better purchase. The outside leg is usually set above the inside leg, with the knee pointed up and out of the crack. If you are either very slim, flexible, or if the crack opens up enough, the arm bar can be replaced with the arm lock, or "chicken

(page opposite)

Bruce Bailey sets an arm lock on the rugged "Twilight Zone" (5.10d), in Yosemite. Note the foot bridged out right and the mammoth chock slotted above his head.

John Sherman photo

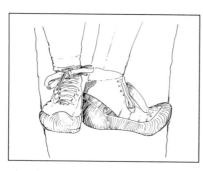

The T-bar

Hand Stacking

wing." Much like the arm bar, you simply fold the forearm back and palm against the opposite side of the crack. If the crack is tight, your elbow will point into the crack; with a slightly wider crack, the elbow will be pointing nearly straight up, with the triceps resting against the rear crack wall. Many times, the natural muscular tension in your arms and a little upper body English will make the arm lock so snug it's hard to even move it. Some climbers swear by the arm lock and use it whenever possible; others only use it to augment the arm bar; and some find it too awkward and only use it to rest. When the crack widens too much to use the heel-toe jam, you must start foot-stacking, the most called-upon stack being the "T-bar."

The best sequence of when to move what is a matter of what the crack dictates, and what process works best for you. Experience is the best and only teacher, but remember the following points. Resist the natural temptation of sticking your body deep into the crack. It may feel more secure, but it inhibits your mobility. So stay outside of the crack as much as possible. And don't thrash. Set each limb solidly, and keep it locked as the others shuffle up. Don't rush, pace yourself, rely on small movements rather than drastic lunging; and never skip the chance to rest. Always scan for face holds inside or outside of the crack. Often a couple of face holds will get you around the nastiest part of an off-width.

Wear sufficient clothing to protect against the inevitable scrapes. Remember that most off-widths are rated for people who know exactly what they are doing. As a beginner you may find even a moderate off-width climb the hardest thing you've ever done. After you have a few under your harness, go back and see what a huge difference experience and technique make.

Hand Stacking

Also known as "Leavittation" (after a pioneer of this technique), hand stacking supplants the strenuous arm bar with a variety of two-handed jamming configurations: fist against hand, hand against hand, fist against fist. This technique should work anywhere that hands can be stacked, and the lower body can at least momentarily support the whole body via knee jams and/or calf locks. Leavittation is particularly efficient on straight-in, off-width cracks so desperate or overhanging that pure arm barring is prohibitive, if not impossible. Only practice can show you what kinds of hand stacks work – there are no rules or "best jam" guidelines. It's the jammed legs that are the real trick.

The basic sequence is: find a hand stack, then a knee lock as high as possible below the hand stack. This "active" leg is soon to bear your full bulk, so work it in as securely as possible. The "passive" leg is heel and toe jamming below, and is mainly a balance point. You must then release the hand stack and establish another above, the high knee-jam supporting your weight, while your abdominals keep you upright. Then repeat the process.

The knee lock is key, tough to master, and is usually where even experienced climbers fail with leavittation. The secret is to keep it as high as possible. For optimum torque, once the knee is completely inside the crack, bend it back so it locks and allows you to bring your foot back out of the crack. The foot is in turn placed against the outside of the crack, supplying a sort of brace effect that allows you to let go with both hands and set up the next hand stack.

A straight-in crack allows a choice for the "active" or jammed knee; the leaning crack does not. If the crack leans right, jam the left knee; if left, jam the right one. Leavittation is a very advanced technique that takes practice to even understand. Its normal application is on off-width cracks at the very top of the scale and of a fairly narrow range of size, though the technique is occasionally fitting on moderate routes and in cracks which fluctuate between sizes.

Squeeze Chimneys and Flares

By definition, any crack too wide to heel-toe jam but only wide enough to barely accept the body is a squeeze chimney. They may be easy to slide into, but usually they are strenuous and almost claustrophobic to ascend. A bottoming, or shallow squeeze chimney is a flare. Once it is too wide to use an arm lock or "chicken wing" with the arms, it's a chimney. These techniques often overlap on a given climb, but we'll look at them separately to focus on the various methods of climbing them.

Squeeze chimneys are climbed using off-width techniques with a few additional tricks and variations. The arm lock is the stand-by for the arms, though a wide arm bar, and even an inverted arm bar (elbow higher than the palm) is often used. You can typically get inside a squeeze chimney, so the arm lock and arm bar variants can be used with both arms. The normal configuration sees the arm lock for the inside arm, and the inverted arm bar for the outside arm. Sometimes, both arms are using the inverted arm bar.

Foot stacking (the T-bar) should be used if at all possible. If the chimney is too wide, press both knees against the front wall, with both feet torqued flat against the back wall. The opposing pressures between knees and feet keep the lower body in place. Like off-width cracks, the lower and upper body move up alternatively.

Many squeeze chimneys are so slim you have to exhale to move up. Most chimneys narrow the farther you enter them, so fight the urge to work deeper – albeit more securely – into

The way is straight, the gate narrow. Robert Finlay bridges up through the "Needle's Eye" (5.8) in the Black Hills of South Dakota. At this juncture, the chimney is moderate and wide enough to march a camel through, but ten feet overhead, the slot narrows and only the chosen can toil on.

Bob Gaines photo

the bowels of the crack and stay toward the outside, where movement is easier. You'll probably find that staying lodged is easy, but moving up is grim duty. Just climb slowly, work it out, and never get frantic.

Flares are wide enough to get inside, but too shallow to do so very far. They can be nasty undertakings, very strenuous and insecure, and technical riddles. Because every flare is a little different, they defy much generic explanation. Still, almost every flare requires the inside arm to be arm locking; and often the purchase of elbow and palm is marginal. The outside hand will exploit any handhold, or at least vigorously palm off the flare to augment the arm lock. The feet are bridging – inside foot back-stepping the back wall, outside foot pressing off any footholds available, or simply frictioning, flat against the face. Sometimes you alternate these tasks between outside and inside feet. The outside foot is key, for it presses the arse and back against the back wall; so the decision which way to face often depends on where the footholds are. Many times you won't know which way to face until you try. If the flare is extremely shallow, very steep, and devoid of footholds, you're looking at a nasty piece of work, where anything goes.

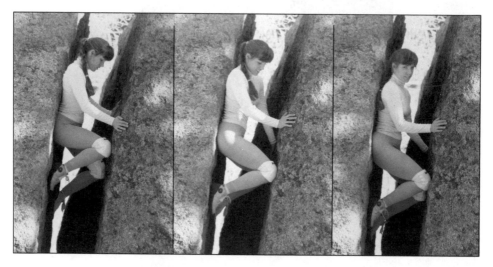

Knee chimney

Chimneys

When cracks widen enough so that they are easily entered, they may lose some degree of security, but they are usually much easier to climb. Knee chimneys are just that: bridging is done between knees and back, variations in size being accommodated by flaring the knees to varying degrees. Movement is a ratcheting affair, with the arm usually in the inverted arm bar position. Knee chimneys are usually secure. Knee pads can prevent painful bruises to the kneecaps and a long-sleeved shirt will protect the shoulders.

When the chimney is wider than the distance between your knee and your foot, you push the feet against one wall and the back against the other. To move up, one foot back-steps off the back wall so your legs form a bridge via opposing pressures. The hands are either pressing off the far wall or are bridged between both walls, like the feet. In either case, the back is released and the legs extended; the torso moves up and the back is again pressed against the back wall. Opposing pressures between hands and back allow the feet to either shuffle up or to exchange positions – front foot now back-stepping, back foot now pressing off the far wall. Always let the legs do the pushing. Foot-back chimneys should never be strenuous for the arms.

If the chimney is wider than the distance between your hips and feet, you can "bridge" it, using one hand and one foot on each wall, each limb pressing directly out. If your purchase is attained by pure friction, this is dicey work, so keep an eye peeled for any footholds or shelves to bridge off of.

In chimneys too big to bridge, it is theoretically possible to use the alarming full body stem: lodge yourself dead horizontal, facing straight down, with both feet on one wall, and both hands on the other – like a clothes rack in a closet. Most expert climbers have done this for a couple of moves somewhere. I've heard climbers claim they had done this on long routes, up vertical shafts for hundreds of feet, and I don't believe a word of it. I can't imagine not falling if you had to do the "clothes rack" for more than a few feet. Don't believe everything you hear. And if something sounds absurd, it probably is.

Foot-back chimney

Liebacking

"Hanging on for dear life" is often the description given for the full-blown, all-out lieback. Fortunately, few liebacks are all-out, but most are athletic and strenuous. Liebacking is perhaps the most exhilarating technique (outside of roofs and dynamics) in the climbing game. You can span amazing sections of rock. It's also the quickest way to find hell in a handbasket for, owing to the great opposing pressures, if your hands fail, you fire off like you're spring-loaded. In its pure form, the technique is used to climb arêtes, cracks in right-angled corners, or cracks which are too shallow for jamming. In its partial form, anytime you lean off a hold you are liebacking, for you are lying back off the face hold, the jug, the edge of the crack, or whatever your hands are on. It's a means to use holds that are other than simple horizontal edges.

The basic motion is: pulling with your hands and pushing with your feet, one in opposition to the other. A typical lieback will find your side flush against the wall. Your hands are clasping the near edge of the crack, and you are liebacking off them. Your feet are pressing against the crack's far edge, are balanced on small holds, are vigorously pushing off a corner's far wall, or maybe are even jammed in the crack. There are many quasi forms of liebacking, but all involve the upper torso leaning off to one side and your arms pulling to create opposing pressure against your feet.

The purest and most typical lieback occurs on a flake leaning against the wall or in a crack in a 90-degree corner – a dihedral.

Your hands are pulling directly out, and your feet are pushing the opposite way, directly against the face or far wall. Since the technique is strenuous, try to keep the arms straight, which, again, lets the skeletal system, rather than the muscles, absorb at least some of the strain. Many times it is possible and desirable to leap-frog the hands, one over the other; but often the top hand will remain on top throughout, shuffling the lower hand up to it, then reaching above with that top hand. On steep liebacks, you'll never want the hands to lose contact with the liebacked edge, so the hands are slid up. Also, leap-frogging your limbs can sometimes get you crossed up, throwing your balance out of wack. Try and keep your feet as low as possible, using any footholds. The closer your feet are to your hands, the more strenuous the lieback becomes.

The lieback

The full-blown or "Frankenstein" lieback is most often found in a steep or overhanging corner. The crack's edge might be rounded or the crack so thin it will accept only fingertips. The opposite wall may be overhung, slanting away and smooth as glass, so your feet gain purchase only through the friction of direct pressure. The "Frankenstein" lieback entails drawing your feet up by your hands and "swinging" into the all-out, liebacking posture. The problem is, not only is this extremely strenuous, but there's often the tendency to swing right out, like a door opening on its hinges. This "barn door" effect can be countered either by increasing the torque to both hands and feet (which makes things more strenuous still), or by bridging the outside foot out and pushing obliquely off the far wall, hoping to stall the swing and regain equilibrium. Sometimes you must momentarily palm off the opposite wall to halt the swing. Sometimes it is possible to jam the inside foot in the crack, keeping the other foot stemmed out wide to provide a hinge-proof base. If you're fortunate, the opposite wall will be peppered with big footholds. If not, it's just you and Frank all the way.

Most liebacks require a clever mix of all these techniques; when to use what is fairly intuitive once you've swung into the lieback. Your body responds automatically to changes in equilibrium and variations in angle, but always try to keep the arms straight. Feel the edge of the lieback as much as possible, and crank off the sharpest, most defined spots.

Look for any stem or rest holds, but don't stop if it's more strenuous than carrying on. Climb aggressively, and don't hang about looking for footholds which aren't readily apparent. The exhortation "go for it!" was invented for the climber swinging into a lieback. Once committed, don't hesitate: power over it quickly.

Stemming

Stemming or "bridging" normally occurs in right-angled or oblique corners, where the crack is non-existent or so thin as to be of little value. Many times it is necessary when the crack momentarily pinches down. Even when the crack is good, your lower body may stem the whole way. In any case, stemming is essentially face climbing in a corner.

Many difficult climbs involve stemming, and the extreme stemming problem can require creative sequences and very improbable, marginal counter-pressures. Consider the stemming corner as an ultra-flared chimney. In its pure form, the feet are pasted on opposite walls, perhaps frictioning, maybe smearing on footholds, but counter-pressuring against themselves and/or the hands. The hands may also be cross-pressuring, palming off the slightest irregularities, or pawing holds. Essentially, your body is like a spring lodged between two sloping walls. The only thing keeping the spring in place is the purchase at both ends, and the tension between. Moving the spring up, then, is the hard part, for this requires the tension to go lax, at least momentarily – yet it never can. Usually it's the diagonal pressure of one hand and one foot that keeps the climber in place, and the climber alternates this bridge in moving up. This can involve a dozen little moves to gain even a meter of upward progress. Sometimes you may actually chimney the corner, back against one wall, feet smearing off the other. You may back-step with one shoe, edge with the other, palm with one hand, and mantle with the other. The possibilities are endless. Flexibility, balance and the ability to exploit any and all features are a stemmer's best tools.

Protecting with Tape

Perfect technique does not eliminate painful hand abrasions altogether. Some cracks are lined with crystals, others require awkward, shallow jamming, notorious for shredding even expert hands; and overhanging fist cracks are almost always good for a few "gobis." A popular solution is taping. There are dozens of taping patterns, none so good to preclude all others (one is illustrated on page 60), but certain tips apply to all taping methods.

First, remove hair from your hands and wrists (and the palms, too, should you have any there). Shaving will work, but singeing the hair off with a low level flame is even better. The tape will adhere well only if you apply a chemical taping base, such as tincture of benzoin or Cramer's Tuf-skin, both available at sporting goods store (although many climbers

(page opposite)

Stem, Jim!
Jim Waugh splays up "Bach's Celebration" (5.12a), at Paradise Forks, Arizona. This three-sided slot is utterly bereft of holds, so full-blown stemming – ratcheting each limb up in turn – is Jim's only hope to celebrate.

Bill Hatcher photo

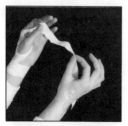

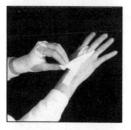

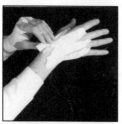

forego this step). Apply the taping base only where the tape will go, otherwise the bald areas will collect dirt and the skin will feel greasy. Also, don't use waterproof tape, only cloth or "coaches' tape" (commonly available in 1 ½-inch width). Following the procedure outlined in the photos, start with half-width strips, pinched at the center, that loop the base of the fingers. Next, bind these to the wrist. Finally, should extra reinforcement be necessary, apply selected lateral strips to tie the finger strips together. As you tape, flex the hand and wrist to stretch the skin, otherwise the tape will limit hand expansion and decrease jamming force. Tape loosely, especially around the wrist. Tight taping cuts circulation and hinders flexibility. Should you already have some "gobis," place a small piece of tape upside down over the abrasion to avoid ripping the scab off and losing your mind when you yank the tape off.

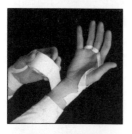

We have reviewed the salient points of physically climbing rock. The psychology and strategy of putting it all together, in conjunction with the process of safe rope management, can be done only after we have a working knowledge of equipment.

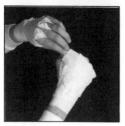

CHAPTER 4

Ropes, Anchors, and Belays

No climber ever gets very good without falling, and the falling climber is quickly killed without a solid, dependable protection system. The protection system combines bombproof anchors, ropes, connecting links, and alert partners to provide a sort of safety net which keeps him from hitting the ground. When you see a climber lashed to the cliff, all the odd-looking widgits and knots and whatnot can look complicated. Actually, the system is quite simple once you understand what the gear is and how it all works.

We see the climber moving up the dark cliff, secured by a rope and partner above. Who got that line up there? Somebody had to go first, and had he fallen, he would have died a horrible death – right? Wrong. The whole point of the rope and the attending gear, along with the hundred years that went into refining both technique and equipment, is to safeguard the climbers in the event of a fall. Rock climbing is not the pastime of nihilists or madmen; and when a world-class climber starts an extreme climb, he knows he will fall dozens, even hundreds of times. And he doesn't expect to get hurt. When the beginner starts up his first climb, the aim should be to have fun, not to cheat death.

In a nutshell: two climbers are tied into their respective ends of a 150- or 165-foot rope. Starting from the ground, one climber secures himself ("anchors") off to a tree, a big block, or perhaps arranges an anchor with some of his specialized gear fitted into a handy crack. In any case, his anchor is not what it should be unless it is *fail-safe*. The climbers then double-check themselves and each other to make sure harnesses, knots and anchors are properly arranged. Having decided on a particular passage, or "route" up the cliff – say a prominent crack – the other climber (the "leader") starts up, scaling the crack using hands and feet. The person on the ground (the "belayer") is meanwhile paying out the rope, using a technique or mechanical device which can stop the rope cold if need be.

Now the leader has gained a difficult section. She removes an appropriate piece of gear from her sling, places it in the crack, tugs it to get a good seating, clips a carabiner (snaplink) through the gear, then clips her rope through the carabiner. The leader now has an anchor which "protects" her for the climbing just overhead. On sport climbs the anchor is usually a bolt. Say she climbs three feet above the anchor and falls. The belayer checks the rope; the leader falls twice the distance she is above the anchor, or six feet. Since the rope stretches, she might fall inches more, but the belayer, lashed to her anchor and holding the fall, doesn't budge. The leader gathers her wits, and tries again.

A question. If the leader was only three feet above the anchor, why did she fall six feet plus the odd extra inches? First, for several reasons, the belayer cannot effectively take in the rope when the leader falls. His duty is to lock the rope off, so when the leader's weight comes onto the rope, the rope is held fast. If the leader is three feet above her anchor – or "protection" – she must first fall three feet to that protection. She still has three feet of slack out, so she falls *three more feet,* past the protection, for a total fall of six feet plus, depending on rope stretch. Hence the equation: the leader falls twice the distance above her last protection – and then some.

Carrying on, the leader places protection as she sees fit, always placing something before a difficult section. Sixty feet up the crack, she might have placed six or eight pieces of protection, depending on the difficulty and how secure she feels. Once the leader gains a convenient place to stop – say a ledge or a stout tree – she in turn arranges an anchor which is *absolutely fail-safe.* In this case, that means an anchor strong enough that, no matter what the other climber does, no matter how far he falls, he cannot cause the anchor to fail or come out. Now it is the leader's turn to "belay," or to take the rope in as the "second" follows the "pitch," or rope length. As the second follows, he removes all the protection which the leader placed, so it may be used on the next pitch. Since the belayer is taking up the rope as the second climbs up to her, the second can only fall as far as the rope stretches, usually only a foot or so, and mere inches if little rope is out. Once the second reaches the leader's anchor, or "belay," he in turn takes over the lead while the erstwhile leader continues belaying, and the process is repeated until the team finishes the route.

This is free climbing; note that the gear is not used for upward progress. The leader does not hang from the gear he places, rather he climbs using only hands and feet. In free climbing, the gear is used *only to safeguard against a fall.* The sport is to climb the rock using your own physical abilities. Rope and gear are what make the process sane and allow you to push your limits, saving your life should you fall off. Since falling has become an integral part of sport climbing, both the system and the gear are very reliable but, once again, it's all in how you use them and the most fundamental item, the rope, is no good if you're not on it or it's not anchored.

(page opposite)

Barry Ward battles up "Twin Crack" (5.12), at Granite Mountain, Arizona. Evolutions in technique and equipment now allow free climbing on what for years remained a sixth class route.

Bill Hatcher photo

THE ROPE

The rope is your lifeline, the primary piece of equipment to any climber. There is not a single serious climber whose life has not been saved by the rope many times over, so obviously modern climbing ropes are extremely reliable. Modern ropes have evolved a long way from the horsehair cords of the Carthaginians and from the dicey hemp lines the pioneers used around Zermatt and other alpine villages, where accounts of ropes snapping were many and tragic. Those early hemp ropes were replaced, first by flax, then with cotton varieties from European-grown fibers. Philippine "manila" and sisal from Mexico in turn succeeded these, and by World War II, a dense, three-strand "balloon" manila and a similar four-strand yachting rope (white line) were the only choices for an alpinist. During the war, Arnold Wexler of the U.S. Bureau of Standards concluded that for strength, elasticity, and durability, nylon was superior to all natural blends. Since 1945, all viable climbing ropes have been fashioned from nylon, or "perlon," a continental trade name for a plastic similar to nylon.

Though there are isolated cases of ropes being cut over sharp edges or chopped by rock fall, *a modern climbing rope has never simply broken from the impact of a fall.* Not in the United States, not in Europe; not anywhere. There is so much overkill built into the system that a rope in good condition has no chance of breaking whatsoever, no matter how severe a fall you take on it.

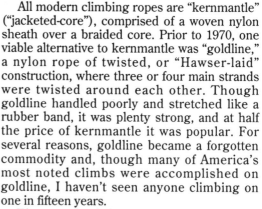

Kernmantle rope

All modern climbing ropes are "kernmantle" ("jacketed-core"), comprised of a woven nylon sheath over a braided core. Prior to 1970, one viable alternative to kernmantle was "goldline," a nylon rope of twisted, or "Hawser-laid" construction, where three or four main strands were twisted around each other. Though goldline handled poorly and stretched like a rubber band, it was plenty strong, and at half the price of kernmantle it was popular. For several reasons, goldline became a forgotten commodity and, though many of America's most noted climbs were accomplished on goldline, I haven't seen anyone climbing on one in fifteen years.

The standard dimensions of a modern climbing rope are 50 meters (165 feet) in length, and 9.5, 10, 10.5, 10.5, or 11 millimeters in diameter. There are 8- to 9-millimeter ropes which are intended to be used in pairs, as we will discuss in later chapters.

For decades, a 150-foot length rope was the standard. You can still purchase one of this length, but many routes have been engineered to require a 165-foot rope and, should you not have one when you need it, you will be cussing yourself for the few dollars saved in buying the shorter line.

Experts have conducted exhaustive studies on the various qualities of kernmantle ropes and have presented complicated graphs and formulas that seem impossible to understand. All the rare terminology and physics actually pertains to basic concepts, easily understood if simply explained. It all starts with the Union Internationale des Associations D'Alpinisme – UIAA – an international organization which sets minimum standards that commercially available rope should meet. Rope manufacturers provide both the UIAA findings and anything else they have been able to independently prove which might give them a marketing edge, but there are only a few specifications which relate directly to performance. The first relates to the number of falls sustained before the rope breaks in a UIAA-simulated drop test.

In this drop test, they tie an 80-kg iron block to the end of a 2.8-meter length of rope. They secure the other end to a fixed anchor, using .3 meters for the anchoring set up. They then raise the iron block 2.5 meters above the anchor point and drop it for a total free-fall of 5 meters. Common sense would tell us that a far longer fall would better gauge a rope's strength, but this is untrue. Kernmantle ropes have fantastic dynamic qualities, meaning they stretch when fallen on. Consequently, the longer the fall, the more rope there is out to absorb the dynamic energy generated by a falling climber. So it's these short falls, where the rope stretches comparatively little, that most stress the rope. Experts all agree that, for many reasons, the UIAA test is more severe than any fall you could possibly take in the field. Indeed, the UIAA simulated fall is so severe that it's about like tying off a dairy cow and marching her off the cliff's edge for a 300-footer. Yet a rope must withstand five UIAA test drops to be approved. Various manufacturers have gone on to make ropes they claim can withstand up to thirteen test falls, but since the UIAA approval means a rope is stronger than you'll ever need, the thirteen fall figure is superfluous, but it may indicate improved durability of the rope in extreme uses. The original kernmantle ropes were approved if they held only two UIAA drops yet, in actual practice, none of these ropes ever broke. So if a two-fall rope never broke, why would you need a thirteen-fall rope? You don't. If a rope is UIAA approved, it will never break in the field. The rest is sophistry.

The next spec is weight, which would be an important consideration if ropes of the same dimension differed much. Of the six leading rope manufacturers, the lightest 11 millimeter rope is 72 grams per meter, the heaviest, 79 grams per meter; so weight is a negligible factor.

"Static" or "working elongation" basically refers to how much a rope stretches when weighted with an 80-kg iron block. The leading ropes vary little here. "Impact force elongation" – how far the rope stretches when fallen on – is far more important, but is seldom listed in the statistics,

Never step on the rope. Debris can work through the sheath to cut and abrade the core. Stepping on someone's rope is an extreme breach of decorum.

Never lend your rope to anyone. Never buy a used rope. They don't fetch much money, and there's probably a good reason why someone wants to deal it. It may have been used to tow a backhoe out of a snowdrift.

Protect your rope from unnecessary exposure to the sun; save for huge falls that result in sheath damage and careless abuse, U.V. rays are the single most destructive force your rope is exposed to, so the more time spent in sunlight, the faster it will deteriorate. Always store your rope in a cool, dry, shady place.

Contrary to common opinion, alcohol, gasoline and other hydrocarbon solvents do not affect nylon chemically; and though you should avoid exposing your rope to any foreign substance, a little gasoline is not disastrous to you rope. Battery acid and other corrosives spell instant death to your line, however.

A certain amount of grime is unavoidable. When the rope becomes obviously dirty, machine wash it in cold or warm water and mild soap. Use the delicate fabric setting and rinse it for two cycles. Avoid the dryer.

Instead, string it up in a shady place, or flake it out on a clean floor and let the water evaporate naturally, normally accomplished in a couple of days.

Periodically inspect the rope for frays and soft spots by folding the rope carefully between your fingers and working it from one end to the other.

probably because it requires very sophisticated equipment to measure this. I.F.E. is a real consideration, since the longer a rope stretches, the farther you fall, which increases the likelihood of hitting something. The available specs from most leading manufacturers vary from about 6 to 7 percent I.F.E. Negligible, you say? Maybe, but the difference might be six inches in a forty-foot fall; and as rope physicist Dennis Turvill has pointed out, "a fall six inches longer can mean the difference between a good bar story and a compound fracture." Hopefully, impact force elongation will soon become a required statistic for all ropes.

"Impact force" pertains to the degree of shock the body receives at the end of a fall. This is crucial, since a greater force means a more jarring, painful stop. The UIAA specifies that the maximum impact force on the climber must be less than 2640 pounds for a single rope. Different brands can vary as much as 25 percent, so some thought should be directed to this statistic.

Another factor is whether a rope has been treated with a waterproofing compound. Compounds differ amongst manufacturers. Some are paraffin-based and come off the rope quickly. The better coatings are of silicone and various fluorochemicals, the latter being the best for durability. Though nothing can keep a rope dry in a deluge, tests prove that coated ropes are 33 percent more abrasion-resistant than uncoated ropes. Also, coating greatly reduces the ability of the rope to absorb damaging U.V. rays; and for these two reasons, coatings do more for a rope's longevity than the number of falls they allegedly hold.

Different sheath characteristics – the tightness of the weave, and whether the sheath slips much – directly affect how a rope handles. Ropes prone to excessive kinking, which are stiff and hold knots poorly, and which get twisted and spin a suspended climber, are really dastardly things to use. Unfortunately, it is difficult to determine a rope's handling characteristics when it is brand new, and there is little objective information which honestly pegs these qualities. Moreover, a rope which in the retail shop handles like silk might prove to be a "corkscrew" once you have used it. The sheath might shift a lot, or it may stiffen or soften up after only moderate use. Ultimately, a climber is left to review the available literature and experiment with other ropes, drawing conclusions accordingly. Fortunately, most of the ropes currently available work very well.

Since any UIAA-approved rope is stronger than you'll ever need, most climbers tend to buy the cheapest UIAA-approved rope they can find, since the majority of climbers don't understand the implications of all the attending statistics. The ideal rope would stretch little when weighted, would have a low impact force, would handle like a mink's pelt, would weigh one pound, would fit in your back pocket and would cost around five dollars. No one rope has all these characteristics. Ropes range in price from $130 to $200. Traditionally, most of the ropes sold in North America were imported from Europe. The popularity of sport climbing has spawned at least four American manufacturers who make good climbing ropes, usually at a lower price than the imported models.

Climbing ropes are both durable and fragile. Despite the astronomical tensile strength of kernmantle ropes, they are made of supple nylon, which is easily damaged when even slightly abused. Since you're hanging your all on the rope, you'll want to pay extremely close attention to the use and care of your lifeline.

Chris Gore, technical consultant for Beal ropes, has laid down the following guidelines for a rope's life expectancy: "A rope should be retired after four years, even if it's used only on holidays. For normal, weekend use: two years. For multi-fall use: three months of constant use or up to a year of part-time use. Any rope suffering a long fall of great severity should be retired immediately." While not definitive, this is certainly sound advice.

A rope bag is an inexpensive and very practical way of storing your rope. There's a lot of garbage rattling around the normal pack, car, or house, and the rope bag protects your cord from these until the moment you start climbing; and the rope is re-bagged once you're done. Some climbers use them to store the slack *during* a climb, but most will find this a bit much. In extreme instances – say, climbing just above a wind-whipped ocean – a rope fed out of a rope bag is a saving grace. For sport climbing, a rope bag (that rolls out into a rope tarp) protects the rope from the dirt, and makes it convenient to move the rope from route to route.

WEBBING

Originally used to batten down gear on PT boats during World War II, nylon webbing (flat rope, or "tape") is an integral part of a climber's equipment. When tied into a loop (forming a "runner" or "sling") its applications range from gear slings and extensions for anchors, to makeshift harnesses, all to be further explained. For now, understand that for fifth class climbing, webbing comes in four widths: 2,

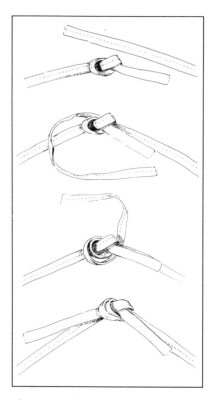

The Ring Bend

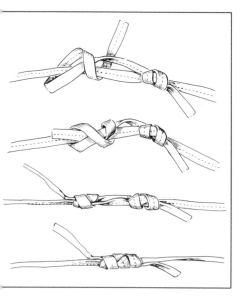

Double Fisherman's

1-, ¹¹⁄₁₆-, and ⅚-inch. This webbing is often times tubular (hollow inside) and is incredibly strong. Utilizing modern fiber technology, super high-strength Spectra webbing is also available.

The most common use for webbing is for quickdraws and runners. Quickdraws come pre-sewn with a carabiner loop on each end, and are used to connect the rope into chocks or bolt anchors. Runners are tied or sewn in single loops made from about four to six feet of 1-, 5⁄8-, or 9⁄16-inch webbing, and are carried over one shoulder and under the opposite arm. The length will vary according to your size. The runner should never be so long that when carried, the bottom hangs below your waist, where it can easily snag on the rock, or even on your foot during a high step. Some climbers also carry double-length runners that are folded in half and then carried over the shoulder. Runners and quickdraws are used somewhere on virtually every climb, and it is a common error not to have enough. Some sources advise you to carry upwards of a dozen runners, but such advice invariably comes from those hawking climbing gear. Most climbers find seven to ten quickdraws and four or five runners more than adequate for all but exceptional cases.

Sewn slings and runners are becoming increasingly popular. The pre-sewn joints dispense with the knot, which is sometimes a hindrance. Their disadvantage is that they cannot be untied and connected with other slings to form a king-sized runner should the need arise, as it will.

Be cautious when using any sewn gear. In their original state the stitching is stronger than the webbing. However, the stitching abrades with use, and the overall strength is significantly reduced. It is a good practice to inspect any sewn webbing periodically. Most climbers carry a collection of both sewn and tied slings.

Webbing is generally sound until, from exposure to U.V. and general wear, it becomes abraded or stiff to the touch. If there's any doubt, pitch it. Though it's exceptionally rare, old slings have broken. And never use a sling you have found or fleeced off the crag. A sling is usually left because someone "bailed," decided to retreat. The runner was secured to an anchor, the rope doubled through the runner, and down they went. To retrieve the rope, they had to pull it through the sling; and pulling even fifty feet of rope through a sling can generate sufficient friction and heat to greatly diminish the strength of the webbing by melting the nylon. Visual inspection can tell you much – faded color or notable stiffness, for instance – but not all. Some climbers like to date their slings with a felt pen, and pitch them after one year's use. Remember to treat your slings with the respect due your rope.

A ring bend or water knot has been the traditional knot to tie runners together. However, nylon webbing is slippery, particularly when new, and it's not unheard of for the ring bend to loosen with time and come untied. A good practice with any gear is to routinely check your knots, especially the ring bend. A much more secure (albeit permanent and bulky) knot for both rope and webbing is the double fisherman's, or grapevine knot. Though it is possible to untie this knot, it becomes increasingly more arduous as the runner is weighted and stressed. Since the grapevine knot is a "cinch" knot – meaning the tighter you pull, the tighter it gets – just a few climbs is usually enough to make this knot more or less impossible to untie. Should any knot prove difficult to untie, some gentle taps with a smooth rock will often loosen it enough to get the fingers in. There is more on runners in Chapter 5: The Art of Leading.

CONNECTING THE CLIMBER TO THE ROPE

For decades, climbers tied the rope directly around their waists. It was a simpler era. Climbers also avoided taking falls. The main disadvantage with the bowline, the standard knot used years ago for tying in, is that it's very uncomfortable when weighted, tending to cut into a climber's side or work up the rib cage when fallen on. The bowline-on-a-coil is a more comfortable variation of the bowline that is worthwhile to know, but rarely used. Disadvantages: the knot uses a lot of rope, is a hindrance on long pitches, and, like the bowline, the bowline-on-a-coil cannot, by definition, be used if there is a need to rappel or anchor to the cliff independently of the rope. Particularly as falling became an accepted side of the sport, and with the advent of tubular webbing and sewn harnesses, the bowline-on-a-coil is almost never seen. Still, it is absolutely secure and works dependably in a pinch. For those reasons alone it is essential to know.

Swami-belt

Occasionally you still see a climber from the seventies climbing in a swami belt, which consists of four or five turns of wide webbing around the waist, secured with a ring bend. The wraps should be snug but not constricting. It takes some practice to tie the ring bend, still keeping the swami snug. A loose swami-belt is hazardous as it can creep up one's torso, inhibiting breathing and crimping the rib cage. The basic swami was originally constructed from 1-inch webbing, but

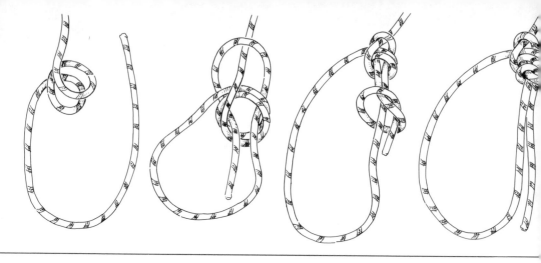

The Bowline with a half-hitch check knot.

as soon as 2-inch webbing was available, everyone switched over to the wider, stronger, and more comfortable webbing. Tie the ring bend with a generous tail – plenty of extra webbing beyond the knot. Once tied, slide the knot around your back, occasionally inspecting it for peace of mind. Falling on a swami or simple rope tie-in is not as uncomfortable as it may sound; with the tightening rope the swami pulls up snugly underneath the rib cage. Hanging for very long on a simple swami is distinctly uncomfortable – even dangerous, however – and most climbers will prefer the comfort and safety of either leg loops or a sewn harness.

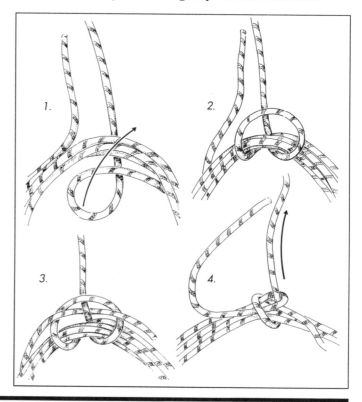

The Bowline-on-a-coil. Finish up with a half-hitch check knot as illustrated above.

Leg Loops

Leg loops are usually made of broad webbing, sewn into channels for each leg and connected in front by a bridge sling, short, and sewn to each channel. In the back, a keeper sling feeds off one leg, goes up and over the swami, and clips into the other leg, keeping the loops from drooping in back. The tie-in passes through both the swami and the bridge sling on the loops. The tie-in knot should be snug to both.

The benefit of leg loops is that whenever you put your weight on the equipment – and the times are many – that weight is taken principally on the legs rather than the back. The varieties of leg loops available are countless: padded, fleece-lined, day-glo colors, some even faced with sham animal hide. But in actual design, they are all fundamentally the same. Make certain they fit correctly: snug, but not constricting when the legs are fully flexed. Put them on and do a few deep knee bends. If they bind the thighs, too tight; if they droop, too loose. Reputable brands are made in sizes from extra small to extra large. One size is bound to fit you perfectly.

When leg loops are used in conjunction with a 2-inch swami you enjoy the strongest tie-in system possible, at least twice as strong as any other link in the climbing chain, including the rope.

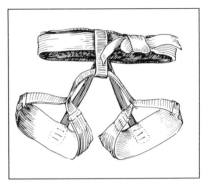

Leg loops and webbing swami belt

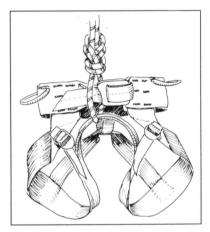

Sewn harness

Harnesses

Anyone who plans to climb more than once or twice should invest in a quality, properly-fitting sewn harness. A harness features a waist strap and leg loops that are sewn into one unit. The harness has come into its own only recently. Though they've been around for twenty-five years, they were of such questionable quality that a popular instruction manual published less than a dozen years ago barely mentioned them. The first batch were cumbersome, uncomfortable, shoddily made, and put withering constriction on genitalia during a fall. Others tended to leave one hanging sideways even upside down after a fall. Present-day harnesses are featherweight, stronger than necessary, and fit so well it's hard to remember you even have one on. There are hundreds to choose from, and with a little shopping it's easy to find the right one. Most manufacturers make several models – for alpine climbing, general rock climbing, and sport climbing; it is the latter two styles that are often the lightest and most comfortable.

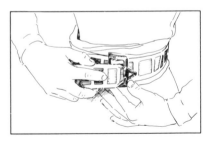

Many harnesses require some special buckling procedure in order for them to be secure, perhaps similar to the double pass-through illustrated here.

A good harness should be easy to put on. During all-around use, it should be comfortable and not feature unnecessary buckles, joints, or any pressure points which can abrade the climber like a burr under the saddle. A good fit is critical to the performance of a harness, but it might be impossible if your physique is even a little off the norm (although manufacturers currently make harnesses specifically for men, women, and kids). You might have to try on several to get the right one. Both for women and men who cannot attain a perfect fit: several manufacturers sell "harnesses" which are actually sewn swami belts and leg loops, sold separately. By buying a component-based combination, you can usually find a perfect fit. A harness is a very personal, specialized piece of gear, so general craftsmanship should reflect this.

Gear racking loops are nice, but if possible, avoid adjustable harnesses which are often overbuilt and feature superfluous buckles and doodads. Many harnesses have individual methods of threading the rope through them for the best tie-in. Likewise, most harnesses have some safety procedure which, if neglected, render the harness potentially dangerous – a double pass-through buckle, for example. Read any instructions carefully, follow them to the letter, and always double-check your harness setup before you leave the ground. There is still another problem. Given the morning coffee, the ready canteen, the hiking and exertion, even the world-class climber will at sometime yearn for bladder relief; and neither the brash nor the bashful find any glory in just "holding it." This presents little problem for your harnessed male. Most harnesses are pretty free up front – aside from the tie-in knot – and a male's plumbing is readily deployed and can normally negotiate these obstacles, even on a wall. For women, special harnesses are available where the leg loops can drop out while the waist belt stays fastened.

One other type of harness bears mentioning, but in almost twenty years of climbing I have never seen someone use a chest harness, in either sport climbing or rescue work. In sport climbing, their applications are few, if any, but there's no harm done if you have surplus cash and want to experiment with one. Supposedly, they are useful on exceptionally overhanging artificial routes, where one spends hours, or days, dangling upside down, or for rope soloing (a risky undertaking for experts only). Chest harnesses have generally been avoided, first because they are needless, and second because upper body mobility is crucial on difficult free climbs.

Tying One On

There are probably a dozen knots suitable for connecting the end of the rope to the swami or harness, but over the years, the figure eight follow-through (Flemish Bend, or double figure eight) has become standard. And for good reason. The figure eight has one of the highest

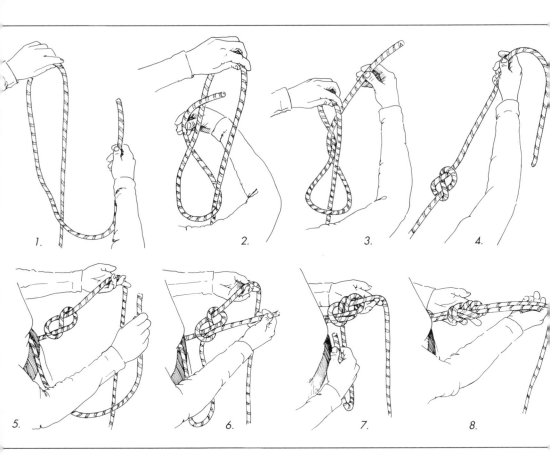

strengths of all climbing knots, it does not have a tendency to come untied, and it is easy to visually inspect. Like the majority of knots used in climbing (there are only about six primary knots, and another ten or so specialty or trick knots), the figure eight follow-through is a "cinch" knot: the tighter you pull, the tighter the knot becomes. Like all knots, the figure eight follow-through must be double-checked before relying on it.

The standard tie-in: the figure eight follow-through. Be sure to loop the rope around both the waist belt or swami and the sling that bridges between the leg loops.

CARABINERS

Also known as biners (bean-ers) or krabs, a carabiner is an aluminum alloy snap-link used to connect various pieces of the climbing chain. They come in three basic designs: oval, D, and asymmetrical D. The D and asymmetrical D have the advantage of greater strength, they open easier when weighted (important in artificial climbing), and the rope flows easier through them. Many climbers always position any D or asymmetrical D carabiner so the gate opens down and away from the rock. That way, the rope feeds through the bigger end. The oval can be positioned with gate up or down, but it's easier to clip the rope in if the

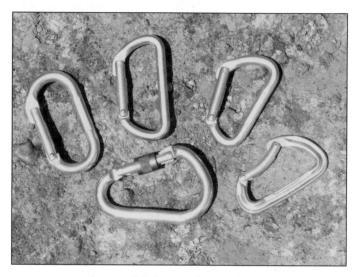

Carabiners (clockwise from the left): oval, D, modified D, bent gate, locking type

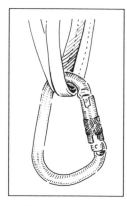

Locking carabiner

gate opens down. Ovals are becoming less and less prominent, but they are still superior for racking wired tapers and for aid climbing. A recent innovation are carabiners with a quickdraw sewn directly into the body, to ensure proper loading on the carabiner and to prevent the quickdraw from unclipping from the carabiner.

Each biner features a spring-loaded gate which opens inward, accepting rope or runner, and which snaps closed when the pressure is released from the gate. All carabiners are designed to be weighted along the major axis – lengthwise – and in this manner, they are exceptionally strong, some with upwards of 5,000 pounds breaking strength. The strength of carabiners is usually marked somewhere on the gate, generally in kilo Newtons (kN). Under no circumstances should the biner ever be set up so there is pressure pulling straight out on the gate, as the biner is then only as strong as the pin upon which the gate rotates – usually under 500 pounds.

Until the climbing explosion in the mid-seventies, it was common to find poorly-machined biners in climbing stores, and one had to use discretion in buying anything but the name-brand carabiners. Commercial competition is now so fierce that a shoddy biner has little chance of making it to the shelves, but inspect before buying just the same. The gate should have fluid action, should pivot strongly on the axis pin, and should mesh perfectly with the mouth of the biner. The finish should be smooth and burr free, and the inside radius of the carabiner must not be too small or it will severely stress the rope. The strength should be at least 4400 pounds (20 kN) with the gate closed, and 1540 pounds (7kN) with the gate open.

Though durable, biners do wear out. Whenever the gate is bent askew, the spring action becomes soft or stiff, or the body becomes noticeably gouged, pitch it. And if you ever drop a carabiner even ten feet, invisible fatigue cracks can result which greatly diminish the strength. Most biners are made of aircraft-quality, 7000 series aluminum alloy, with a useful life span exceeding ten years. But effects from normal work hardening can shorten the life span. Metal fatigue is a much-bandied word that is usually misinterpreted. Metal does not get tired. The term metal fatigue refers to cracks in the material that develops over time with repeated loading of the carabiner. And if the carabiner is cracked, you obviously pitch it. Corrosion is the arch foe of aluminum, and manifests in a white powdery dust. Climbers active on sea cliffs should take special note of this. If there's ever any doubt that the carabiner is defective, just pitch it. If you don't, you'll inevitably find yourself at a crux with only one biner left – the dubious one. You'll clip that old, corroded, creaking krab into the anchor and cry a river because you were too cheap or stupid not to have retired a piece of gear whose time was up.

It's not unheard of for a carabiner to mysteriously come open at the worst possibly time. Whenever this is even a remote possibility, use two carabiners and turn them so the gates are opposing – so they can only open in opposite directions. A special "locking" carabiner was designed to safeguard against unwanted opening. It features a threaded or spring-loaded sleeve which fits over the mouth of the krab and prohibits its opening. Always use a locking carabiner for attaching your belay/rappel device to your harness. It's also a sound idea to clip into key anchors with a locking carabiner, or two carabiners with gates opposed, though many climbers don't bother doing so.

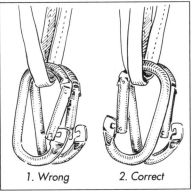

1. Wrong   2. Correct

Secure carabiners against unwanted opening:

1. the wrong way

2. gates in opposition

Gaining popularity is the "dogleg," or "bent-gate" biner. The gate is bowed in, and when depressed, gives a wider gate opening than other biners. The real advantage is when you're desperate and eye-to-eye with fixed protection. With the bent-gate krab you can slap the rope into the bowed gate; a little pressure and a jerk and the biner is clipped. Unfortunately, because the rope clips in so easily, it also unclips easily; so bent gate carabiners can be dangerous, particularly if the rope is running across the gate. More on carabiners and quickdraws in the next chapter.

Black Diamond Equipment has offered this advice per carabiner maintenance: "If gates are a bit sticky, cross pressure on the gate while open can straighten slightly. A dry silicone at the hinge, then blowing clean with gas station hose, works wonders (for gate action). This also works well with the lock ring or sleeve on locking biners. Don't use oil."

ANCHORS

The anchor is the fail-safe spot to which we attach ourselves; it is the single most important part of the climbing protection system. Normally this is to secure ourselves to the cliff, but not always. Commencing a climb, we may choose to "tie off" (anchor to) a tree or block on the ground. Anchors furnished by the terrain are called natural anchors, be they trees, chockstones, horns, or whatever. Artificial anchors are provided by specially-designed climbing hardware which exploit cracks and hollows in the rock. When the rock is barren of both natural anchors and cracks, a climber may drill a hole in the rock and place a bolt – a permanent anchor.

Anchors (say a sling wrapped around a tree) which can withstand force from any angle are called multidirectional anchors. Anchors such as runners over horns or flakes are only good for downward pull and these are called directional anchors.

NATURAL ANCHORS

Runners are vital in exploiting natural protection and can be looped around or over anything that can provide a solid anchor: knobs, spikes, flakes, through blocks, over chockstones, around trees, or other fixed objects. Sometimes it is handy to have a double runner (12 feet, carried in a double loop over your shoulder), though many climbers choose to simply tie or loop two normal-length runners together. Runners simply looped over protuberances can be

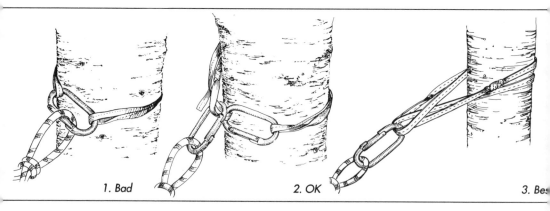

1. Bad   2. OK   3. Bes

ANCHORING TO A TREE:
1. Incorrect. This stresses the relatively weak gate of the carabiner.

2. Better, but the sling is overly stressed.

3. Best, especially when used with a locking biner.

marginal – fine for downward pull, but susceptible to slipping or being lifted off from lateral pull or rope drag. Whenever possible, tie the knob (or horn, spike, etc.) off by forming a slipknot in the runner, and cinching it snug. With flakes, pull the runner down behind the flake to where it is lodged between the flake and the wall. If all else fails, clip a piece of gear onto the bottom of the runner. A little extra weight can keep a runner from simply sliding off.

Common sense and sober judgement are necessary in determining if a natural anchor is good, or something less. With most climbers, a little experience makes this question pretty cut and dried. You usually know if a chockstone is loose, or whether a sling will slip off a knob, but not always. You wouldn't bother to place an anchor if you didn't need one, so always test the rock or tree or whatever if there are any doubts as to its strength. With potentially loose chockstones or flakes, test them gingerly, lest you pull them off on yourself or someone below.

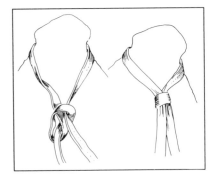

Slinging a horn with a slipknot on a runner

ARTIFICIAL ANCHORS – Nuts

Also known as chockstones, or simply chocks, nuts are metal wedges of various sizes and designs, strung with cable or rope, which fit into constrictions or cavities in the rock. Except for the more difficult artificial climbs, nuts have all but replaced pitons as the means of securing anchors in the rock. Prior to 1970, pitons were the standard way to obtain anchors. Pitons were originally made of soft iron, and because removal could ruin them, they were usually left "fixed" in the crack. American ingenuity came up with almost indestructible chrome-moly steel pitons around 1958. With these there evolved the American ethic of always removing your pitons, leaving the crack "clean" for the next party, not leaving a string of fixed pitons to aid and mark the way for later ascents. This provided for high adventure and, for those later ascents, a feeling similar to the pioneers who first climbed a route. But the new pitons really brutalized the rock. Repeated placement and removal had ruined more than one climb, leaving huge and unsightly "piton scars" – literally holes blasted into the rock – and nuts came to replace pitons none too soon. To the climber, there is aesthetic allure to a perfect crack rifling into the sky. That we can now climb these without ravishing their form is a testament to how far climbing has come. Nuts cause no damage to the stone; and many climbers find that "clean climbing" is a much more artistic and satisfying way to climb than hammering their way to the summit, or chasing a line of bolts up a face.

Tradition says that the modern chock evolved from the British technique of tying off natural chockstones in the cracks. This led to placing chockstones in the cracks and stringing runners over them. Next came machine nuts (found along the railroad tracks below the British crags) through which rope was slung. Sometime in the sixties someone began making nuts particularly for rock climbing. The first nuts were crude and had limited applications but once the wide use of nuts caught on in the early 1970s, the designs steadily improved to where now, in most cases, nuts can provide better anchors than driven pitons ever could.

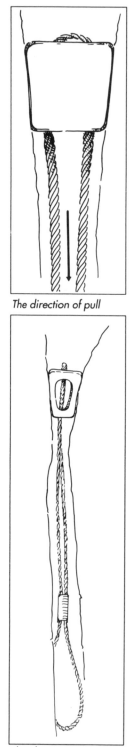

The direction of pull

The classic taper

When weighted, a nut will lodge in the narrowing slot in which it is placed. Obviously, a nut is placed with a certain direction of pull in mind, usually straight down. In some instances, a nut is placed so the direction of pull is straight out, or even straight up (explained later). Whatever the placement, the loop of sling or cable issuing from the nut can be considered an arrow which, when extended from the nut, clearly shows where the direction of pull should be.

Nuts are placed in a wide variety of cracks and hollows, so they come in many shapes and sizes. Still, nuts are basically variations of two themes: tapers, or stoppers; and hexentrics, or hexes. Both are designed to slot into constrictions, or bottlenecks in the crack. Placing a sound nut is relatively easy with a little practice, but keep these points in mind: 1) Try to select the nut which best matches the taper of the crack. 2) Set the nut so maximum surface area is on the rock (you don't want the nut lodged on just a few crystals). 3) Remember that usually – but not always – a bigger nut is more secure than a smaller one, if you have a choice. 4) Make sure the rock is solid where you set the nut. 5) Place the nut no deeper than is necessary to meet the above criteria. To do otherwise only makes removal difficult; it does not make the nut more secure. More tricks used in placing nuts will be further reviewed in Chapter 5: The Art of Leading. For now, we will examine the different types of nuts.

Tapers

These are made by dozens of different manufacturers, each giving a little different look to the one timeless design. The first tapers were much wider than they were thick. Now, virtually all tapers have adopted a boxier shape, better for several reasons, especially endwise placements. They vary from thumbnail-sized micros strung with what appears to be piano wire, to weighty, inch-and-a-half bombers strung with special "Spectra" cord which, pound for pound is "stronger than steel." Originally, all but the smallest tapers were strung with rope. Now, swaged cable has replaced rope for all but the largest-sized tapers. The cable gives us several advantages. It is generally stronger than rope of corresponding size. The stiff cable allows easier placement. Where a taper strung with rope will droop when held, the wired nut is like a knife which can be slotted with one hand; and the stiff cable allows a few inches of extra reach which can sometimes make an important difference.

Variations on the taper follow four basic patterns: the straight taper, the curved taper, the offset taper, and the micro brass or steel taper.

The straight taper is the original design. Even the smallest ones are stronger than one would think. The wider, or "face sides" are flat, and tapered down at the same angle. These are most useful in a crack whose sides taper uniformly, and where the slot best matches the taper of the nut. A good match means a good fit, and again, a good fit

Tapers

means most of the surface area of the nut is on the rock. A common error is to try to place the biggest taper the crack will accept. Much more important is finding the placement that seats solidly in the crack. The obvious bottleneck leaves little to chance; the nut locks in as if the crack was made for it, and the lip of the crack pinches off to prevent an outward pull from dislodging the nut. But when the crack is flared, or convoluted, or shallow, it often takes some fiddling to find the best placement – or any placement. All but the smallest tapers can be placed endwise as well, so try whatever works best. The better tapers feature slightly beveled edges which makes them easier to both place and remove. The rounded edges also increase purchase in marginal edge-contact placements. The two ends of the wire cable are secured with a swage (a piece of metal which is compressed around the cable), over which a rubber shrink-tube swage cover is secured, creating a very secure loop. Most manufacturers will in some manner color-code the sizes in its line. With practice, you will learn what color corresponds to what sized nut, and can then grab the right one quickly – a boon when the going's grim.

The curved taper has virtually replaced the straight taper in the medium to large range. One side is concave, the other convex. The theory is that most tapers are placed where the sides of the crack vary slightly. When placed and yanked on, the curved taper does a quasi-camming action on the convex side until it rotates into the best spot. The top of the concave side is milled flat, which with the camming action on the other side results in a three-point foundation once seated. They work especially well when the constriction is gently curved. This sounds confusing, even to me, but simply place a curved taper and all will be clear.

The curved taper can also be placed endwise, both ends forming a straight taper as thick as the next widest nut; so you have the best of both worlds. The curve of the taper varies with each manufacturer. When the curving is less pronounced, they are generally easier to remove.

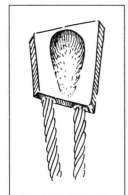

Offset taper

A useful variation to the taper is the offset, available only in small sizes, and tapered on all sides, forming an asymmetrical trapezoid. I didn't understand that either. Basically, one edge is thicker than the other – or "offset." (Better get one and look at it.) These offsets are perfect for flaring cracks which narrow in the back, in which a straight or curved taper will find scant purchase. Be warned, however, that offsets are less forgiving in marginal placements, and unless you've got most of the surface area firmly locked, offsets can "pop" quicker than you can say "watch me." Originally viewed as a specialty item for use on big artificial routes, many free climbers carry a few for those "oddball" placements, where nothing else works quite as well.

Tapers are made in remarkably small sizes, most often "straight taper" in profile. The super-thin but strong cable on these tiny nuts is either silver-soldered or cast with the nut, resulting in cable strengths that exceed those of the body of the nut. Some are made of hard brass, even stainless steel; others are cast from "investment cast" brass. In a fall, the harder brass and stainless tends to break the surrounding rock away if the rock is poor. The investment brass is somewhat malleable, so it is less likely to break the rock and seats well owing to increased friction and bite. When the rock is diamond hard, the malleable brass taper may deform and shear through the placement, so there's a trade-off involved. Most practiced climbers carry both kinds and vary use according to the need.

A manufacturer of these tiny tapers, Wild Country, offers the following advice: "The limiting factor with small nuts is not their lower strength, but rather their small surface area which concentrates the impact of a fall so intensely that when they fail, it is likely because they rip out, not through broken wires." Be aware, though, that with long use, the cable usually frays beneath the head of the nut.

There are other modifications on the taper that you'll see as well. The faces of some of the smaller tapers have been gouged out to form a teardrop cutaway, or a scoop. This supposedly adds purchase when the nut is placed between a cluster of crystals. Other tapers have been filed this way and that, are banana-shaped, squat, tall, titanium, plastic, even wooden. But they all work by being slotted into a constriction and weighted in the direction of the cable or cordage.

Hexentrics

Hexentrics

Six-sided and barrel-shaped, hexentrics – or simply "hexes" – are good for wide cracks, bottlenecks, and when the crack is more suited for a round (as opposed to tapered) nut. The sides are shaped so they can be wedged in three different attitudes, camming fairly well even in parallel-sided cracks. Placed endwise, both ends are tapered, and the hex is slotted like a big taper. Since Chouinard Equipment (now Black Diamond Equipment) introduced them in 1971 they have steadily evolved. The newest batch feature angled sidewalls for better endwise placements.

Since the introduction of spring-loaded camming devices (SLCDs), hexes, long the only viable nut for wide cracks, have almost disappeared, but not altogether. For the true bottleneck placement, a bomber hex is still the strongest nut in town. Not one has ever broken in use. They are relatively inexpensive, and many times can find better purchase than any high-tech SLCDs. Consequently, most climbers carry a selection on their rack. They come in ten sizes.

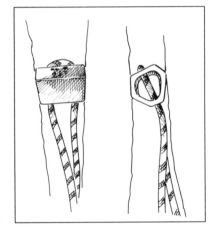

Hexentrics, placed as a chock (left), and as a cam (right)

Lowe Tri-cams

Many climbers have considered this odd-looking nut just a piece of esoterica, but some climbers swear by them. The design creates a tripod with two parallel camming rails flat against one side of the crack or pocket, and the fulcrum point on the other. They're uniquely good in horizontal placements, providing both cam and wedging action. Tri-cams also work well in desert sandstone, the point digging

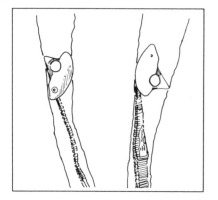

Tri-cams, placed as a chock (left), and as a cam (right)

into the soft rock. In certain shallow pocket placements, they have no peer. They come in eleven sizes.

Stringing your nuts

All but the smallest hexes and tapers are made to accept a length of rope rather than a swaged cable. This is particularly useful in hexentrics because it allows an unrestricted camming action of the nut. Originally, both tapers and hexentrics were strung with various dimensions of nylon rope. Once Spectra cord hit the market, everyone shifted to it because it proved to be much stronger than nylon of the same size. Presently, most nuts machined to accept cordage have holes drilled for the standard 5.5-mm Spectra line. Gemini, a blend of Spectra and Kevlar, allows light and durable use of the otherwise slippery Spectra. Both fiber blends are available in 5.5-mm for chock cord and in flat stock for runners and quick draws.

Use the double or triple fisherman's to secure the cord because it is a knot that is relatively permanent. (Note: the manufacturer recommends use of the triple fisherman's for Spectra cord.) Keep the knot near the carabiner end of the loop so that it does not interfere with the nut placement and, by its stiffness, tends to keep the loop open to accept a biner readily.

Removing Nuts

Removing, or "cleaning" nuts is sometimes nasty work, especially if they've been fallen on. The best strategy in cleaning any nut is to first examine the placement with an eye toward simply reversing the path by which the nut was placed. Sometimes, just a tap with a carabiner can jar a set nut free. If the nut cannot be wiggled loose and lifted out, a moderate upward jerk will often free it.

If the nut is buried deep in a crack, you may have to really yard on it. Be warned that this can bend any cable which, done repeatedly, can not only ruin the nut's symmetry but weaken the cable; and you can actually break the cable on the smaller tapers. Always keep an eye peeled for frays in the cable, especially around the swage, and above the holes in the top of the nut. The broken strand not only diminishes strength, but these "wild hairs" can prick the fingers something ferocious. When this occurs, just pitch them.

As an aid to tapping out well-lodged nuts, cleaning tools are made in a dozen different forms, all thin and blade-shaped and all invaluable in cleaning a lodged taper. A little experimentation will show just how to pry and tap out stubborn nuts. If all else fails, set the cleaning tool against the nut and tap it with a rock, large chock, or other object to set the nut free. Make sure to attach a keeper sling to your cleaning tool: ⅛-inch diameter nylon accessory cord will do.

With visions of a shiv buried in their belly, some climbers are loath to carry what is essentially a blunt knife, fearing a fall might somehow result in a puncture from the cleaning tool. Though I've never once heard of this happening, more than a few climbers are not looking to be first. Whatever, tapers are often left on climbs when a cleaning tool would more often than not have gotten the nut free.

SPRING-LOADED CAMMING DEVICES

In 1967, Greg Lowe invented the first camming device for protecting rock climbs. Greg's version was a bust, but it got the concept out there. Finally, in 1978, Ray Jardine improved upon the concept and started marketing "Friends," and climbing has never been the same.

Friends work so well that when they first came out many past rock masters thought they were a means of cheating.

Climbs which for twenty years were feared owing to poor protection were now reduced to mere physical endeavors. Friends had taken the horror right out of them, for you could place a Friend whenever you wanted, and the placement was generally bomber. No longer did a climber cast off on a rugged lead hoping he could get in good nuts, and hoping the nuts were somewhere near the crux. Now you could throw in a Friend whenever the going got tough. And they were dead easy to place. Gone forever were the days when a climber was greasing out of an overhanging crack, trying to wiggle a hex in where the crack just wouldn't have it and there was no going on without it.

Spring-Loaded Camming Devices (from the left): Black Diamond Camalot, Metolious TCU, H.B. Quad Cam, Wild Country Flexible Friend, regular Friend.

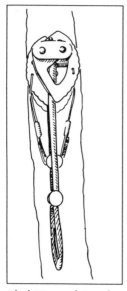

Black Diamond Camalot in a typical parallel-sided placement.

The great benefit of spring-loaded camming devices (SLCDs) is that the crack need not constrict to afford a placement. In fact, a parallel-sided crack is where a SLCD is best placed and where all other nuts fail to work even remotely as well. Since Friends first hit the market, they have been copied by everyone with a machine shop; now there are Camalots, TCUs, Quad Cams, Aliens, Big Dudes and others. Some, like TCUs (three cam units), are designed specifically for thin cracks. They have three rather than four cams, and their lower profile allows a better range of protection in narrow cracks and pockets, but the lack of a fourth cam sacrifices some strength and stability. Camalots feature a double axis for the cams, resulting in a wider range of application for SLCDs of the same size. Flexible Friends supplant the rigid stem with a cable stem, giving it a lower profile for thin cracks, and making it far better for horizontal placements. Still, SLCDs all work on the same principal.

Wild Country, the manufacturer of Friends, has offered the following advice regarding SLCDs, but the advice is so sound that it applies to all protection. Parenthetical additions are mine. "The security of climbing protection has always depended on the experience and knowledge of the climber placing it. Climbing hardware is only a tool, and knowledge about how the tool works properly is important to achieving its greatest performance. With this knowledge, if you have to make a risky gear placement, you'll do so out of intelligence and not out of ignorance. Per SLCDs: always align stem and cams in the direction of loading (i.e., direction of pull). Don't offset the cams – they have little holding power that way. Realign the cams evenly. Avoid a "tipped" placement, where the cams are placed wide open, and rocking on the cam tips. In such a position there is little room for further expansion, and stability is poor. Always use a sling long enough to ensure you won't move the SLCD by climbing past it. (All SLCDs have the tendency to either "walk" in, or walk out of the crack when even nominal rope drag is pulling on them. A sling connected to the end of the SLCD alleviates the problem.) Don't allow the cams to invert – inverted cams won't hold. Don't stuff a "too large" SLCD into an undersized placement; it may make removal difficult. (It may make removal impossible. Ideally, the cams should be zero to fifty percent deployed, with the device placed in the most uniformly parallel section of the crack. You

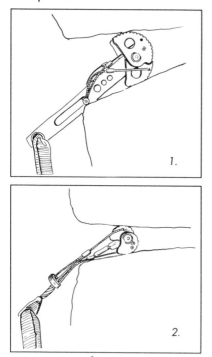

1.

2.

1. Incorrect use of a rigid-stem Friend in a horizontal placement risks shearing the stem.
2. It's much safer to use a flexible-stem unit.

must reduce the cam ratio to pull out the SLCD. If you force the SLCD into an undersized placement, you've torqued the cams to their minimum displacement. Since they are spring-loaded, the cams are never passive, so you can't simply slide the SLCD out, and you have no way of reducing the profile any further because it's already at its minimum. So you've just lost an expensive piece of gear.) Never place a rigid-stem SLCD so that the stem is not aligned with the direction of pull; especially avoid placements where the stem is loaded over an edge, where a fall can either bend or break the unit. Referring to placements when the stem is not in the direction of pull: bottoming cracks should be avoided as they make cleaning (removal) difficult and may hinder stem alignment during a fall. Flexible Friends will work in such positions, but stems aligned in the direction of pull are always more secure. (And what happens when you encounter a flared or bottoming crack and you can't avoid it? You try to place a taper or a hex. If impossible, you place a SLCD with a flexible shaft and hope it doesn't rip out.) Always regard flexible stems as less predictable than rigid stems. ("Predictable" here means the rigid stem SLCDs rip out less frequently when fallen on.) Four camming surfaces are generally more secure than three. (Sometimes the crack is too shallow to "sink" the SLCD, so one or more cams are hanging out of the crack. Such placements are very suspect.)

These remarks apply to all SLCDs, save one. Black Diamond's Camalots can be placed in their fully open, or "umbrella" configuration – essentially placed like a hex. A hex will generally be better here, but the Camalot has this capacity. Other SLCDs do not.

The twin-axle Camalots are the only SLCDs that can be used as a passive chock.

Sliding Nuts

There is a last, specialized genre of protection that combines aspects of the taper and the SLCD. They all share some form of inverted taper that is fixed to a cable. A second taper, inverted the other way, slides up and down the face of the first taper, controlled by a spring loaded cable. Owing to the sliding taper, the device has a variable range and can conform to the exact dimensions of the placement. In rather fast-paced evolution, the first of these units, Sliders, led to Quickies, Rock 'n Rollers, LoweBalls, and Cobras, among others. Though this is esoteric and specialized equipment, they all work like magic in narrow, shallow, parallel-sided fissures.

A million words and as many photos are both poor substitutes for grabbing a handful of nuts and going to a crag to practice placing them. Find several cracks at ground level and experiment to find how the aforementioned principals work, how to spot the best placements and learn what nut best fits where. Clip a runner into them, step on them, pull on them, discover just how good, or bad, they are. And don't expect expertise in an afternoon. Better than twenty years have gone into refining the modern nut, and statistically, an experienced climber not given to rashness has little chance of hurting himself. But there is no sport on the face of the earth less forgiving to him who makes a major mistake or oversight in regard to safety. You can get killed in a real

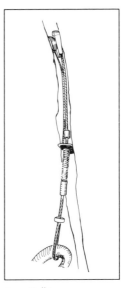

LoweBall in use.

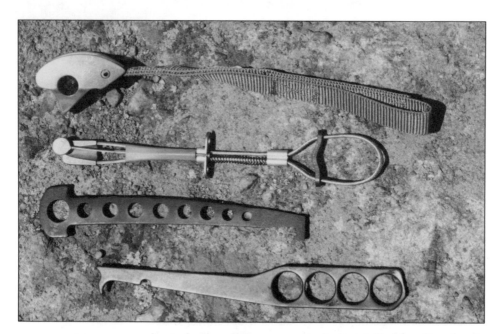

From top to bottom:

Lowe Tri-cam, LoweBall, a couple of cleaning tools

hurry by ignoring any aspect of proper climbing. So when it comes time to test your own judgement on whether a nut is good – whether you should trust your life to it – do so only after you feel confident you can make the right decision. And the only way for a novice to gain this confidence is to practice nutcraft where it doesn't count – near the ground.

Wide Crack Anchors

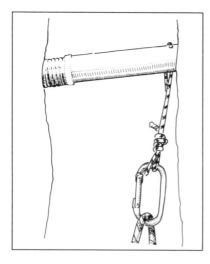

The BigBro is available in sizes to fit up to a 12-inch crack.

Wide cracks – those over four or five inches – have traditionally proved difficult to provide anchorage. Large "tube" chocks that appeared in the early seventies replaced the huge pitons that hitherto had provided a semblance of security. The tubes required a slight constriction to work well, however, and with the introduction of Friends, backyard machine shops produced monster Friends. Now commercially available as Big Dudes, these SLCDs, while heavy, bulky, and certainly expensive, still provide good security in the wider cracks. Also available for wide cracks is the BigBro, a tube that works best in parallel-sided cracks, is incredibly strong, compact, and less costly. A push button releases the spring-loaded inner sleeve, the tube is bridged across to both sides of the crack, and a threaded ring is spun to lock it all to size. A sling on one end provides the means to clip in.

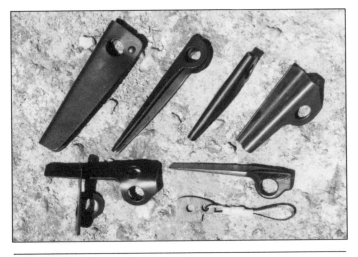

PITONS (clockwise from top left):

Angles give a three-point contact to the rock – the back, or "spine," and the two edges of the channel. Three sizes are shown here (top left).

Designed and produced by Ed Leeper, Leeper pins (top right) are much cherished by sixth class aficionados. The Z-shaped cross-section and offset eye give added bite in vertical cracks and enable other pitons – often small angles – to be stacked in the Z's breech.

The archetypal piton is the forged Lost Arrow (middle right), the eye centered and at a right angle to the blade. Heftier than blades and bugaboos, Lost Arrows are fashioned after the original John Salathe design.

The smallest piton is the RURP: Realized Ultimate Reality Piton. The RURP (bottom right) is only used in extreme artificial climbing, and is useful in incipient seams where its thin profile can chisel in, many times creating its own placement. Since RURPs are often impossible to remove, a wire loop ensures their continued use when fixed.

Bugaboos (horizontal, lower left) and knifeblades (vertical, lower left) are of the same design, bugaboos being thicker than the slender knifeblades. The right-angle eye allows placement in corners.

All these pitons are available in a variety of sizes.

PITONS

Pitons ("pins" or "pegs") are steel devices, usually spike-shaped, which are hammered into cracks to secure anchors. The shapes are many, but every modern piton has an eye through which a carabiner is clipped. A recreational climber today might frequent a popular sport climbing area for five years and never hear the ring of a piton being driven. Chocks, SLCDs, and bolts have made pitons unnecessary in almost all cases. But for big artificial climbs, and now and again in free climbing, pitons still have their place. Regardless, the ranks of climbers experienced in placing pitons is shrinking, and the number of accidents as a result of misplaced trust in fixed piton anchors shows the need for developing pitoning skills.

Prior to World War II, pitons were made of malleable soft iron so they could conform to the crack. Even one placement would maul their shape, and they were usually left in situ, or "fixed," since removal would destroy them. The most common soft steel piton today's climber will run across is the ring-angle, a pin of channel design with a welded ring. Obviously these are very old, and in addition to being of questionable security, the welded ring design may fail at relatively low loads. There really is no practical way to test such pitons. It's best to assume them to be worthless.

In 1946, a Swiss expatriate named John Salathe hand-tooled pegs from Model-T axle stock for the first ascent of Lost Arrow Spire in Yosemite Valley. Tradition says these Salathe pins were the first ever made from hard steel. In the fifties, Chuck Wilts invented the "knife-blade," a wafer-thin peg he fashioned from chrome molybdenum ("chrome-moly") steel. Like Salathe's, these hard steel pins could withstand repeated placement and removal, enabling climbers to scale multi-day climbs with a limited selection, rather than lugging a duffel bag full of soft iron. In the late fifties, Yvon Chouinard began manufacturing chrome moly pitons in his mom's back yard. He quickly expanded and by the early sixties any climber could purchase state-of-the-art chrome-moly pitons. That the first ascent of Yosemite's mightiest walls corresponded with the availability of good pitons was no fluke. While every other facet of climbing technology has steadily evolved, pitons have changed little in the last twenty-five years – neither in design or construction. Chouinard had it down by 1962.

Various European manufacturers still market pitons, but in the United States, what was Chouinard Equipment – now known as Black Diamond – has totally locked this limited market, and is the only company making them on any kind of scale. Black Diamond makes pitons in four different shapes. Each model is either stamped or forged of alloy steel, and, for better or worse, all are far more enduring than the hardest granite.

As mentioned, pitons are virtually never used in sport climbing. The one exception is climbers making first ascents. It is rare even for them to use them, but in the case of a hole or a thin, parallel-sided crack, sometimes only a piton can secure the desired protection, although in most cases nowadays, leading climbers just place bolts where they can't get in good chock protection (dreadfully, sometimes even where they can). To preserve the rock and avoid future climbers having to place the piton, it is always left fixed. Never remove a piton from an established free climb. It's there for a reason. To adequately judge the security of a fixed piton, however, one must have experience in placing them, and a hammer. Most piton hammers have a forged steel head attached to a wooden handle which absorbs the vibrations better than a metal handle. Hammers weigh in around 24 ounces and last for many years.

Choose the piton whose shape best corresponds to the crack. Insert the piton by hand. Ideally it should enter about 75 percent of its length before you start hammering. Drive it to the hilt. As you hammer it home, a rising ring – like a scale on a xylophone – usually means a sound piton. When you have the choice between placements in a horizontal and vertical crack, the horizontal peg is often better. In such horizontal placements the eye of the piton should always be positioned down. When placing pitons straight up, use the longest pin that will fit. These placements are often better than you would think.

To remove the pin, knock the piton back and forth along the axis of the crack as far as it will go until it's loose, then snatch it as it loosens. If the pin is stubborn and requires extensive hammering to remove, clip a sling into the eye so if it comes out while hammering, you won't drop it. If it's loose, yet still won't come out, try prying with the hammer pick through the eye.

Since the unnecessary use of pitons is frowned upon in virtually every climbing area, how does one practice their use? Basic pitoning is a pretty straightforward technique, but you should try your hand before heading onto a climb where you expect to place them. Most climbing areas have rock outcrops which, owing to poor rock or whatever, no one climbs on. Often such cliffs are some distance from the central climbing area, which is all the better. Any scrappy crag will do, so long as it has some cracks in it. Find some privacy and experiment, but never place pins on established clean routes.

BOLTS

When there are no cracks for traditional nuts or pitons, a climber can retreat, ignore the need for an anchor and simply "go for it," or drill a hole into the blank stone and hammer in a bolt – a permanent anchor.

The use of bolts has been one of the most controversial issues in the climbing game. Slowly but surely most climbers have begun to accept a proliferation of bolts, especially at the sport climbing areas. Most climbers have the intuitive understanding that artistic climbing is to follow a weakness up a given cliff. You work with what nature has provided. There is something inherently distasteful about changing the

Bolts of various types: The two contraction-type bolts at the bottom of the picture at left are typical of the ¼-inch anchors found on many routes. They clearly are not as strong or durable as the modern ⅜-inch bolts pictured. Carabiner for scale.

medium to fit our need, and bolting does just that. Bolting has been called "the murder of the impossible" because with the bolt, you can climb anything, anywhere. We can hammer one in the underside of a glass-smooth ceiling if we want to. But should we? We clear the land because we need a place to hang our hat. But we don't need to climb. We choose to. So what do we do when we come across an otherwise unclimbable section of rock? It has always been a question when the rock, in its natural state, is either unclimbable or too dangerous to try, whether it's okay to permanently alter it – by placing a bolt – so that we can climb it. Well, that depends . . .

Say there is a 2,000-foot crack that blanks out for thirty feet. Surely it is okay to drill a few bolts for the blank stretch if it means putting together a 2,000-foot dandy. But what if the blank section is 100 feet long and requires eight bolts? What if the blank section is 1,000 feet long and requires 80 bolts? And what if all 2,000 feet are blank? And what if the 2,000-foot wall is featured with plentiful holds but few cracks and would tender a face climb of the first order if we only took the time to install the requisite bolts – say 200? Bolting is compromising the rock – there's no way around that. So where do we draw the line? Should we draw the line?

This is a philosophical question that the beginner need not face but should be aware of from the start. The question is reserved for those who make first ascents – the first people to establish a climbing route. For these pioneers, the excitement of discovery has motivated climbers since the first man stood on top of the first mountain. As today's pacesetters look ever harder for new lines, they increasingly face the bolting question. This is not the venue to pass judgement on the pros and cons of bolting. Climbing's allure is that everyone is left to decide for himself. There are no governing bodies, thank God. The flip side is that when a climber places a bolt he impacts the world of all climbers for all time.

The bolt has been an integral part of American climbing for over fifty years. Many of America's best climbs have dozens of bolts. Most face climbs wouldn't exist, or would be suicidal, without bolt anchors. As you get immersed in climbing you will quickly learn how bolts are "at once a blessing and a curse," as Yosemite legend Royal Robbins said. For now, let's see just what they are and how they work.

First is the hole. Holes were traditionally drilled by hammering on a drill bit held by a rolled steel sleeve/holder. By hammering the holder and twisting it at the same time, the hole is accomplished, taking up to half an hour for a 1½-inch-deep hole drilled in hard granite – even longer in dense limestone. For years this tedious drilling deterred excessive bolting, but the introduction of lightweight battery- and gasoline-powered electric drills has changed all that, with thirty seconds for a hole.

For decades, the ¼-inch diameter bolt was standard. As more and more of these sheared off unexpectedly, ⅜- and ½-inch bolts have come to replace the old ¼-inchers. The bolt is nail-like, and may be of several types: the contraction bolt has a split flange which is squeezed together as it's driven in the narrow hole. The expansion bolt expands a surrounding sleeve (either as it is driven in or after it is set) by wrenching down the head. Some of the best bolt anchors simply combine a threaded bolt with epoxy that is stronger than the rock.

Carabiners can then be clipped to the bolt hanger, a strip of bent metal that is usually secured by a nut screwed onto the bolt. Other bolts are like normal machine bolts, and the hanger is already affixed when the bolt is driven home. Most of the new ⅜-inch bolts have a minimum strength of 4,000 pounds, but the older, ¼-inch bolts hold significantly less.

A beginner should not worry about the mechanics of placing a bolt. You never place bolts on existing routes, so you'll never need that "skill" until you're an expert doing first ascents; and many experts never do first ascents. For general sport climbing you need only know how to judge the condition of a bolt on an existing route. There is no absolutely reliable way to test in situ bolts, but plenty of reasons to want to. Here are some suggestions:

Always consider a ¼-inch bolt suspect. They are no longer placed as anchors, though they are commonly found on existing routes, and any you come across are bound to be old.

Make sure the hanger is flush to the wall, not a "spinner," where the hanger spins around. This means the hole was drilled too shallow for the bolt stud. And don't try to "fix" the spinner by hammering on it. Had that been possible the first party would have sunk it. Further hammering will only damage the shank and the head. So never hit an existing bolt with a hammer.

Commercially-made hangers are made of stainless steel, good for over 4,000 pounds. Beware of homemade hangers. Most are fashioned from inferior aluminum or steel angle stock, prone to work-hardening, eventual brittleness, and failure. Chances are the climber who made the hanger doesn't even know the alloy used or the strength of the hanger.

If the bolt is a "screw-head," make sure the nut is snug and the threads are in good shape. If the threads are denuded or stripped, the nut has little resistance and can pop off under surprisingly low impact force. If the bolt is a "buttonhead" or looks like a machine bolt, again see if it's snugly set, and free of fatigue cracks.

If the bolt is bent, or looks to be set in an oblique hole, beware! Rust is another thing to look for. Discoloration is natural enough, but a lot of rust denotes a "coffin nail," and you know what those are used for.

Use common sense. If the bolt looks funky, don't trust it. And always back up a bolt with a nut if possible. A perfect bolt is nearly impossible to pull out, even from an astronomical fall. But be careful: there are a lot of bad bolts out there.

HOW SAFE ARE THOSE FIXED ANCHORS?

An aged bolt anchor placed in rock soft enough for the wind to quickly erode. Obviously someone was foolish enough to use this for an anchor.

Dan Langmade photo

Besides bolts, many popular climbs have fixed nuts and/or pitons. Gear is expensive, so the gear usually was not left on purpose, but because someone couldn't remove it. But not always. Fatigue, terror, and inexperience often keep a person from really trying to clean a stubborn nut. So never trust them outright. With nuts, first check the placement. Is it good? If so, has the nut been mauled by greedy hammers? Has the cable been torn by people trying to force it out? If it checks out, it's probably okay, but back it up anyway.

Inspect all fixed pitons closely. A piton which Herman Munster couldn't clean with a nine-pound sledge becomes, after the winter freeze and thaw, loose as a tent stake in peat. Check that it's firmly placed. To test a fixed piton well, a piton hammer is a necessity; a couple of good blows along the axis of the crack will give a good indication of how tightly it has been placed. Follow up with blows to set the pin. Keeping in mind that few climbers test fixed pitons, it's advisable either to carry a hammer, test the pin inadequately with blows from the heaviest nut you have, or treat the fixed pin as worthless; it probably is. Often the eye is cracked, and if you can't back it up, it's a judgement call. Sometimes larger fixed angles will be more secure if treated like a chockstone and wrapped with sling. If you know a route features a lot of fixed pitons, carrying a hammer and testing the pitons is the only way to intelligently gauge your security.

A triangular sling configuration, sometimes called the American triangle, is commonly seen when two fixed anchors are side by side – two bolts on a smooth wall, two pitons driven into a horizontal crack, etc. A sling is fed through the two anchors, which form two points of the triangle. The third point of the triangle is where the rope or biner passes through the sling, at the bottom of the setup. There probably is not a cliff in America that doesn't sport this configuration, most likely as a popular, fixed rappel point. Considering that the physics are all wrong with this setup – it actually increases the load on each anchor – it's a wonder more of these rigs don't fail. As with other fixed anchors, you may well find an abundance of slings threaded through the anchor, climbers not realizing that it's not the

The American Triangle

slings that present the danger, rather the triangular rigging that so stresses the anchor.

Obviously, when the anchors are truly bombproof, it doesn't much matter how you tie them off. But anything shy of big new bolts should not be subjected to such inward loading as caused by a triangle. Even the stoutest fixed pins will work loose after awhile, and to use the American triangle to connect passive anchors is to invite disaster.

The solution is easy. Tie the anchors off individually and rappel or belay from two or more slings; or equalize the force on them with the sliding knot.

Fixed SLCDs are rare but not unheard of. The cheapest ones are $45, so everyone and his brother has probably tried to clean it. Make sure the sling or cable is in good shape before trusting it.

Fixed slings should never be trusted blindly; hidden damage may spell disaster for anyone who does not instead examine what the sling is attached to and re-rig the anchor accordingly. Most climbers try to clean fixed slings just to get that trash off the cliff.

TYING INTO THE ANCHOR

You must first uncoil, or "flake out," the rope. Find the end, then feed out the line in a neat stack, making sure not to bury the end. You now have a bottom and top of the pile, and, to avoid tangles, you always draw the rope from the top. Now you're at the bottom of the cliff, harnessed, booted up, tied into the rope and chomping at the bit. If the belay site is at all exposed, or if the leader significantly outweighs the belayer, you have to rig a bombproof anchor before the climb starts. You look for a natural anchor – a stout tree or a large block. You could use the rope to tie these off, but you'll go with slings. Better to get tree sap on a two-dollar piece of webbing than the rope. And the anchor is often weighted, pulled on, jerked about, so you'll let the sling take any abuse. The rope is plenty strong for this, but why scuff it up if you don't have to?

The double overhand

Once you have arranged a natural anchor, you must tie into it. Since you are already tied into the end of the rope, you must use a knot for the middle of the rope. For this purpose, either of two knots, the double overhand or the double figure eight, provide the strength and ease of tying to make their use exclusive of any other for the main tie-in to the anchor. The double overhand is the simplest knot imaginable, but once weighted can be a bearcat to untie. The double figure eight is better; it's strong and easy to untie.

A tie-in knot that is quick and easy to tie, easy to adjust for length once tied, and unties easily is naturally a knot welcomed by climbers. The clove hitch is such a knot. It is particularly useful in constructing multi-nut

The double figure eight

anchors. The tradeoff for all this utility is less strength than other knots. Clove hitches reportedly slip at around 1,000 pounds of load. This slipping can actually improve equalization of the load between the anchors, and help absorb energy from a leader fall, but may not be good for the rope. Clove hitches also have a tendency to work loose. Be sure they are kept tight at the bottom of the carabiner, away from the gate.

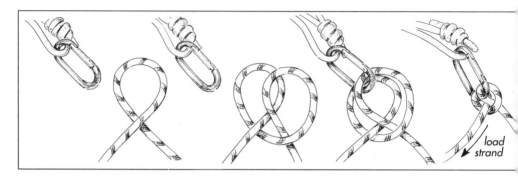

load strand

The clove hitch

The reliability of a clove hitch can be improved by using a locking carabiner. I need to make an esoteric point here about clove hitches. The load strand of the rope coming from the clove hitch should be aligned near the spine of the carabiner, and away from the gate, or you sacrifice nearly one third of the carabiner's strength. The clove hitch should not be used as the sole tie-in knot; the wise climber uses a figure eight somewhere in the anchor system. I have never seen a properly-tied clove hitch failing in any climbing situation, though I've heard of it happening. Likewise, carabiner failure is almost unheard of as well. Still, you might as well be apprised of the considerations.

Knot now in hand, be certain never to tie off an anchor with only one non-locking carabiner. That is simply relying too much on a piece of equipment that can easily hide flaws. Besides which, the gate might get torqued open by a bight of rope. A slim chance, granted, but you won't be taking any chances, so you use two carabiners, gates opposed, or a locking carabiner (with the gate locked, of course).

If there is no substantial natural anchor – a tree, block, or large bush – you must construct an artificial anchor using nuts. The first rule with anchors is never use only one nut. Never. Most experienced climbers don't consider an anchor secure until they have set a minimum of three good nuts.

Multi-nut Anchors

Constructing a multi-nut anchor will at first take some time and trouble, but a trained eye and the knack for finding propitious nut slots – both a result of experience – quickly make this routine. Climbers are called on to do this many times each outing, so the training comes quickly. When setting an anchor system, always consider the following details:

• Find a spot that provides convenient anchor placements. Take a moment to plan the entire system. Analyze the situation and prepare the anchors for any possible direction of pull.

• Keep the system simple, so it is quick to set and easy to double-check and keep tabs on. Use the minimal amount of gear to safely and efficiently do the job.

• As mentioned, remember that any anchor is only as strong as the rock it is set in.

• Make sure the anchor system is Solid, Redundant, Equalized, and allows No Extension, or SRENE. (This acronym is somewhat modified from one used by the American Mountain Guides Association.)

This all can sound overly technical and complicated, but in fact all of these concepts are based on common sense and simple mechanical laws that are usually self-evident once you gain experience. Still, let us look closer at the fundamental concepts behind SRENE:

Solid means just that. The individual anchors and the system as a whole must be bombproof, able to stop a rogue elephant, without question.

Redundancy generally means placing three or four solid anchors (more if the anchors are less than ideal). Never use only one nut. Never. Most experienced climbers don't consider an anchor secure until they have set a minimum of three good nuts. Two bombproof anchors is the absolute minimum. In emergencies, climbers occasionally will use a single bolt, bush, or tied-off boulder for an anchor, but secure backup anchors will greatly reduce the chance of a catastrophe. Redundancy should exist through the entire anchor system: all anchors, slings and carabiners should be backed up. Redundancy also can include setting anchors in more than one crack system, to avoid relying on a single rock feature.

Equalization distributes the load equally between the various anchors in the system, to increase the overall strength of the system and to reduce the chance of a single anchor pulling out under stress.

No extension means that if one of the anchors in the system should fail, the system will not suddenly become slack and drop the climber a short distance, shock-loading the remaining anchors.

The first step is to locate where you want to belay – what physical location is best for tending the line, what affords the best stance, what allows use of the remaining gear on your rack, etc. If adequate anchor placements aren't available, consider moving the station higher if possible, or lower if necessary. Often, you won't have a choice. There will only be a small shelf, or one crack. In that case, you look for the best, most obvious big nut you can arrange. Most belay anchors

---

SRENE

Solid
Redundant
Equalized
No Extension

are built around one atomic bombproof nut – a primary anchor. If there is more than one such placement, go with the one that is more handily located, ideally about chest level, where you can remain standing, can hang the rack, and can keep an eye on the whole works. Sometimes, you'll have to rig the anchor at your feet, or off to one side, or wherever the good placements are, then tie yourself off with slack enough to get back in position to belay (always tying off taut and in line with the direction of pull). Whatever the situation is, the first priority is to sink that first, bombproof nut. If you're at a dicey stance, you might want to clip into this piece before you finish rigging the belay anchor.

The second step is to shore up the primary nut with secondary anchors. Set one nut to oppose the primary nut and create a multi-directional placement, then set at least two more pieces in the downward direction to back up the primary bomber. Remember that you want an efficient anchor, not simply one that will bear the most impact. That means the nuts should be straightforward to place and remove, and should be as centrally located as possible; a

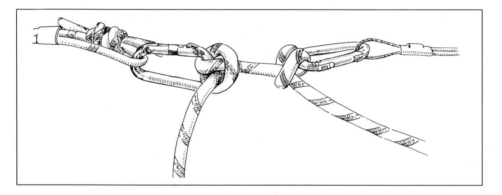

Using a clove hitch to tie two nuts in opposition.

nice, tight grouping, as opposed to a baffling web of nuts crisscrossing the station. Once that first, primary nut is set, try to rig the secondary anchors in close proximity, but not so close that they are cramped or virtually on top of each other. If the rock is less than perfect quality, you may want to spread the anchors out to preserve redundancy. Don't put all your eggs in one basket. Be sure the one closest to you (first to be loaded in event of an upward pull) is multi-directional.

Personally, I like to place a minimum of four pieces, three in the downward direction and one upward, opposing the primary anchor – no matter how inviolate the placements seem individually. Sometimes, three are enough, and sometimes that's all you'll get. Anything less is a crap shoot.

Lastly, you must connect the various components of the system together so they function as one unit. In many cases, this is the most critical, and difficult, part of the whole procedure. Several possibilities exist for connecting the anchors. In the best situation, the belayer will tie tightly to a bombproof multi-directional anchor set near his or her waist, then tie in to two more bombproof downward anchors placed above the first, with the belayer's body in line between the anchors and the anticipated direction of pull. It's a good idea to tie into the most bombproof anchor with a figure eight knot, while clove hitches should suffice for the remaining anchors. It takes some practice to learn just how to feather the clove hitches so the whole rig is more or less under equal tension. This popular rope tie-in is usually the quickest method, requires the least amount of extra gear, and is used ten to one over all other setups.

Equalizing the Anchor

Once you have set the nuts, equalizing the system provides the greatest strength from the anchors. Equalizing the anchors is especially important if the anchors are anything less than bombproof, so all force is distributed evenly between the various placements. Very often, however, anchors are rigged whereby one set of opposing nuts provides a backup for another set of opposing nuts – so although both sets are tied securely together, strictly speaking they are not perfectly equalized.

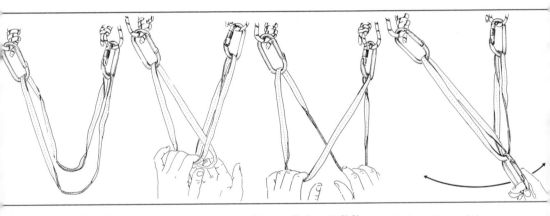

To distribute the force, use a self-equalizing "sliding knot," and clip into the sling. Make sure you put the proper twist in the sling so you're still connected into the sling if one of the anchors fails. And once the anchor is all set up, apply some tension in the direction of pull and scrutinize it like an engineer. Often you will want to make some small finishing adjustments to get the system just as you want it. All components of the anchor should have all the slack removed, usually accomplished by cinching up the clove hitches. More elaborate methods of equalizing an anchor are possible; these listed are the most common modes.

Self-equalizing slider knot. Remember to double up the tie-in carabiner!

SLCDs are very useful in rigging anchors because you can jockey the SLCD around to an ideal location, rather than hoping for bottlenecks or constrictions in the right place.

Horizontal Cracks

Depending on the cliff, at least some of the time we're left to rig anchors in horizontal cracks. At least part of the

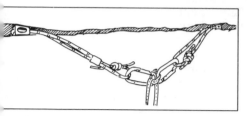

system is built on opposing placements, where the direction of pull is toward the middle. But often the best single nut is the one set for a direct, outward pull. With a taper or hex, you find a slot, wiggle the nut in, and move it horizontally to where the lip of the crack is narrower than the depths. When pulled straight out, the rock would have to break away for the nut to fail. Of course SLCDs have simplified this process, for you only need a reasonable crack to arrange the anchor as you see fit.

Opposing nuts rigged with a sling tied into a clove hitch.

A Few Thoughts

The anchor is the foundation of safe climbing. A poor anchor is like jogging on the freeway – you won't last long. There is no mystery to rigging a sound one. If there is ever any doubt, double up the anchor. While three nuts are often adequate, it's not uncommon to see an anchor with four, even five nuts, all equalized. When the crack is thin, forcing the use of smaller cabled tapers, place more rather than fewer. Trusting an anchor rigged completely from micro nuts is petrifying duty, and should only happen in extreme emergencies, never out of choice. SLCDs have proven their utility, but many climbers avoid rigging anchors completely from mechanical devices, particularly for top-rope situations, where the weighting and unweighting can cause the SLCD to walk around. There's nothing like a bomber "passive" (non-mechanical) nut buried in a bottleneck. Come hell or high water, that nut's going nowhere. There are situations in climbing where you may take a calculated risk, but never with the anchor. The topic of rock climbing anchors is covered in more depth in my book Climbing Anchors.

THE BELAY

Belaying – the technique of managing the rope to safeguard a climber against a fall – is the most important responsibility climbers routinely face. We will look carefully at each aspect of the belaying system, but first, here's a brief overview.

The belayer passes the rope through a belay device and clips it into a locking carabiner attached to his harness. He feeds out or takes in rope as needed to keep the climber safe. The belayer locks the rope off if the climber falls, and might lower the climber back to the ground at the end of the climb. A belayer keeps excess slack out of the rope, but doesn't allow the rope to pull down on the leader, nor does he "hoist" a top-roped climber up the route. The responsible belayer double-checks the leader's and his own harness buckles, the anchor setup, belay device, locking biner, and tie-in knots before either leaves the ground. The belayer is responsible for the safety of the person climbing. He must be proficient, and he must stay focused on the climber. The belayer should situate himself in a secure stance so he can't trip over his own feet, say, and pull the leader off. Finally, he should stack the rope to feed nicely, preferably not in the dirt, before the climber sets off.

When belaying a leader, the belayer feeds out rope through the belay device, or "belays" (belay devices will be discussed more fully later). Both his anchor and location are generically called "the belay," or "belay station." You climb in stages called "pitches," which usually refers to the distance between belay stations, something less than a rope length. A pitch is rarely a whole rope length, since you often stop short at a ledge, a good stance or crack which offers a convenient place to belay. A bombproof anchor is far more important than stretching out a lead simply to make it longer. If you pass obvious belay stances, you often end up wasting time constructing an anchor in a poor crack or at an awkward locale.

Belaying is the technique of not only paying out the rope, but holding it fast should your partner fall. The entire protection system of rock climbing depends on the certainty of both the belay anchor and the belayer to do their job: to stop the climber should he or she fall, and to remain fastened to the cliff. It is very rare that both the belay and anchor should fail and it's into the beyond if they do. That is why extreme vigilance is always paid to both the anchor and belay.

The mechanics of belaying are basic; consequently, some climbers pay less than perfect attention to the task. Don't fall into this dangerous trap, for a belayer literally holds his partner's life in his hands. A cavalier attitude toward the importance of the belay or the anchors will get someone killed in a hurry. The process is fundamental and the technique is simple and reliable. Still, forty percent of all fatal climbing accidents in Yosemite are due to mistakes and failures in the belay chain. Consequently, the importance of a sound belay system cannot be overstated.

There are two ends of the rope: your end, which you are tied into and which is tied off to the anchor, and the "live" end, which goes to the person climbing. The rope is fed through a belay device and locking carabiner attached to your waist and grasped firmly in each hand. The "live" end going to the climber is handled by the "guide" hand. The "brake" hand holds the rope on the other side of the belay device. When the climber is leading away from you, the guide hand feeds the rope out, pulling it through the belay device; when the climber is ascending up to you, the guide hand pulls in the slack as the climber ascends. As the rope is reeled in, it passes through the belay device to the brake hand which, too, is pulling in slack – the brake hand pulling the rope away, the guide hand pulling it toward you, always keeping the rope snug through the device.

Belaying a climber leading away from you is fairly simple: the guide hand shuffles out the rope in little tugs, the payed-out rope moving smoothly through the belay device and the brake hand on the other side. Taking the rope up, or belaying a climber "in" is a little tricky at first, and involves a three-part sequence. The guide hand is extended away from the waist. It clasps the rope and pulls it in. Simultaneously, the brake hand is pulling out, clasping the rope and pulling it

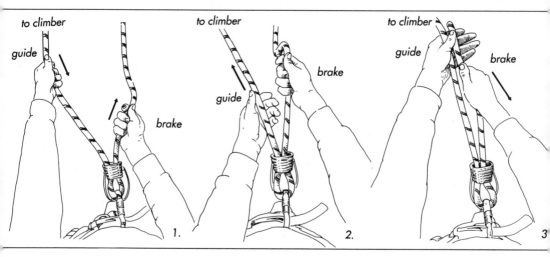

to climber guide brake 1.

to climber guide brake 2.

to climber guide brake 3

BELAYING

Taking rope in:

1. Both hands grasping tightly, the rope is fed through the device.

2. The guide hand slides up,

3. clasps both ends of the rope above the other hand to allow the brake hand to slide down, and the series begins again.

away from your body as it passes through your belay device. That's the first stroke: the guide hand pulls in, the brake hand pulls out. At the end of that stroke, the guide hand is at the belay device, and the brake hand extended out from the device.

Part two requires the brake hand to momentarily hold fast while the guide hand slides back out along the live end. When the arm is fully extended, the guide hand – still holding the rope on that side – reaches across and grabs the brake hand rope above the brake hand.

Part three involves the brake hand sliding back to the belay device and the process is repeated: guide hand pulls in, brake hand pulls out. Guide hand extends, grabs both sides, brake hand slides back. This procedure sounds complicated but is very simple to perform. It is the best way to belay and still observe the absolute rule: the brake hand never leaves the rope. Not only does it never leave the rope, your fingers are always curled around it, ready to clench hard when necessary.

A fall is checked by bending the rope across the belay device with your brake hand, which collapses the belay device onto the locking carabiner and locks the rope fast. When you try to belay the rope in, never letting your brake hand leave the clenched position, you'll see there is only one way to do so – the way just described.

The ability to stop a falling climber depends on several things. You must not be caught unaware. Your attention must remain focused on the climber with whose life you are entrusted. When a climber falls, your brake hand must quickly bend the rope across the belay device (extending the brake hand at a 45-degree angle away from the device), causing the friction to increase and the rope to automatically lock up. Properly performed, most falls can be held with little effort. In time, this reaction will become instinctive. To efficiently arrest a fall, you must be properly braced,

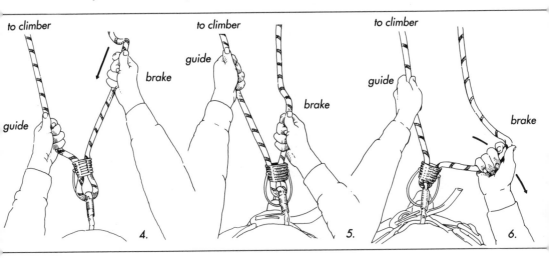

anticipating both the impact force and the direction of pull caused by the falling climber. But all of this is of little value if you are not properly anchored. To say it again: the anchor is the backbone of the safety system. It, beyond anything, must be secure!

On sport routes and top-roped climbs, the belayer often lowers the climber back to the ground at the end of the route. A retreating leader may also need to be lowered to the ground, or to the belay. To lower a climber, first lock the rope off by bending it across the belay device. Next, lean back, or "sit into" the rope to give the climber tension. Place both hands on the brake side of the rope and slowly but fluidly lower the climber to the ground. When the climber reaches the ground, slowly ease her onto her feet. (For a more detailed discussion of lowering, see Chapter 7: Sport Climbing.)

When you start a climb, the belayer should be located close to, if not right at, the base of the rock; and always be tied taut to the belay anchor. If there is any slack between belayer and anchor, a long fall can jerk the belayer off his feet and thrash him around until he comes taut to the anchor. The rope, meanwhile, can be ripped from his hands, resulting in disaster. Every fall generates force in one direction – the direction of pull. Always station yourself in a direct line between the direction of pull and the anchor. If you don't, the force of the fall may drag you there anyway,

BELAYING

Letting rope out:

4, 5. Both hands grasping tightly, the rope is fed through the device.

6. The braking action: the brake hand bends the rope across the belay device.

and you might forfeit the belay – and the leader's life – during the flight. Remember ABC: Anchor-Belayer-Climber.

To clarify, consider these examples. You're tied off to a tree ten feet away from the cliff, but you're belaying several feet to the side of the start of the climb. If the leader falls, you can plot the ideal direction of pull as a straight line from the tree to her first anchor. If you're not also in line with that pull – because you are some ways off to the side – the impact will, perforce, drag you in line. If you are in line, but have tied the anchor off with a lot of slack, you will probably be dragged toward (or even up) the cliff until the rope becomes taut to the anchor. In both instances the leader has fallen that much farther. The belay is of little value while you are bouncing over the ground, and it's perilous to get banged

ANALYZING A
BELAY STATION:

1, 2. Two sets of opposing nut anchors, secured with clove hitches, except

3. Figure eight knot, for maximum security.

4. Belayer's brake hand.

5. Guiding biner attached to the harness holds the leader's end of the rope in place.

6. The direction of pull should the leader fall.

7. The tie-in from the waist goes down to a non-directional anchor. (Ideally, the belayer should be in a direct line between this anchor tie-in and the direction of pull so that she does not get pulled out of place should the leader fall. Here, as often happens, the anchors lie to the side of the belayer's stance.)

against the cliff, for the sudden force can jar your brake hand off the rope. If you're set up correctly, catching a fall is an effortless and routine event.

If you must arrange your anchor on the cliff, try to rig it directly below the start of the climb. This puts the direction of pull straight up, which is far less awkward than having to compensate for a belay coming in from the side, which forces the belayer into an oblique angle. The stance is of key importance to a ground belay rigged on the cliff – that, and a taut tie-off to the anchor. The short tie-off keeps you from being lifted off the ground. Since a fall will draw you toward the cliff, many belayers like to keep one leg braced against the wall, acting as a shock absorber in the event of a fall. If you're belaying safely on the ground and your partner does not significantly outweigh you, you may want to forego the anchor to avoid becoming a target for rockfall.

Belay Devices

Many types of belay devices are currently available. Most work by creating friction on the rope so the belayer can easily hold the force generated in a fall. A belay using a device has commonly been called a "static" belay, as the rope is locked tight in the device in the event of a fall (several of the devices actually let a few inches of the rope slip through them before they lock). Since most belay devices are normally clipped to the front of a harness, the term "static belay" is an overstatement. The rope is indeed locked fast in the device when stopping a fall, but you'd have to be a twenty-ton Roman statue to keep your torso from moving with the pull. The main value of a belay device is that it requires very little strength to hold even the longest possible fall, and there's little chance of it ever failing, or the belayer suffering abrasions or rope burns – if the whole system is properly rigged. When the disparity of weight is substantial between belayer and leader, belay devices really shine over the age-old hip belay (to be explained later). For two years I did most of my climbing with a woman whom I outweighed by over one hundred pounds. I fell dozens of times, and she always caught me effortlessly, and never got a scratch.

Following are a few of the most popular devices. The first belay device was the Sticht Plate, invented by a German engineer in the early 1970s. The plate is a 4-ounce aluminum disk with one or two channel holes machined through it. A bight of rope is passed through one of the channels and clipped through a locking carabiner attached to your harness or swami. (Two opposing-gated regular biners will also work, though not as conveniently). The plate has a keeper loop which, when clipped into the carabiner, keeps the plate from floating out away from the waist. Since the plate will sometimes lock up when you don't want it to, some plates have a spring on the back to prohibit this. Using two carabiners to attach the rope to your harness also helps prevent the plate from locking up, and provides smoother belaying and rappelling.

Sticht plates come in all manner of sizes and dimensions for use with 9-, 10-, and 11-mm rope, and other configurations for double ropes. A plate with two 11-mm slots is probably the most versatile for belaying and rappelling.

There are also micro versions of the Sticht plate which work exactly like the Sticht, are as strong, and weigh less than one ounce. They are often too small for 11-mm ropes, and usually overheat quickly.

The Lowe Tuber, Black Diamond Air Traffic Controller (ATC), and Trango Pyramid are cone- or pyramid-shaped tubes that are light, feed rope a bit more smoothly than a flat plate belay device, and have more surface area for heat dissipation. A bight of rope passes in and around a locking carabiner and back out the tube. During a fall, the tube, like the Sticht plate, locks the rope off at the biner. The amount of working friction depends on what end of the tube you have against the locking biner. For belaying with 9-mm or smaller ropes, the small end of the device should be toward the carabiner. With larger ropes the device will feed rope more smoothly with the large end of the tube toward the carabiner. For rappelling, the small end should be toward the carabiner, unless the rock angle is low and you're using two large diameter ropes, in which case the large end should be toward the carabiner. Like the Sticht plate, a keeper loop holds the Tuber, ATC or Pyramid close to the biner. This style of belay device is currently the most popular.

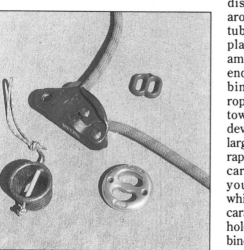

Various belay devices, including (with rope) the Petzl GriGri.

Some climbers belay with a figure eight rappel device. It is acceptable to belay a top-roped climber with the rope arranged in the figure eight as you would for rappelling, but this setup does not provide enough friction for belaying a leader. The smaller hole on most figure eights is designed for a bight of rope to be passed through and clipped into a locking carabiner, like you would rig a belay plate. This is the only safe way to belay a leader with a figure eight.

Someone was bound to create a device that automatically locks up the rope in the event of a fall, whether your brake hand is on the rope or not. The Petzl Gri Gri and the Salewa Antz are two such products. Both devices come with extensive instructions about their safe usage, and both require some practice for a climber to become proficient with them. These self-locking belay devices are excellent when you're being belayed by a novice. They're also great for sport climbing, when the climber is spending a lot of time hanging on the rope to work out moves. Both devices must be properly rigged, however, or the climber can hit the deck if he falls.

Long used by stevedores to tether onerous loads on the docks, the Munter hitch is a handy alternative to devices, for it only requires a special carabiner attached to your harness or swami. Knowing the Munter hitch could prove to be essential if you ever drop your belay device. When Swiss climber Werner Munter introduced this hitch to climbing – claiming the invention – the UIAA conducted extensive tests, gave it thumbs up, and it has steadily caught on ever since. During the fall, the brake hand goes out, and the hitch locks on itself. Use a carabiner with a large opening-an oversized pear-shaped biner with a locking gate – with the Munter hitch. The mouth on a regular, or even a D carabiner, is not wide enough to keep the hitch from binding when you switch from taking in to feeding out rope, or vice versa. Most

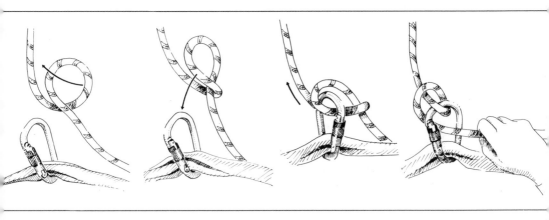

climbers who have tried the Munter hitch have found it to work quite well. The action is good, the setup instantaneous, and you don't have to carry a device, even if it only weighs an ounce. There is a tendency for the rope to get excessively kinked, however. And a word of caution: since the rope is continually running through the biner, the action can unscrew the sleeve on a locking biner, so crank the sleeve tight before belaying, and keep an eye on it.

THE MUNTER HITCH:

1. Twist rope
2. Twist again
3. Clip doubled rope in
4. and pull up and out.

Another word of caution: belay devices perform only as well as you know how to use them, and a good belay is safe only if you observe the rules we've laid down. The belay anchor must be inviolate; always tie in taut to the belay anchor; get in line with, and anticipate the direction of pull; maintain a good brace or stance; stay alert; and the absolute rule – never take your brake hand off the rope, lest your belay prove lethal to your partner and, perhaps, to yourself.

The Hip Belay

With the advent of modern-day belay devices, the hip belay has become all but obsolete. However, it is essential to know how to belay with little or no equipment in case you accidentally drop your gear. The hip belay is also the quickest belay to set up for short stretches of belaying on fourth class terrain. It was the primary belay method for decades, and works quite well when performed correctly. A belay device substantially increases the margin of safety, however.

Hip belaying is similar to belaying with a device, with your body substituting for the device. As before, you have two ends of rope: your end, and the live end which goes to the climber. The rope is wrapped around your waist and grasped firmly in each hand. The live end is handled by the guide hand, and the brake hand holds the rope on your other side. Feed the rope out with your guide hand, pulling it around your waist and through the brake hand on your other side.

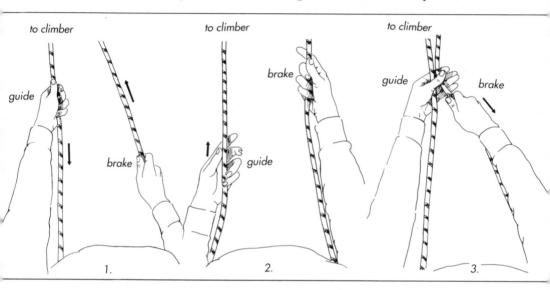

to climber

guide

brake

1.

to climber

brake

guide

2.

to climber

guide

brake

3.

THE HIP BELAY

Taking rope in:

1. Both hands grasping tightly, the rope is fed around the back.

2. The guide hand slides up,

3. clasps both ends of the rope above the other hand to allow the brake hand to slide down, and the series begins again.

Take the rope in, using the same three-step sequence that you do with a belay device. The guide hand pulls in while the brake hand pulls out. The guide hand extends and grabs both sides of rope. Finally, the brake hand slides back and the guide hand drops the brake rope. Again, the absolute rule is to keep the brake hand on the rope.

When using the hip belay there is a remote chance that the rope can be lifted over your back – if the guide hand is somehow jerked loose from the rope. A "guiding biner" solves this. Clip a biner into your swami belt or harness near the guide hand. The live end is then taken up or paid out through the biner, and even if the guide hand comes loose, the line still goes around the back to the brake hand. You will quickly learn that the guide hand is no more than a guide and does little to stop the fall. It's the friction around the waist and the brake hand coming across the opposite hip that accomplish the brake.

When the pull is straight up, many climbers pass the rope under their butt instead of around their waist. Even with the guide biner, the straight up pull will often draw the rope up one's back, which is quite sensitive and fairly lean. So your bottom – with the rope running under it – is a better and more secure cushion when belaying for the upward pull. In any event, always wear a shirt, and keep it tucked in unless you want some "galley slave"-like scars.

On paper, the hip belay sounds both strenuous and painful, and it's easy to envision a long fall sawing you in half or striping you with bone-deep rope burns. Neither should happen. Much of the impact force is absorbed by the rope, which stretches quite a bit, by the equipment the rope is running through, by the belay anchor, and finally, by the belayer. And the friction afforded by your back or bottom, plus

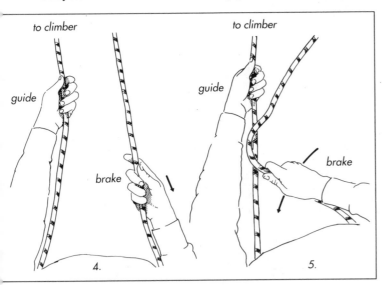

THE HIP BELAY
(Continued)
4. Letting rope out.
5. The braking action: the brake hand wraps the rope around the waist.

the natural dampening effect of your body is such that – if the system is rigged and executed correctly – a grandma could hold a baker's apprentice on the biggest fall he could take.

Beginners frequently develop a penchant for belaying one way, always using the same brake hand. Situations arise which will require you to belay with one hand or the other, so practice belaying both ways from the start.

The hip belay has been described as a "dynamic" belay in several recent articles and manuals, and this is a misnomer. Years ago, when the old hemp ropes would snap under high impacts, several authorities suggested letting a little rope intentionally slip through the hands to ease the shock on the hemp – a true "dynamic" belay. I'd wager this was never accomplished, though, because once the rope gets to speed, the hands haven't been made that can simply crimp it to a stop. The recent re-invention of the term "dynamic belay" simply refers to inherent give in the system, and in no way harks back to the diabolical suggestion of letting some line smoke through your hands in a misguided attempt to ease the fall.

The Art of Leading

Most veterans admit that climbing doesn't really start until you cast off on the lead. You can boulder around enchanted forests and follow a leader up the world's greatest rock climbs, but the moment you're the first on the rope, it's suddenly real in an altogether different way. Everything is magnified manyfold, as now you're playing for keeps. The decisions are all yours – as are the rewards and the consequences. Whether that first lead is up a razor-cut crack at the base of El Capitan, or on some filthy slab in a scrapheap quarry, the feeling of command and the special demands are always the same. It's no longer just an exhilarating physical challenge, but a creative problem-solving design requiring a lot of intangible things and with the penalty of injury, or even death, for a major oversight.

Because leading is a procedure involving equipment and an applied system, we can nail down certain objective realities, at least in a generic sense. But the deeper we go, the greyer it all becomes. It's like discussing a fine painting or a classic wine: if you talk long enough, you'll be babbling regardless of your expertise. Every climb, like every canvas, every wine, is a little different, and very little applies to one and all. Every climber is ultimately self-taught. We can open the way a bit, suggesting what fine leading is about, and not about, and ever stressing safety, but more than that must not be expected from an instruction manual. A professional guide can take you a bit further in preparing for those first leads, but when you do take the sharp end, it's just you and the rock.

The First Lead

Ideally, you will have taken a climbing course and had the fundamentals drummed into you by a competent instructor. You will have spent time placing nuts, rigging and equalizing anchors, so when you grab the lead, you don't have nagging doubts about your ability to do the basic things safely. You will have complemented your practical experience by reading this manual, or one like it. And you will have served at least a brief apprenticeship following an experienced leader up a host of climbs, becoming familiar with the nuances which a book, or even the best personal instruction, cannot impart. And ideally I would be a Sultan on a South Pacific Island with no duties save to count my trunkful of black pearls. We don't live in an ideal world, and many first-time leaders have little experience. Some have no

(page opposite)

Diane French and Rolando Garibotti on "The Contest," Eldorado Canyon, Colorado

Beth Wald photo

experience. Others can't be bothered with instruction and don't want to follow anyone, anywhere. They'll lead from day one and thank you very much for your advice. I don't suggest this latter tactic. It's a quick way to get hurt. You don't want to learn leading through trial and error. A first-time leader should know the whole procedure well before stepping out as boss. But either way, you'll have to decide what it is you want to lead.

Guidebooks

Picture a cliff, a quarter-mile long and 300 feet high. Folks first started climbing there in 1950, and the cliff has become a favorite for rock climbers. Since the first climber discovered the first way up the cliff, exploration has been steady until now there are over 300 different ways – or "routes" – up the wall. How do we know this? Since 1950, each route was recorded and later published in a guidebook. A guidebook lists first ascents – the names and dates of the first people to climb a given route.

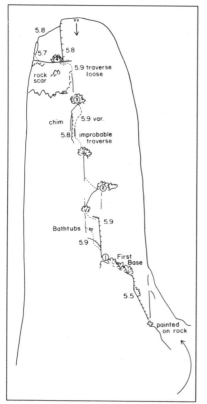

Typical guidebook topo

Each route is named and rated by the first ascenders and, by the time a route makes it into print, it's usually had enough ascents that the rating is fairly objective, arrived at by consensus. Most guidebooks have several master photos, or topographic drawings, with lines superimposed to show the various routes, or at least prominent features allowing one to find specific climbs by reference. A guidebook is indispensable – to experts, who want to know where the hardest routes are, and to beginners, who yearn for easy ground, and everyone in between. It allows us to pick a route that best suits our taste and expertise. Many guides have a quality rating, or at least a list of recommended routes; so a visiting climber can spend a few days and know he's tasted some of the best the crag has to offer. A guide is particularly important for the beginning leader, who can use all the guidance he can get.

The early guides used photos and written descriptions. In the mid-seventies the written description was replaced by the "topo," or topographic guide. A topo is simply a minimal blueprint of the climb – really just a detailed line drawing – featuring prominent features, belay locations, the type of climbing (liebacking, etc.), and the difficulty, all rendered in a facile set of symbols. This graphic representation of cliffs and their climbs is the most precise and convenient means of route description, easily understood and capable of crossing language barriers. Every topo guide has a key at the beginning to clarify the symbols, though most are obvious.

Topos are normally more detailed than the prose guides but are still in truncated form, so it takes some experience to learn how to read them at a glance. Though rare, some guides still use prose descriptions, so become familiar with both formats. Many times the guidebook is bulky, so climbers often photocopy the topos and carry a page instead of a book..

Choose a route well within your abilities for that first lead. Most every cliff has a classic easy route which hundreds of people have broken in on. Whatever you choose, be certain the protection is sound, that you are at least somewhat adept in the techniques involved, and that the route is straightforward, requiring no unusual shenanigans or special skills. A direct, easy climb – that's what you want. If the first lead proves too easy, no one's stopping you from hopping right back onto something a little stiffer. Getting in over your head on your first lead is a horrible and potentially dangerous experience, and may color, if not end, your climbing career. Take it slow. Cut loose only when you know what's happening.

The Rack

The collection of gear the climber takes up the climb is called the rack. There are two considerations: what gear to take, and how to take, or "rack" it.

Once you have decided on a climb, the guidebook should tell you the requisite equipment needed for safe passage. If it doesn't, you're left to eyeball the route and estimate what's needed. A "standard" rack may be the catch-all rack that works for 80 percent of the routes at 80 percent of the areas (not counting the clip-and-go sport routes). This consists of a complete set of "wires" – cabled micro tapers to tapers of about an inch across, a progressively-sized selection of SLCDs to about two or three inches, five or six over-the-shoulder-length runners, seven or so quickdraws, carabiners for each nut carried (and a few extra as well), and a nut tool to remove stuck nuts. In any case, climbers routinely ask around to get the lowdown – what's the best rack, is there any hidden placement and where is it, and does a certain nut work best at the crux? One can waste considerable time getting such advice, which is sometimes contradictory because everyone

Racking methods

does things a little differently. Also, the suggested rack is often a little "thin," so use your own judgement. The suggested rack normally refers only to sizes encountered, not spelling out the nuts by brand names. Learn to translate this relative to the gear you own. And remember: it's better to take more than you need than less.

"ON BELAY?" The question the climber asks before he proceeds.

"BELAY ON" The response the belayer tells the climber when his belay is set and ready.

"CLIMBING" What the climber says to the belayer indicating the climber is starting to climb.

"CLIMB" The belayer's response that he's ready to belay the rope, proceeding to do so as the climber advances.

"SLACK" A command to the belayer to let out some rope, give slack.

"UP ROPE" A command to the belayer to take in the rope, pull up the slack.

"TENSION" or **"TAKE"** A command to the belayer to hold the climber on tension by holding the belay fast.

"LOWER" A command to the belayer that the climber is ready to be lowered.

"WATCH ME" Commands the belayer to pay close attention, expect or be prepared for a fall.

"FALLING!" The climber is falling—a statement of fact.

"BELAY OFF" The climber's signal to the belayer that he has anchored himself and that the belayer's responsibility to belay should end.

"OFF BELAY!" The belayer's response to the climber that the belay has ended.

"ROCK!" Akin to yelling "Fore" on a golf course. Rocks are coming down; take cover.

"ROPE!" A rope is coming down; watch for it.

There are two methods to rack gear, or "hardware": on a gear sling worn over the shoulder, or on gear loops on the side of your harness. Either method works, but on steep and overhanging climbs, gear on a shoulder sling will follow gravity and slip around your back, making quick access difficult, and putting more of the weight on your hands. Gear racked on a harness hangs directly over both hips, and depending on your free hand, you may discover the desired nut on the opposite hip, requiring an awkward reach and some fumbling to even unclip it.

Whatever method you choose, gear should be racked systematically according to size, in an order you have memorized for ready access. Rack small nuts up front, progressively bigger going back. SLCDs and medium to large hexes are racked individually – one biner for each nut. Clip the carabiner in so the gate is facing the body and opens from the top. This way the thumb will naturally go to the gate and you can lift the nut straight off, rather than having to twist it about, opening the gate with your fingers. Wired nuts are racked in bunches, from micro-nuts on up, perhaps six on one biner. How they are clipped onto your rack depends on how you want them. Some climbers unclip the appropriate bunch, fit the nut of choice, unclip it from the bunch and return the remainder to the rack. Others know at first glance what nut they want and remove it individually from the sling or harness. (If you're wrong, it's better to have had the whole bunch in hand for an easy second try.) If you remove wires individually, rack the carabiner gate out, so you can lift the nut out, instead of back and under. If you remove the whole bunch, rack the biner so the gate faces your body. Free biners should be racked together, either in front of or behind the nuts. (Additional equipment will be explained later.)

Starting Out

You've picked a route and you know where it goes. You're racked up, tied in and breathing fire, but who's that tending your line? A cousin sprung from reform school to whom you explained the fundamentals on the hike in? No, sir! You must have full confidence that your belayer will catch you if you fall. If you can, get an experienced climber to belay you for that first lead. He can give valuable coaching from below, and can critique your lead once done. Moreover, you know he can belay, can catch any fall you'll take, which frees your mind to concentrate on the lead.

A standardized protocol of communication removes any doubt as to what the leader and the belayer are doing, are expected to do, are asked to do, and are warned to do. It is described at left. When you anticipate being unable to hear each other because of river noise, say, work out your own protocol in rope tugs before the leader starts the pitch. Maybe three sharp tugs from the leader would mean you can take him off belay and two sharp tugs from the leader means you can climb. In such difficult situations it is the responsibility of the belayer to be particularly sensitive to the rope so the climber has the proper amount of slack or tension.

Before you start up, study the rock above. Spot any key holds, obvious features, or nut placements. Climb up mentally, imagining the required techniques. On easy climbs, the sequence is usually no mystery – just a matter of execution, so picture yourself doing the moves, then go at it.

The first section above the ground is crucial because if you fall there, you hit the deck. So climb no higher than you feel comfortable jumping off from, then set your first nut. (All gear placed to protect the leader is called "protection," or simply "pro.") Make certain that first pro is especially good, and that it can handle a bit of an outward tug. And make certain your belayer knows you're clipped in. To the first pro, the belay is worthless as you aren't clipped into anything. Now you're plugged in, and the system is operative. If the pro seems questionable, double it up – place two or even three nuts until you *know* something will stop your fall. At the outset, the leader must always calculate how far he has to fall to hit the ground or a ledge on the route, and he should always have some pro in to preclude this. Up higher, once you have several nuts in – providing they're good – "decking out" is no longer a concern. But "rope drag" is.

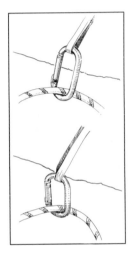

Protection: The Direction of Pull

As a leader, you must continually assess the direction the rope will pull on all the protection below you, should you fall. Until you can, you won't be a safe leader. Though it sounds confusing, the concept is easy.

Rarely does a climb follow a perfectly straight line. Even cracks curve and snake around, so the rope to some extent

Top: Stressing a carabiner sideways over an edge is weak and wrong.

Bottom: It's much better to use a longer sling.

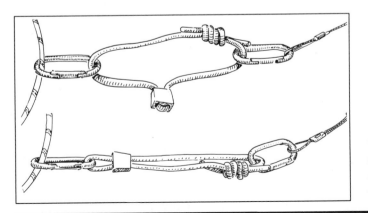

Top: Incorrect use of a nut sling as a runner

Bottom: A much stronger way

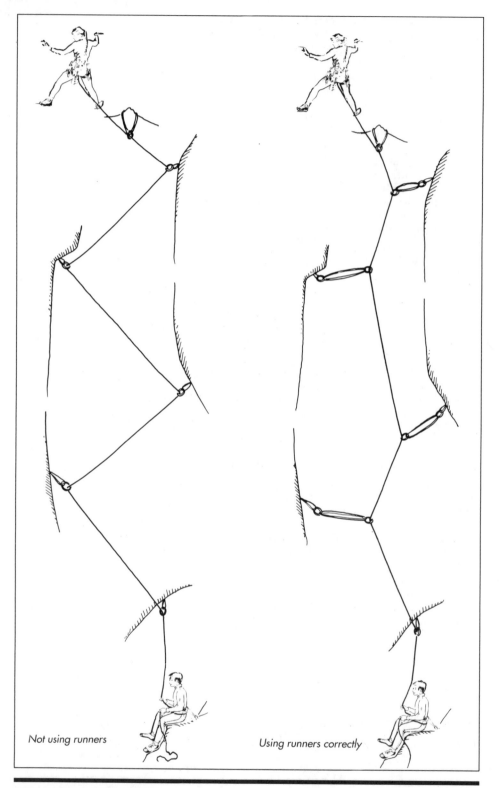

Not using runners

Using runners correctly

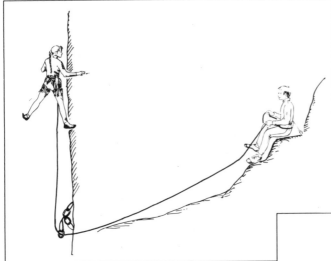

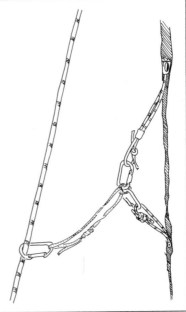

has to bend about according to the contour of the crack your pro is in. To ably predict the direction of pull, a leader must be conscious of the various forces on *the entire system*. When you fall, the rope comes tight and the transmission of force pulls all the protection toward the middle, toward an imaginary straight line between leader and belayer. Pro not placed directly in that line is subject to considerable sideways and upward pull, and can easily be wrenched free if you have not compensated for the oblique force. So when the route zig-zags around, there are certain things we do.

You always want the rope to follow as straight a line as possible, even if all your protection is from bolts (which cannot be wrenched free from sideways forces). The more crooks the rope makes, the greater the friction – the "rope drag" – which in degrees, is like the belayer holding you back. An experienced leader imagines a plumb line between the belayer and the end of the first pitch, and arranges protection so the rope follows that line as closely as possible. When protection is by necessity placed to the side of the plumb line, we attach runners to the pro which, in effect, extends the protection toward the imaginary line. The drawback with runners is that they increase the potential fall twice the length of the runner. For this reason, and because the runner is like a free tether and can move, rather than being just a fixed point, it is very rare that someone will attach a runner bigger than the normal length worn over the shoulder. If the runner is well off to the side, and a fall will still transmit lateral force on the nut, either set the nut with a firm downward jerk, or place an oppositional

Use of a multi-directional anchor to prevent the rope from lifting the protection from the crack

(page opposite)

Using slings to allow the rope to run freely and keep the protection properly aligned

QUICK-DRAWS
Top: shoulder-length
tripled

Bottom: sewn sling

Clipping into wired nuts:

Top: Never thread sling
material directly into a
wire; with a solid fall
the wire will slice
right on through!

Middle: Never clip into
an anchor that has any
stiffness to it (like a wire)
with two carabiners;
a twist in the rope can
pull the nut free or
force the biners to
unclip themselves.

Bottom: Correct use of
the quick-draw, with
rope-end biner gate
down and out to easily
accept the rope.

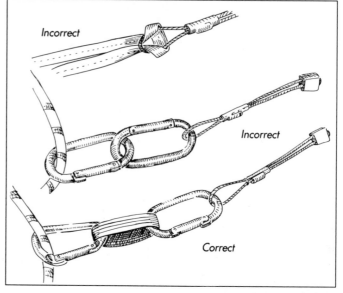

Incorrect

Incorrect

Correct

nut beneath it to form a multi-directional protection. The theory is simple: you are not just trailing a rope, but dragging it through your protection. Runners keep that drag at a minimum, and keep the nuts in place.

When clipping into fixed protection or cabled nuts, even if they're placed in a direct line, it's advisable to use quick-draws. Quick-draws are small, sewn runners, fashioned from either 1-inch or 9/16-inch tubular webbing and harbor two carabiners, one for the pro, one for the rope. Quick-draws are short, so they don't appreciably increase the potential fall, and they really facilitate the rope running smoothly. Moreover, cabled nuts are stiff, and when clipped off with single (or even double) biners, can be lifted from the crack by rope drag. Quick-draws prevent this. Some climbers prefer to rack their shoulder slings as quick-draws by tripling the loops; this allows one to easily extend the quick-draws to a full-sized runner as required. Standard quickdraws, however, are lighter and much less bulky.

As you climb, try to avoid having the rope run directly between your legs – it's better to trail it over a leg; in the event of a fall there is then less danger of the tightening rope flipping you over backwards and increasing the chance of a head injury.

When to Place Protection

There is no hard-and-fast rule concerning when to place protection or when to simply carry on. Experienced climbers place pro when they need it. To the beginning leader the experience is all new and he might not know when he needs pro; he is likely to think he always needs it. You definitely want sound protection at the start of a pitch, and before any hard, or "crux" section. Anticipate the crux; place protection when you can, not counting on the hope that you can slot something fifteen feet higher at the hard move. Whenever you encounter an obvious bottleneck or are resting on a big hold, slot a nut – no matter how easy the climbing is. If the climbing feels manageable and you feel good, go ten or fifteen feet between nuts and feel the thrill and freedom of the lead. But always be aware of ledges or features you may hit should you fall, and protect yourself accordingly. Avoid the temptation to "run the rope out," going long distances between protection, even if the climbing is clearly easy. Once you are a good judge of both your own prowess and the

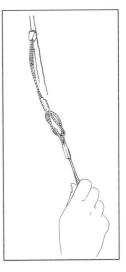

Using two wires woven together to reach a good placement

Rope clenched in gritted teeth, Todd Skinner grapples to clip a bolt on the muscular "Calling All the Heroes" (5.13d), Hueco Tanks, Texas. Extremely strenuous climbs like this are the domain of the world-class cragsman, and few hear the call to tackle such leads. In the case of "Calling All the Heroes," few are heroes; most fail.

Bill Hatcher photo

terrain encountered, do whatever you like. But the beginning leader will rarely want to go more than about fifteen feet between nuts. That's only eight nuts for a 135-foot pitch, which isn't excessive by any count.

If one hand is holding you to the rock, clipping in can be trying. The universal method is: reach down below your tie-in, pull up a loop and hold it in your teeth; reach down for more slack, then clip in. Sounds odd, but there's not a leader alive who doesn't do this. Sometimes fixed protection is found in awkward positions and can be very strenuous even to clip. Climbers sometimes rig quick-draws with one end clipped to a shoulder sling and the other clipped through the lead rope. At a desperate clip, just unclip from the gear sling and clip the fixed pro, and your rope is clipped in as well. If you discover the fixed pro is good enough, you're set. If it's bad, you're no worse off.

Bent-gate carabiners, though great to clip a rope into, should only be used for that purpose. Don't use them to clip into a bolt, fixed pin, or wired nut. Even quickdraws can bind and open the gate all too easily. Watch them.

Route Finding

Part of learning to be a good leader is knowing what makes a bad one – knowing how climbers defeat themselves – and avoiding these needless mistakes. Good climbing requires you to use available holds the easiest way; good route-finding requires you to keep to the easiest holds. Follow the line of least resistance, not wandering onto more difficult rock on the flanks. Route finding is part instinct, part experience (which you might not be long on). Study the topo and compare it against what you see. Locate salient features, like bushes or roofs, and know where the hard parts are in relation to them. The topo should tell you this information – i.e., that the section above the bush is hard, that the crux is after the crack peters out. Get yourself prepared *before* you start by memorizing all the given information.

If you feel you have wandered off the route, look for the signs: chalk marks, boot marks, fixed protection, broken flakes or holds. On popular routes, the texture and color of the rock is often different, smoother and lighter than bordering stone, because hundreds of shoes have paddled over every hold, probably for many years. With crack climbs, the route is often obvious. Face climbs are more nebulous.

Cruxes: The Hard Parts

Even easy climbs have cruxes, sections harder than the rest. You will recognize them because the holds will suddenly run out, the crack will thin, widen, get shallow, or the angle will bulge. Don't climb mechanically, but with all your savvy. Recognize the crux before you are on it. Set a good nut, or several nuts. Study the holds or crack and plot a likely strategy; but once you have committed yourself to it, improvise if your theory is wrong and climb aggressively.

Bracing for impact, Labuddy Willoughby whistles off "Old Legends Die" (5.13b), Hueco Tanks, Texas. Note how Labuddy maintains body control, which greatly minimizes potential injury. Labuddy was unscathed and later completed the climb.

Beth Wald photo

Use whatever works best, and easiest, which sometimes is an improbable sequence. If a fall seems possible, or likely, make certain your pro is solid, and observe what, if anything, you will hit if you come off. If everything checks out, alert your belayer and go after it. No leader wants to fall, and you don't start up something without some hope of succeeding. The fact that success is not a given defines the challenge in climbing. But the fear of falling prohibits one's best effort and if everything checks out the fears are groundless. Falling is part of sport climbing. Good protection and realistic judgement keeps the sport sane.

Falling

Fifty years ago the incontrovertible rule was: the leader must never fall. The equipment was unreliable, and there was always the chance of the rope breaking. Present-day gear is remarkably sound, and while no one wants to fall, controlled falling has become standard practice for virtually all active sport climbers. Many leading climbers don't feel they have pushed themselves until they have logged some "air time." Indeed, you can never discover your limits unless you exceed them. Climbers routinely do, and the smart ones rarely get a scratch, even from twenty-foot falls. This relaxed attitude is not due entirely to the gear, however. Climbers have become expert in calculating the risks and potential consequences, and people have learned how to fall.

There are only two issues involved when you commit yourself to a potential fall: is the protection adequate to hold the longest possible fall, and what will you hit should you fall? The belay is never in question because you simply don't climb

Sayonara! Chasing his fleeting shadow, Hidataka Suzuki sails off the lip of the extremely overhanging "Your Mamma" (5.12c/d), in Eldorado Canyon, Colorado. However daunting, the climber was held fast and he grazed nothing but mountain air in a fall routine to experts.

Bob Horan photo

with someone who can't hold your fall unless you're a lunatic. If the pro is sound and the rock steep and smooth, it's fairly common to see a climber spend a whole afternoon falling off a difficult route. However, if the protection is dubious and there's something to hit, it's very rare to see a climber carry on unless he is virtually certain he will not fall. It's not the act of falling, but the consequences which are the issue. Climbing and protecting are separate skills, each of which keeps you alive, so for any lead – especially the first – don't challenge yourself in both at the same time. The beginning leader should avoid falling at all costs, but the possibility will arise and both his and the expert's concerns are the same: the security of the pro, and what he might hit if he loses it.

Falling is an art. When you fall, you need to maintain body control, to stay facing the rock, and to avoid tumbling. On a slab, you slide down on your feet, both hands pressing off the slab, keeping your chest and head far away from the surface. Keep your legs bent and spread apart, cat-like. The rope stretches considerably, so the jolt is less than you might think. I caught a partner on a fifty-footer on a steep slab which did nothing but wear his shoes out prematurely. He stayed relaxed, and just slid down on his feet, balancing with his hands – like a high-angle slide. I saw another person take the same fall, freeze up, and start tumbling. He needlessly broke a wrist.

On vertical climbs, you don't slide, but plummet – and very quickly. Remember to keep your legs a little extended and bent, so at impact they absorb the force like shock absorbers. Don't freeze up or go limp. That only invites injury. The screaming, rag-doll fall is worse still. The flailing arms will invariably smack something.

When you have traversed away from protection, a fall will swing you, pendulum fashion. The cat-like stance is your only hope to avoid tumbling. Be prepared for your weight coming onto the rope, which otherwise can wrench you askew, even spin you like a top. Remember, pendulum falls are dangerous no matter your posture or agility. Slamming into a corner from twenty feet to the side is almost the same as falling twenty feet straight down and smacking a ledge on your side.

Even a long fall happens so fast that you don't have time to think. All the stories about a person's life flashing before his eyes are pure bunk. You only have time to react. Often it's the shorter, eight to 10-foot falls which are the real wrenchers, where little rope is out, and the rope stretches less than on a longer fall. But whatever the length, don't freeze up, stay relaxed, facing the wall, legs and arms bent, and you'll usually not be hurt if your calculations were right.

After a fall of more than twenty feet, the rope suffers appreciable fiber elongation and structural deformation, much of which is recovered in time. After a longish fall, lower down and wait at least ten minutes for the rope to recover some of its stretch. The knot will absorb up to thirty percent of the impact force, so after lowering down, tie into your anchor with a sling and loosen the knot.

Often you will know you're going to fall before you do: you're bunched up and can't move; your fingers or toes are buttering off the holds; or your strength is ebbing fast. Warn your belayer, and don't panic. Fall as gracefully as you can. Not to impress anyone, but to keep your form. The person who falls out of control may have popped unexpectedly, but more likely panicked once airborne – a sure recipe for trouble. Don't underestimate even the smallest fall. A fall can break bones and even kill you if it goes wrong, so calculating and reacting to the consequences is extremely important. This is something a manual can only suggest.

Loose Rock

Most climbs of any length have at least some loose or rotten rock and the two are quite different, though the dangers are real in both cases. Loose rock doesn't necessarily mean the rock quality is poor. A flake, chockstone, block, or hold might be diamond-hard but still ready to go if you so much as breathe on it. Common sense is your best guide here. Delicately test suspect holds (if you have to use them) by tapping them with the heel of your hand, or kicking them with your foot. The sound can tell you a lot. Try to avoid them if at all possible. Arrange your protection so the rope goes around them. If there is a chance of them coming off, warn your belayer.

Rotten rock, crumbly and decomposing, is a nightmare. Every hold, every flake, every nut is suspect because you simply don't know what will hold and what won't. It's all instinct and judgement. Stay clear of such routes until you have the experience to know you shouldn't climb them anyway. If you dislodge rocks onto the rope, inspect the whole rope at the first opportunity. A bounding stone can chop even a new rope in a heartbeat.

Protecting the Second

The leader is responsible for the second's well-being as well as his own. He's got to do more than just warn the belayer of rockfall, or tell him he's about to fall. He must

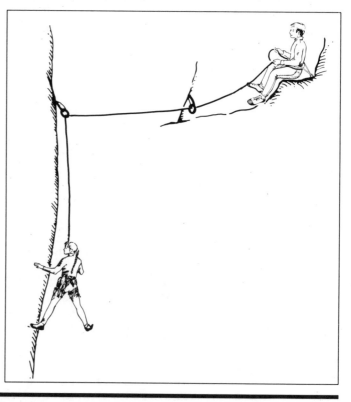

It is the leader's responsibility to ensure that the second does not have to follow a crux traverse without protection – usually simply a matter of putting in pro **after** the crux.

protect the second with the same acumen as he protects himself. This is most essential on traverses, where the leader moves sideways off a piece of protection. Note that when the leader reaches a traverse, he slots a nut that protects him going sideways. When the second follows, he cleans that nut and if he falls off, he'll swing all the way to the next nut. When the rope runs dead horizontal, it's very hard to keep from tumbling if you fall, so a leader should always protect at regular intervals – for his and his partner's safety.

Leading on the Face

Aside from what's already been said, it's a slippery task trying to explain the alchemy of leading a difficult face climb. But maybe the following will help.

A good face climber is a master of strategy. The first step is to break the climb down to sections between obvious footholds or rest stops. That way you can concentrate on one section at a time, and climb a succession of short climbs, rather than one long and ghastly one. Before a crux section, arrange pro you are certain is sound so you can concentrate on the moves, not the consequences. Get on a foothold and scrutinize the face. Spot the best holds, and break the section down to body lengths. Keep reducing each section down to the last visible hold. Then construct a mental sequence and visualize yourself climbing it. If it's too strenuous to pause very long, size up the holds, and cast off. On strenuous leads, you have to be aggressive and really go after it; but never abandon your form. Look at the baseball player who goes with a grand slam swing: instead of trying to stroke the ball, he tries to murder it. He's overanxious, and usually returns to the pine hailed by boos. Savvy, alertness, and controlled aggression are all vague terms that apply to leading a hard face.

Learning to downclimb is particularly important to the face climber. If you know you can reverse a section, than you minimize the potential danger and fear. Successful leaders will often venture out several times to gain the confidence to eventually go for it, gaining familiarity with each effort, and further reducing the hard section to the last, crux move. Hard face climbs are often not reversible, and eventually you will have to go for it, anyway. But climbing up and down can often help a leader settle in and muster the needed resolve.

Leading Crack Climbs

We have discussed the necessary techniques for climbing cracks – but the fact is, often the hardest part of leading a crack is not the climbing, but arranging the protection. When the climbing is strenuous, the leader finds himself hanging from a questionable jam and desperately trying to place a nut. Here are a few tricks to remember.

On thin to medium-sized cracks, don't plug up the best jams with protection. A "honed" leader will often opt for a smaller nut which fits into constrictions between the bigger, better jams.

You will normally place protection above your hands. Sometimes, if the only good nut slots are where your fingers are, you will place a nut below your hands, slotting it just after you have removed your fingers. Try to set these nuts quickly, as often you are hanging on in a crunched-up position, with a bent arm, which is more strenuous than the straight arm hang.

Be conscious that your feet don't get entangled in the rope. If your foot gets caught under both the rope and the nut, an upward step can lift your nut from the crack.

When the crack is parallel-sided and strenuous, go with SLCD's, which are much faster to place, and usually better.

Utilize all rest opportunities, and get a good nut in while you're there. Arrange sound protection before any crux section of liebacking or jamming, and if it's safe, power over the section without stopping. Hanging on in the middle of a crux section to get added protection in is often the wrong tactic, and can result in a fall you wouldn't have taken if you'd powered on.

Husband your energy. Don't use brute strength unless you need to. Stay relaxed, and try to get into a rhythm, a groove. Never thrash.

Setting the Belay

Once you have completed the first lead, you must rig an anchor to belay the second climber up. The anchor, of course, must be atomic bombproof unless you wish to risk getting ripped off the wall if the second falls. There are countless different possible belay constructs, all dictated by what the climb affords. As mentioned, always stop at an obvious ledge or belay spot. Try to rig the anchor directly above the line of ascent, so you can belay in line with the direction of pull. If you're on a ledge, tie yourself off with enough slack so you can belay at the lip of the ledge. This facilitates easy rope handling and communication, and keeps the rope from running over a potentially sharp edge. You'll usually choose to sit, facing out and down, but you can stand if you have a good brace. Just make certain you are tied off taut to the belay. If not, a fall could drag you right over the lip. Not good.

If the belay is on a small ledge or stance, you'll belay facing the anchor. Tie in with enough slack so you can lean back.

Rig the rope so it comes up, runs through the anchor, then back to you. Belaying through the anchor puts the load directly on the hardware so (for the hundredth time) the anchor must be stout. Also, the force of a fall will draw you directly toward the wall, so remained braced.

Belaying through the anchor is not a requirement. Climbers do so as it is usually safer and always more comfortable. The anchor, rather than your waist, takes the bulk of the force during a fall. If for some reason you cannot get an anchor to your utmost satisfaction – which does

(photo opposite)

A HANGING BELAY

1. Nuts held in opposition by clove hitches tied into a sling.

2. A clove hitch in the rope ties the first anchor set in opposition to a series of downward-pull nuts and also connects to 3.

3. A main figure eight tie-in for the belayer. Note that this all leaves her a bit below the upward-pull nuts, not the ideal situation, but certainly acceptable since any upward movement forced by a leader fall would soon be checked by the nuts.

4. Hanging her weight on the anchors is only practical at this small station and adds counterweight security to the belay.

5. The leader has wisely run the rope through a good downward-pull anchor at the belay to direct the impact force away from the belayer's waist.

6. The extra rope has been carefully lap-coiled across a sling to prevent it being caught by the wind or a flake below.

happen – you should probably belay right off your waist. When the second climber falls, the force is not extreme, and if you're properly braced and ready, your torso can absorb the force, often with no help from the anchor at all.

Some climbers argue that you should never belay through the anchor because it loads the system unnecessarily. They would rather the torso absorb at least some of the force, saving the anchor for a backup. But for me and thousands of others, the anchor is not a backup but the whole shooting match, and all the talk about saving or guarding the anchor is balderdash. Anyone who has climbed a big wall knows that if your anchor isn't good enough to belay through, it's not an anchor at all, but a lethal liability.

Sometimes there are no belay ledges, or stances, or even good footholds. Here you must construct a "sling," or "hanging" belay. Many hanging belays feature permanent anchors – bolts, pitons, or both. If you have to construct an artificial anchor, observe the rules we've gone over. Once the anchor is all equalized, tie yourself off with enough slack so you can hang at, but not below the hardware – and not so far out that you can't easily reach the anchor if need be. You normally belay through the anchor on a hanging belay.

If you're wearing neither leg loops or a harness, you should carry a belay seat ("butt-bag") to sit in. Hanging off a swami is uncomfortable and rough on your back and kidneys. If you don't have a belay seat, create a loop of rope to sit on by tying the free rope back under your butt and to the anchor. Anything but hanging directly off your back. Whatever construct you end up in, always pay close attention to the rope. As you belay it in, keep it organized; stack it neatly. Don't let it loop down onto the rock below unless it can't get in the second's way, and there are absolutely no knobs or flakes for it to snag on. Never flip the slack into a deep crevice or behind a narrow flake. If there's anything for it to snag on, it will. If need be, loop the slack over your lap (lap-coiling) or through a sling, thus keeping it out of potential snares. This is essential with sea-cliff climbing.

If you climb long enough, you'll probably lose a rope due to a hang-up, even if you're paying close attention. Strong winds, common on north faces, can blow the unattended rope exactly where you don't want it.

Changing Leads

Once the second has followed the pitch, having cleaned all the protection you put in, the first thing he does upon gaining the belay is to tie himself off – *before* he is taken off belay. And he should tie into more than one biner. Pull out the topo. Eyeball the hell out of the next lead and re-rack the gear accordingly. Don't take off with an unorganized rack because you won't want to fumble with the gear in an awkward position above. Relax. And don't take off until you have gone through the ceremony of figuring out as much as you can from below. Discuss questions and strategy with

Todd Skinner and Steve Petro climb the difficult (5.12c) "Psychedelic Psycho," in Fremont Canyon, Wyoming. The belayer pays close watch to the slack lest it loop down into the drink.

Bill Hatcher photo

your partner. All this can take only a few minutes once you get the hang of it.

Though your anchor is bomb-proof, there's no need to prove it is, so get a few nuts in immediately off the belay. Falling directly onto the belay is a worst-case scenario. With a hip belay it is misery and possible disaster. The belay devices will do the job, but the force can sprain backs and slam the belayer into the wall hard enough to knock him cold. Even a short fall onto the belay transmits to both belayer and the anchor forces in excess of a thousand pounds – and there is always the chance you might land on the belayer, somehow jarring his brake hand free, in which case you'll plummet to the end of the rope or to the ground, whichever comes first. So even if the climbing is simple, get some pro in straightaway. To do otherwise is to violate a rule as fundamental as never removing your brake hand from the belay rope.

If you are not "swinging leads," and the second intends to follow every pitch, you face several options – depending on the nature of the belay station. If you're on a good ledge, you can both tie into the anchor with slings looped through your

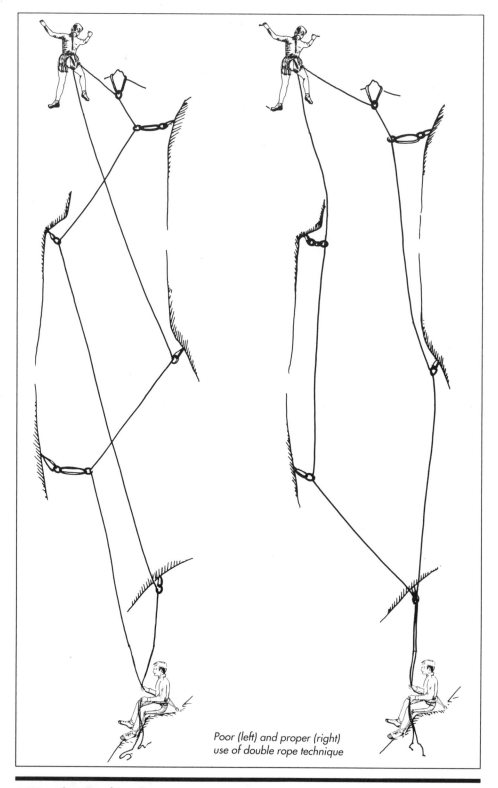

*Poor (left) and proper (right)
use of double rope technique*

harnesses. The leader unties from the anchor and ties the second in as he was tied in. That gives the leader a free rope, and he's set to go. On small stances or hanging belays this can be an enormous hassle, and you will often choose to simply change ends – untying your knots and swapping ends. Remember that you will at least briefly be untied from the rope, so make certain that your sling tie-ins are secure, and fastened with at least two biners to an equalized point.

If you are a party of three, it is easiest for the third climber to climb last on a second rope that is trailed by the second climber. At the belay, the third is tied off, and the free end is trailed again on the following lead. If the third climber wishes to lead a pitch, he is simply put on belay, clipped through the anchor, and off he goes. If for some reason he wants to go second, you are looking at some weird rope shenanigans, untying and knot-switching, which is more hassle than it's worth, but possible using the aforesaid techniques. If the route wanders, it is the second's job to clip the third's rope through key nuts to check any drastic sideways falls. The third climber must then remove the pro his rope has been clipped through.

Double Rope Technique

Most Europeans and many British climbers lead on two 9-mm ropes. For several reasons, the technique has never fully caught on in America. Managing a single 10.5-mm lead rope is easier. There is less weight for the leader to drag behind him, and the belayer's task is easier as well. Since American climbs tend to follow straight lines, the single 10.5-mm rope has remained the standard. The advantages of using double ropes are these:

1) When a route wanders, a single rope will zigzag extravagantly through the protection, and a hundred runners can't eliminate rope drag. By using two different-colored 9-mm ropes, you can clip one line through protection on the left and one on the right, each rope running somewhat parallel and straight – or at least avoiding the drastic jags of a single rope. 2) When the climber leading on a single rope pulls up a loop to clip in, he's adding distance to a potential fall at twice the length of the pulled-up loop. With double ropes, if the top pro should fail, or if the climber falls just before clipping in, the extra loop is not added to the fall since the other line is clipped in below, and he will come onto it first. 3) When the protection is poor, you can stack or duplicate placements, distributing the force of a fall between two nuts and two ropes, reducing impact on both. 4) On horizontal traverses, a single rope must go sideways with the line of protection. With double ropes, providing that the leader was able to climb above the traverse before belaying, one of the ropes can be left unclipped from the traverse protection, so the rope runs up and across to the belayer, instead of dead horizontal – much better if the second should fall. 5) Perhaps the most important advantage is for those

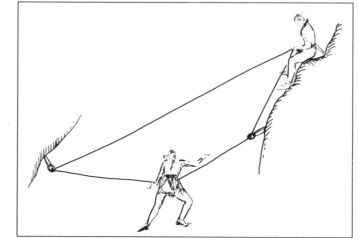

Protecting the second on a traverse with double ropes by belaying from both sides. The far anchor, remaining fixed, need only be as good as a sling through a fixed pin to secure the relatively gentle force of the falling second.

Whenever two ropes are run through one anchor they should be clipped into separate carabiners.

who climb regularly on sharp-edged rock like limestone, quartzite, or gneiss, where it is possible that a single rope could be cut during a fall. I've only heard once of a fall that resulted in a severed rope, but for those climbers frequenting areas where it is even conceivable, double ropes are a solution.

As the leader places pro, he will forewarn the belayer which rope he is going to clip in: "Slack on the yellow," for example. And herein lies the single biggest disadvantage with double ropes: their great potential for snarling and snagging – not only on rock features, but on themselves. A hip belay with double ropes is tricky business, requiring the lines to be fed out or drawn in alternately. With the belay devices, it's often hard to keep both lines running smoothly and ordered in a tidy pile. The lines can likewise become crossed in or behind the device. These problems are manageable with experience, so make sure you have some before belaying on double lines.

Twin Ropes

A recent technique involves leading on two 8.8-mm ropes, using them as one rope, clipping both lines into the protection, though through separate biners. Aside from reducing the chance of total rope failure through cutting over an edge, and the ability to make full-length rappels, there seems little else to recommend using twin ropes. A single strand of 8.8-mm rope does not pass the regular UIAA test. It does pass the "half-rope" test, which substitutes a 50-kg dropped weight for one weighing 80 kg. Because it holds seven such falls, climbers have started using the 8.8-mm lines for double rope technique as well. With either twin or double ropes, it is safe practice to clip the first couple anchors off the belay with both ropes to safeguard against the high impact force of the leader falling close to the belay. With the thinner twin ropes, this practice should be continued until well into the lead to provide plenty of rope to absorb any fall.

Twin rope technique, and using 8.8-mm ropes as double ropes, are as yet unestablished practices, used only by experts in specialized situations. Time will render the verdict. For the novice, it's best to stick with the older, less complicated methods.

Retreat and Self-Rescue

No climber has a 100 percent success ratio. Unexpected dangers, sore hands, hornets, apathy, no water, rain storms – the causes are many that may force a team off the cliff. There are two considerations when retreating: getting down unscathed, and doing so without leaving all your gear behind.

The most common practice is simply to lower the leader down to the belay. Oftentimes, if the leader doesn't fancy the pitch, the second will try his hand before the team throws the towel in altogether. If the decision is made to retreat, you will lower down, removing all the protection between the lowering point and the belay. This means that if what you are lowering off should fail, you will fall a very long way, so make certain whatever you lower off is bombproof. A good rule is to never lower off one nut. Back it up and equalize it, if necessary. And don't try to save a biner by running the rope through a runner threaded through the lower-off anchor. The generated friction on weighted nylon can saw right through it. Better to lose a piece of gear than your life. Dozens of climbers have thought otherwise, and paid dearly.

If you (as leader) have more than half the rope out, you cannot return to the belay straight off because the rope won't reach. (Clearly, if you're 90 feet above the belay, you need 180 feet of rope to lower back to it, and the longest ropes are 165 feet.) One choice is to downclimb to a point where you have sufficient rope to lower off. The other choice is to lower down past the halfway point, taking pro out as you descend, and do the following: Arrange an anchor that is bombproof, and tie off to it with slings threaded through your harness or swami. Before you untie and pull the rope through, tie the rope off. You don't want it getting away from you, which

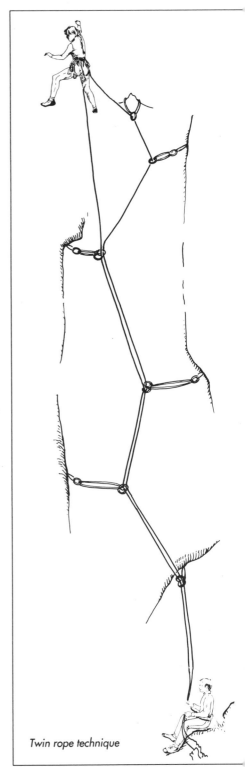

Twin rope technique

would leave you marooned. Once you've pulled it through the top anchor, tie back in, take up the slack, and lower back down.

If the leader is hurt or unconscious, you as belayer should try to lower him down, hopefully to a ledge. If there is not enough rope, you have little option but to tie him off, a procedure that may require innovation and the use of a prusik or Bachmann knot (discussed in the next chapter) in order to free yourself from the belay, then retreat for help (providing you have another rope) – or yell for it. And fast. An injured climber should not be left dangling. It constricts circulation, inhibits breathing, and his head will invariably be drooping in an abnormal attitude. Such a scenario is a true emergency and should be treated as one. A rescue team will have to climb up to him, establish an anchor, and lower him off on another free rope or come down from the top, whichever is easier. Such a procedure requires at least one other climber and two more ropes. So you'll need help, no matter who you are. The chief concern is to get the injured climber down quickly. It's usually much faster to simply leave all the gear behind, retrieving it when someone's health is not at stake.

If you are on exceptionally steep rock and left dangling from the wall after a fall, you should have foreseen the possibility. The belayer is left to tie you off. Wise leaders take another rope to pull back in with, or lead on double ropes for the same purpose. If you are on a single rope, you can often initiate enough swing – by flopping about in space – to pendulum back to the wall. If you can't, you're in a fine mess, and extracting yourself is quite involved. Hopefully there is some lesser-angled rock below that you can lower to. If not, these are your options: try to hand-over-hand the rope back to the last nut, having the belayer reel the slack in once you've clasped the nut. This is nearly impossible, but it has been done. You can use a prusik or Bachmann knot setup to climb back up to the last nut (explained in Chapter 6: *Getting Down*), or you can wait for a rescue. Someone will have to climb up to you, toss you a rope, and pull you back into the wall. If any of these scenarios are even remotely possible, trail another rope so you can get back to the cliff. Anyone who doesn't almost deserves the consequent hassles.

There is another method of retreat, involving rappelling off an anchor, that we will discuss in the next chapter.

By predicting the possibilities you can avoid the consequences. You can never predict a rainstorm or a case of the "willies," so expect at some time to "bail off" a climb. Just never bail off one nut, or lower down with your rope running through slings.

The Fear of Leading

Justified fear is a shrewd advisor, but groundless fear is self-defeating and can exhaust you. If you are terrified, quickly take stock of your situation. Is the belay good? It better be. That's a given. Is the protection adequate? If so, you might be confusing exhilaration with fear – which is common to beginners. Get on a foothold and settle down. Relax. If you know you're safe yet still feel like fouling your britches, write it off to the jitters. If you eventually learn that you just can't adjust to the vertical environment, you might be in the wrong sport. Climbing's not for everyone.

Relaxation is essential in any exacting work. While telling someone to just relax is simple enough, beginning leaders often say, "Here I am, 100 feet up a vertical cliff, trembling on a little foothold with my rope clipped through a few pieces of wire. How am I supposed to relax?!" First, avoid things which cause a leader to panic. Never rush. Loss of concentration leads to poor self-control and frantic climbing. Try to climb in a measured, self-contained manner. You're not in a race. Be realistic about the difficulties and hazards. If you're nervous, ask yourself why. Assess the problems. If the risks are imagined, you can usually talk yourself down. If they are real, you must retain self-control. If you don't, you short-circuit any rational response, and you might get hurt as a direct result of being afraid to get hurt.

The Psychology of Success

Climbers have long recognized the link between mental attitude and physical performance, and there's a lot of talk bandied about concerning visualization, imaging, zen breathing, et al. These disciplines can greatly magnify one's performance, but remember this: they're all ineffective if you can't unleash the tiger in your heart; and that's something that just can't be taught or acquired. Likewise, your mental attitude reflects your physical capabilities, and there are times that, even with the heart of a tiger, you still can't chin yourself on a burnished limestone wart, and there's no sense in telling yourself you can. The value of the mental exercises is to amplify your actual capabilities and to keep your mind from thwarting your full potential.

The important breakthroughs in climbing have not occurred because someone came along with stronger fingers and better boots. They occurred because someone had a new idea about what was possible, believed in himself, and had the fortitude to see it through. It all started with an idea, a belief.

The starting point to successful climbing is a positive attitude, an honest belief that you are going to give it your best shot, and that you have a chance at succeeding if all goes well. You cannot talk yourself into doing something you don't really want to do (or know you don't have a snowball's chance in hell of doing). A positive attitude can bolster your resolve, but not create it. So on the day of an important climb, on the drive up to the cliff, while hiking to the base, we start programming our minds, telling ourselves that we can do what we set out to do if we believe it. We nip fear in the bud.

The next phase is to reduce our thoughts to the task at hand, eliminating extraneous ideas, emotions, small talk, distraction. Switch off the ghetto blaster and focus on the climb. Get relaxed. Concentrate. The mind is capable of doing many things at once, but only one well. Don't split your attention or derail it with things which won't further your immediate aim.

Before and during the climb, visualize yourself doing the moves, climbing smoothly and in complete control. The word "imaging" is popular just now, but it's the same old thing – and very effective: the basketball player visualizing the ball piercing the hoop with the game-winning shot, the climber seeing himself liebacking over the crux bulge. A climber might study the crux and preview several different sequences in his mind before the most probable one clicks a mental light on.

Throughout the whole process you are verbally telling yourself – silently and out loud – that you will succeed. This is no more than self-hypnosis or auto-suggestion, and can have remarkable impact on the receptive mind. When effectively done, you are programming the subconscious, where much of the reservations originate.

The ultimate performer is the one who climbs "unconsciously." Not like a zombie, but one whose conscious, rational mind is not continually checking the upward flow with negative thoughts and is only a distant observer. It's a trance-like state that only recognizes the task at hand. The will is crystallized, the attention needled down to a tiny

Todd Skinner frees the 21st pitch (5.11c) of El Capitan's Salathe Wall while partner Paul Piana belays atop El Cap Spire.

Bill Hatcher photo

section of space and time, and when you're climbing, the only thing that can hold you back is a true physical impossibility.

Some climbers are so keen to succeed that they defeat themselves by trying too hard. To these climbers, the mental disciplines are particularly effective, for they can instill the control and discipline that their natural gusto would have otherwise negated. The old notion that "the tiger hunts in absolute peace" best illustrates this point.

On the exceptionally difficult crux, all the mental games must conclude before you start. The most difficult climbs require a tenacity and degree of effort almost unheard of in any other sport. The mental games are remarkably effective as a beginning ritual, but once you swing into that double overhanging lieback, or onto that bald and bulging face, it's no time to be talking to yourself or imagining anything. It's all focused effort.

A realistic goal, a strong desire, correct programming through visualization, verbal and nonverbal self-commands, and the focus, control, and tenacity to execute the task – that's what you're after.

Climbing with Style

On the face of it, it is debatable that the fashion in which we go about climbing rocks is of any consequence to anyone. We just want to get up safely, and if we ignore decorum here and there, who cares? But a funny thing happens once we are even moderately skilled. Simply getting up at all costs is not very satisfying. We slowly realize that the way we get up is both the means and the end. Virtually anyone who sticks with climbing comes to this conclusion. To understand current mores, let's look at where they originated.

In the classic *Ropes, Knots, and Slings for Climbers*, Walt Wheelock talks about the "Golden Age" of climbing, centered in and around Zermatt, a century ago. "A rope was only to be used as a belay, not as a climbing aid. One just did not put his weight on the rope if he were a worthy member of the Alpine Club. It could be used to aid a descent and in the case of emergency or for safety, but each climber was expected to climb his own peak."

This "fair play" trend continued until climbers, in their search for new and harder routes, began using equipment for direct assistance. First were pendulums and tension traverses, essentially leaning and swinging off the rope to move sideways over blank or unclimbable rock. Soon climbers were constructing ladders of pitons into which they would clip runged rope stirrups, or "etriers," stepping up and slamming home each new piton in turn. This "direct aid" technique allowed passage over rock otherwise impossible using only hands and feet. The eventual refinement of this technique led to the first ascents of the finest pure rock walls in the world – in Yosemite Valley, California. And as the standards rose in aid (or "artificial") climbing, so did those in free climbing.

In the U.S. and England, free climbing and aid climbing were always considered different and distinctive forms. With

aid climbing, you used gear as your means of ascent –
anything goes. With free climbing, you never used the gear
except to safeguard against a fall, and even the slightest
infraction – resting on a piton, stepping on a bolt – meant you
were not free climbing, but aid climbing. This attitude is
based on the concept that artificial and free climbing are
distinct pursuits. One is mechanical, the other athletic. No
one argued that free climbing was the purer form, and active
climbers stuck by the rules, for a game without rules is
meaningless. From the beginning (when alpinists shunned
assistance from the hemp), climbers were aware that
runaway technology (and dependence on it) would dilute the
challenge, so the elements of style were upheld to preserve
it. Even on routes requiring extensive aid climbing, pioneers
would push the free climbing to the limit before breaking out
the etriers as a last resort.

The rules of free climbing, unofficial as they were,
brought several points to bear. The spirit of adventure and
exploration was the very stuff that animated climbing.
Furthermore, since one could conceivably hammer their way
up any rock wall using aid techniques, free climbing would
have to display some element of honesty and fair play –
sportsmanship, if you will – lest the two forms become
blurred, and the distinctions insignificant. Some big climbs
were obviously aid routes, and were approached accordingly.
But when there was some doubt, climbers harked back to
the original alpinists, when the climber was expected to
"climb his own peak," not by hanging on the rope or pitons,
but through his own physical prowess and skill.

On a prospective free route, an honest free climber
avoided anything which could reduce the adventure and
challenge: he wouldn't descend the climb first, inspecting the
rock for available holds, placing protection in the crux
sections, chipping footholds, or anything else which could
make his ascent easier, or give him unnatural advantage
before he had actually taken the lead. He would start from
the ground and deal with obstacles as he encountered them
– "on sight." If he fell off, he would lower back to the belay
and try again, rather than hang on the protection before
carrying on. If he was a real stickler, he would pull the rope
through the protection and lead it from the ground. If it
simply couldn't be free climbed, then aid climb it they did –
and right on their heels there would be others trying to free
it, often succeeding.

Leading climbers stuck fast to the "on sight" philosophy,
though as early as 1960, people were pre-inspecting leads on
rappel and placing bolts for ready protection once they
decided to lead the climb. But these efforts were generally
considered "cheating" and were avoided by most leading
climbers. By 1975, the hardest climbs were so severe that
climbers often had to return several times before they could
do them legitimately – climbing from belay to belay with no
falls and no assistance from the gear. By 1980, the top climbs

were still harder, requiring weeks, even months before a "hardman" could make it in one go. To reduce the time spent, climbers started top-roping (belaying from above) the climbs before leading them, pre-placing pro to make the eventual lead less strenuous and dangerous, and rehearsing the moves while hanging on gear (hangdogging), and in several pitiful instances, manufacturing holds where there were none. Presently, the hardest free routes are sometimes dangerous, but because the climbers have memorized every toe hold, every crystal, every thumb position, they are far less adventures than remarkable examples of rock gymnastics. The ultimate goal of any climber is still to climb the route as though the rope was not there – climbing the route without falls on the first attempt. However, today's hardest routes are so extreme that most find the old rules impractical, if not passé, but you do eventually have to climb the route from bottom to top, no falls, to claim a "free," or "redpoint" ascent. The methods used to get there, the how of it all, are immaterial if they serve the end of the "honest" free ascent. So, at least, says the new-wave ace. There are a handful of traditionalists who still say any divergence from the old norms is an earmark of a "yellow" climber. Both schools have a point, and the issue remains an ethical quagmire, as it should.

So what does this all mean to the novice? Not much. In fact, it means precious little to anyone save the world-class climber who has his whole existence invested in rock climbing and little else. The novice should approach a climb trying to carry out the old norms, not resting on the protection unless he has to, realizing that top climbers bend the rules because their game is really a different thing altogether. And while the old "on-sight" rules have been somewhat abridged by the cutting edge, even they observe two absolute edicts: never place new bolts on existing routes, and never chisel holds into the rock. These edicts are the only rules which have sure ethical import, because they can directly, and permanently, affect someone else's experience. A route is public property, and once a route is established, it is no one else's task to change it to their liking. Can you imagine going to the Getty museum and taking hammer and chisel to a Grecian frieze, hammering off the odd mole, straightening an aquiline nose, until you had it just as you liked? You'd be ushered out behind the shed where the big fellas would rearrange *your* features.

As long as you climb with nuts, you are totally free to do as you choose, and nobody is going to care much. Most climbers find that respecting the old rules is more satisfying than making a joke of them. A novice should concern himself with routes that will challenge him, but which he can do without hang-dogging or pre-inspecting. Unfortunately many climbers, even novices, feel pressure to climb high-number routes, and they sacrifice every trace of style in trying routes beyond their ability. When they finally manage to hang and yard their way up a route they're the first to tell everyone they did, neglecting the ticklish details of style. You haven't "done" a route until you've freed it; don't be ashamed to include the bald truth when reporting your accomplishments, so your integrity will never be questioned. Most climbers find it more rewarding to climb several routes within their ability than to spend all day falling up one over their head. If you stick with climbing you will discover all this for yourself; and if you find yourself hanging on the protection, no need to tell the priest. Just realize you're not climbing as well as you might be.

Free Soloing

By definition, you are free soloing anytime you climb without a rope, regardless of the difficulty. The common usage, however, refers to a climber who is scaling a fifth-class climb where a rope and equipment are usually employed. Yet the free soloer has neither. He has only a pair of shoes, a chalk bag, and the prowess he brings to the cliffside. Since the penalty for a fall is almost certain death on a route of any length, even experts will question the sanity of the campaign. To the person not given to risk-taking, even the most passionate explanation will ring hollow. Remember, free soloing is rarely a reckless practice – rather a very calculated, conscious act. And it's a matter of degree. The chances of a 5.12 climber falling off minimal 5.10 terrain are remote, but still possible. Yet the nervy aficionado will sometimes push the gamble ever closer to his all-out limit till he is virtually doing a high-wire act above infinity, where a moment's lapse in concentration, an imprecise toe placement, a fractured rugosity, and the reaper falls. To the novice witnessing this first hand, it seems the purest madness. Why do it? You should certainly not attempt it to find out why. The few who regularly practice free soloing are inevitably experts who technically know exactly what they are doing, and intuitively know exactly why.

What the free soloer craves is either raw intensity, or the joy and freedom that comes from mastery. If he craves notoriety for his feats he is motivated by sham values and may pay for his vanity. The reasons to free solo must come from the heart and be monitored by an icy, analytical mind. Anything else courts disaster. We all climb, amongst other reasons, because it is exciting. So when the free soloer ups the ante to include all the marbles, you can imagine how the thrill is magnified. Foolish? Perhaps, but an element of tomfoolery runs through the very skein of any climbing. The free soloer has simply pushed things to their ultimate expression. His rewards, in terms of intensity of experience, are the greatest. And so are the penalties. Amazingly enough, very few free soloing accidents ever occur. This is a clear testament that the practice is undertaken by experts in a very measured and sober way. Ultimately, free soloing is a distinctively personal affair, and even daily practitioners discourage the practice, as they should. There is certainly no reason for the recreational climber to ever even consider it.

Getting Down

Every climb ends in a descent, so climbers must be well-versed in going down. Depending on the situation, the options for getting down from a climb include walking off, downclimbing, rappelling, and lowering. (Downclimbing and rappelling are covered in this chapter, and lowering is addressed in Chapter 7: *Sport Climbing*.) There is an inevitable chicken and egg syndrome with this chapter, in that I'm introducing terms and practices which, at the outset, you might never have heard of. If at first mention you do not thoroughly grasp what is being laid down, rest assured that by the end of the chapter we will have clarified what we were obliged to merely touch upon in these first paragraphs.

Understand that the tools and techniques for descending are fairly straightforward, but the cost of a major mistake can be your life. Good judgement, attention to details, awareness of hazards, and diligent double-checking will keep you healthy climbing and descending. Remember, even a momentary lapse of concentration can end in tragedy. Until you're confident that you can safely get back down to the ground under a variety of situations, you don't belong on the rocks without a qualified guide.

First and foremost, always have a plan for the descent before going up on a route. On sport routes, getting down may require only climbing to a double bolt anchor and lowering to the ground (soon described). Descending longer routes can be complicated, devious and dangerous. Innumerable epics have been suffered because a party neglected to do their homework per the descent. Most guidebooks include information on getting down from the routes; fellow climbers may also be a source of route and descent knowledge. If no information is available about the descent, scope the cliff from the ground. Look for places to walk or climb down, or established rappel anchors. If you can't find an obvious descent, it's sometimes best to rappel the route you climbed to avoid going irreversibly down into unknown terrain-which has happened more times that one might expect. In a popular area you can most likely get rescued. Pull this stunt a little ways off the beaten track, and it's dust to dust.

Climbers must also know how to improvise a descent for those unavoidable retreats. Sport climbers need only know how to retreat from a bolt in the middle of a pitch, while those who do longer routes must be capable of, and prepared for, a multi-pitch retreat. There is not one single climber in the history of the sport who has enjoyed a 100% success rate on long climbs. In most cases, the more long routes a climber has bagged, the more times he has also found himself descending a route for reasons ranging from falling stones to ebbing desire. He lives to again mount the high crag simply because he knows how to safely retreat.

Walking down should be the first option if the walk-off is easy, though frequently climbers will lower or rappel instead for convenience. Walking down is normally simple business, though not always. Be mindful not to cut down too soon to avoid getting "cliffed"; and use good judgement to find the path of least resistance.

DOWNCLIMBING

Should rappelling prove unsafe or impractical, you will most likely have to downclimb off. Competent downclimbing is essential to descend gullies, slabs, chimneys, or any stretch of rock encountered once the climb is over. Unless the rappel route is very straightforward, most experienced climbers will opt to climb down off a crag if a realistic route is available. And even when the rappel route is a simple task, climbers will still climb off. It's often faster, and their fate is in their own hands, not dependent on equipment. Downclimbing can be as fun and challenging as climbing up. Almost without exception, downclimbing is done without a rope since the terrain is usually fairly easy. If you haven't made the descent before you probably have little or no knowledge of the terrain below, so be very careful.Hopefully you at least scoped the decent from the ground so you have some idea where you're headed. The downclimbing route must be free of loose or rotten rock. If it isn't, no one should be in a position to be hit by rockfall. It is generally best to keep the party close together so falling stones cannot build momentum, and the first one down can forewarn those behind of particular danger spots. Don't be afraid to pull out the rope and rappel or belay if things get too hairy. Never solo down anything you don't feel absolutely confident about. Likewise, never coerce your partners to down-solo anything they aren't comfortable with. Instead, be the first to offer a rope for your partners.

If you're the stronger partner you should go down first to find the most logical route, and to spot your less experienced partners through the dicey stretches (provided you have a good stance!). Again, try to stay close together so any dropped rocks can't gain "wrecking ball" speed before nailing someone; so both climbers have ready assistance if someone gets into trouble; and so the team doesn't get separated.

If you rope up to downclimb, the weaker climber goes first, with a top rope, placing protection for the stronger partner to "down-lead" on (hopefully the "weaker" partner knows how to place good protection). Rappelling is almost always a safer and quicker option than down-leading, though.

On lower-angled downclimbing, face out so you can see where you're going, and lean back to the wall with one or both arms as needed for balance. As the angle steepens, you'll reach a point where it becomes easier to turn in and face the rock, peering past your hip or between your legs for directions. A little experience and all the nuances will come clear.

The ability to downclimb safely and fast is a handy skill. You can outrun approaching storms, avoid unnecessary rappels and, providing you use common sense, have a fun time doing so. If you start down the wrong gully or shoulder, though, it can get nasty. Against my better instincts I thrashed down a manzanita-choked gully east of Basket Dome in Yosemite Valley, and Lord Jim with a chainsaw couldn't have reversed it. Five hours and a thousand weeping punctures later we finally gained the valley floor, and I've been careful what I head down ever since.

RAPPELLING

A million postcards feature a colorfully clad climber "roping down" the sheer crag, bounding in arcs, meters off the wall, a waterfall cascading in the background. To the layman, the image embodies everything quixotic about climbing, though there is no climbing involved. Beginning climbers are anxious to try, though this zeal usually falters as they backpedal toward the precipitous lip. Climbing manuals are quick to state how experienced climbers hate rappelling. In reality, most climbers don't really mind rappelling, though they avoid it if possible. There is the uncoiling of ropes, setting anchors and sometimes leaving gear behind, and the spooky task of absolutely trusting the gear, rarely with any backup. If the rappels are long and involved, including many anchor transfers and a lot of eerie dangling on the gear, even the best climbers will walk a long way to avoid the hassles. But any way you stack it, if you're going to climb, you're likewise going to have to rappel – and a lot.

"Abseil" (European), "rappel" (American), "roping down" – call it what you want, it all involves using friction to descend a rope.

Statistically, rappelling is climbing's second most dangerous process, close on the heels of leader accidents. A climber's bulk is continuously stressing the equipment, and if any link in the weighted chain should fail, the result is disastrous. Equipment failure, anchors pulling, knots coming untied, and a host of human errors – usually avoidable – have caused many rappelling tragedies. Consequently, assiduous attention must be paid to every aspect of the procedure, starting with choosing the best rappel route.

The Line of Descent

The first question is: where are you rappelling to? If you're simply heading for the ground and can see that the rope reaches, your task is relatively simple. If you have to make more than a single rappel to reach the ground or your destination, make certain of several things. Are you descending to a ledge, a stance, or what? Do the ropes reach, and if so, what will be the next anchor? Do you have the necessary gear to rig an anchor? Many times rappel routes are established featuring fixed anchors; other times they are not. Numerous climbs end at a place from which you can walk off. If not, the way down often rappels the route just climbed. You know the topography, the ledges, the anchors. There is no mystery to it.

If you want to descend a virgin stretch of rock, requiring numerous rappels, you have no way of knowing if there are adequate ledges and anchors. Even if you have inspected it with a telescope and can spot a big ledge, you still have no idea how good the anchors might be. Unless you carry a huge bolt kit, you are committing yourself to a real crap-shoot that could leave you stranded. I highly advise you to pass on such an expedition.

For normal sport climbing, you need to know the place you're heading for, that there is an anchor or the possibility of getting one, that the same is available below – all the way to the ground – and that your rope will reach every rappel point/anchor in turn. Most guidebooks supply this information, but more often than not your judgement about a situation is what will get you down safely. At popular crags it is a good idea to ask around if you have any doubts about the descent. When in total doubt, rappel an established route, preferably the route you've just climbed – if you have to rappel at all.

ANCHORS

A bomb-proof anchor is the foundation of sane climbing, never more true than with a rappel anchor. Yet several times every year climbers – if not entire teams – are killed because of failed rappel anchors. Very occasionally these tragedies are due to acts of God – trees inexplicably coming uprooted, or several bolts or pitons popping mysteriously – but more often than not the accidents occurred because someone chose to save equipment and chance it with a suspect anchor. Is the anchor unquestionably sound? It has to be. Go with an indisputable natural anchor whenever possible – a towering ponderosa pine, for instance. With an artificial anchor, a minimum of two nuts, bolts, or pitons are obligatory. Three, even four, different points are sometimes called for, depending on the quality of the placements.

Look the rappel anchors over good. Again, at least two bombproof anchors should be established at rappel stations, and they should conform to the "SRENE" standard: Solid,

Redundant, Equalized, and allow No Extension. "Solid" refers to the comparative security of the individual nuts, bolts, etc... "Redundant" simply means that you have a number of solid anchors. "Equalized" refers to the process of equally spreading the stress of a rappel over the various component parts of the anchor (explained in detail in Chapter 4: Ropes, Anchors, and Belays). "No extension" means that if one of the anchors should pull, there is no slack in the system that would allow the rappeller's body weight to suddenly shock-load onto the remaining anchors.

If the anchors are anything less than bomber, back them up if possible, and make sure everything is well-equalized. Avoid the American Triangle (pictured on page 92), especially if the anchors are suspect. Occasionally, rappel anchors consist of a single tree or set of slings on a rock feature, but climbers should back up anchors whenever possible. Anchor failure will likely kill you and your partner, so don't be cheap with your lives! If you use a tree, it's usually best to run the rope through a sling rather than around the tree; otherwise, you might damage your rope or the tree, or your rope could get stuck.

Fixed Anchors

Inspect fixed anchors as if your life depends on them, because it most assuredly does. Rusty pitons and bolts are particularly suspect. When in doubt, back up the existing anchor or place your own. The cost of a good nut is a small price to pay to see your children grow up, and all those who follow will benefit by your sacrifice.

At popular climbing areas bolt anchors are sometimes connected by a chain. Never simply loop your rope around the chain. If a link or bolt hanger breaks, the rope will slip right off the chain. That happened 1,000 feet up El Capitan, and three young men died. I never better understood the significance of the word grief as when I saw friends of the stricken three milling around El Cap meadow, their faces long as doom and asking how come. There is no reason anyone should ever have to repeat their fate.

Many times, fixed anchor slings will come equipped with a heavy metal ring, like a medallion, through which you can feed the rope. These rappel rings are nice to pull a rope through and are usually quite strong – the cast aluminum ones are the best – but beware the welded steel ones. A new nylon runner threaded through the eyes or hangers of the anchor isn't given to invisible cracks or work hardening. I've heard of those rings breaking, but I've never heard of a new runner breaking on a rappel. Not once.

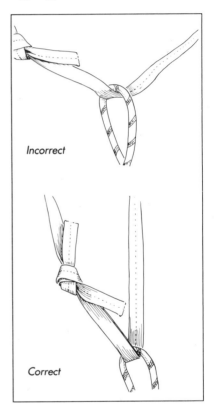

Incorrect

Correct

Anchor slings should be arranged to hang at less than a 90-degree angle (bottom) to maintain their maximum strength. The weight of the rappeller unduly loads the broadly-slung configuration illustrated at top.

Most often on fixed rappel anchors, the individual placements – be they nuts (rare), pitons, or bolts – have a host of runners threaded through them from past rappels. If you're relying on fixed slings (left by previous parties), check every inch of them to make sure they haven't suffered from too much UV radiation (sunbleached), or been chewed by rats or other varmints. Especially check the part of the slings hidden from view, and inspect any rappel rings or links. Add a sling if any question exists about the condition of the existing slings, and add a chock or two if the other anchors don't look positively bombproof. It's your life you're dealing with here, so don't get into the bad habit of trusting whatever fixed gear exists.

The rope is retrieved by pulling it through the slings, and the process can cause enough friction to greatly reduce the strength of the slings, and occasionally even burn straight through them. Recently, some old slings taken from rappel anchors were tested for tensile strength, and it's reassuring to know that many of these slings were stronger than expected. Figures indicate that if there are more than four slings in place, there is little chance of all of them breaking. However, wear from the elements, cutting on sharp bolt hangers, and friction burns all factor in to greatly diminish a runner's strength, so the importance of backing up suspect slings cannot be overstated.

Wherever the anchor is, you are obliged to rappel directly below it. Gravity deems it so. A weight on the end of a string hangs directly below the string's anchor – the plumb line. After you have descended a ways, you can traverse around a bit, but a slip might set you on a dangerous, sideways tumble. So if you have to rig your own anchor, do so directly above (or as close as possible to) where you plan to descend; and don't deviate more than necessary.

Barring special circumstances, you will always rappel on a doubled rope, or ropes, which are retrieved by pulling them through the anchor slings. To facilitate this retrieval, the point where the rope runs through the slings is of vital concern. If you are on a smooth wall, it makes little difference. On a ledge, if the anchor is low, the slings should ideally extend just over the lip of the ledge, so the rope is not bent over a sharp or angled edge. Even the smoothest rappeller will bounce on the rope, which will abrade over an edge, leaving a pile of sheath fiber on the rock. A sharp edge may even cut into the rope. Be keenly aware of what the rope runs over – avoiding, blunting, or even padding any hazards. And make certain the rope is not running through – or even near – any notches, cracks, flakes, or knobs. When it comes time to retrieve the ropes, they will invariably get lodged in these features. And of course inspect the ledge for loose or rotten rock. The action of a rappel can dislodge them, and when you are pulling the ropes down, the free end can whisk loose rocks directly onto you.

On a big ledge you can't extend a runner over the edge, since no one carries twenty-foot slings with them. So if the anchor is located some way back from the lip of the ledge, rig the anchor as high as you can above that ledge – say at eye level. This reduces the angle at which the rope passes over the edge, decreasing the friction on the sheath during the descent and on the whole line when you eventually pull it through the anchor. When the rope makes a sharp bend, it tends to bind on the lip, on itself, even in the slings, and retrieval is difficult, sometimes impossible. If this is unavoidable, have the first person down try to pull the ropes from below before the other climbers rappel. Ideally the ropes will have fluid action through the slings, but expect some friction. A nylon rope running over nylon slings will generate friction no matter what the setup. If the ropes won't budge,try leaving two biners through the slings. If this doesn't reduce the friction enough for retrieval, you'll have to improvise, possibly tying all your slings together so they extend farther out. And don't carry on until the ropes can be pulled from below.

Setting the Ropes

If you are making a short rappel, where one doubled rope will do, thread one end through the anchor slings, match it with the other end, and draw both strands of the rope through your hands, with one end passing through the slings until you have the middle of the rope anchored at the slings. Be careful that you accurately find the middle of the rope so you won't come up short. Some ropes have a middle mark, which is more convenient for finding the middle. Do not drag the rope over the slings as you set up the rappel. The friction will burn them. Rather, gingerly draw the rope through, an arm's length at a time, or better yet, pull the rope through a carabiner that is clipped above the slings. If the rappel is longer than half a rope length, tie two ropes together. The old standard knot for doing this is the double fisherman's, or grapevine knot (page 68), but it's rugged duty to untie after being loaded. Probably the most overkill knot commonly used is a figure eight knot backed up by two grapevines. Regardless, it is relatively easy to untie after weighting, and works well with ropes of different diameters. A simple and quick method is to tie the ropes together with an double overhand knot. Do not use this knot for ropes of substantially different diameters, however. The double overhand creates the smallest knot profile, which decreases the chances of getting your rope stuck. A convenient knot is a square knot backed up on each side by a grapevine. The square knot makes the whole thing easy to untie after loading, while the grapevines secure the square knot.

Naturally, the knot will be on one side of the anchor. Note this, and remember which rope you must pull to retrieve the ropes. Pulling the wrong rope entails trying to pull the knot through the slings, which is impossible 99% of the time, and

(above and below)
Double overhand knot

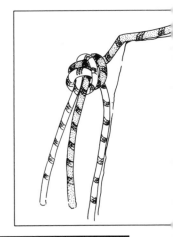

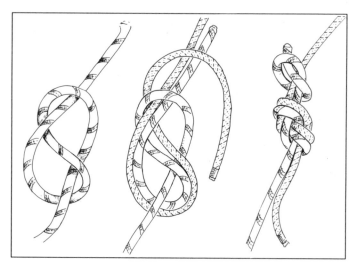

often hopelessly binds or twists the rope in the slings. Then you're stuck and may have to reclimb the pitch to retrieve the line.

To toss the ropes down, both lines should be neatly piled with ends on top. Normally, you will grab the ends and coil a forty- or fifty-foot section of doubled rope and throw this off. This quarter-coil has some heft, and the momentum of the tossed line is usually enough to drag down the remaining line. To get a rope down a broken cliff, where danger of hangup is real, try lap coiling, then tossing the upper half of the rope first, following with the lap-coiled ends.

Carefully inspect the rock below for anything the rope can be snagged on. Gauge your throw to avoid them if possible, even if you must pitch the rope some way to the side. It should straighten out once you start down. If the ropes get bound on some feature – a bush, for instance – and you cannot pull them back up for another toss, you'll have to straighten them out during the rappel. This happens. Never rappel below a snag in your rope; you will rarely be able to untangle it from below, and you could pull a rock down on yourself trying.

If there is doubt the ropes will reach, knot the ends – and for extra assurance, clip an old carabiner through that.

You must make certain that the rope reaches the ground or the next anchor. You can normally verify this visually. If not, it's a good idea to tie a "stopper knot" in the end of each rope so you can't rappel off the ends of the rope. This is especially important during bad weather, when it's dark, or if you're lacking experience. Most climbers do this as a matter of course, for rappelling off the end of the rope is not unheard of, and is usually disastrous. The stopper knot does increase the possibility of getting the rope stuck, particularly if it's windy and the rope is blowing sideways. Some people prefer to tie the ends of the ropes together with a figure eight knot, but I've found that this prevents kinks from untwisting at the end of the rope (and every rappel produces kinks).

Tossing the rope

RAPPEL BRAKES: RAPPEL DEVICES

Rappel devices generate friction on the rope to help control the descent. Properly rigged, rappelling is not strenuous, and the speed of your descent is easily controlled by one hand. A variety of devices are currently available. The most useful are compact, light and also double for belaying. Most rappel/belay devices create friction when a bight of rope is passed through a slot and clipped into a locking carabiner.

The figure eight descender remains the overall favorite. If you buy a figure eight, make sure it's good to at least 3,000 pounds, and buy the lightest one you can.

Some of the other devices, particularly the flat plate variety (such as the Sticht plate) tend to bind and give a jerky rappel. This problem can be remedied by clipping into the rope with two carabiners rather than one.

Figure Eight

To rig the figure eight, pull a bight of the rappel rope through the big hole and loop it around the stem, then clip the small hole into your harness with either a locking biner, or two regular biners, gates opposed.

Another option is, instead of looping the rope around the stem of the device, simply clip it through the biner(s) connecting the device to your harness. On single ropes, you

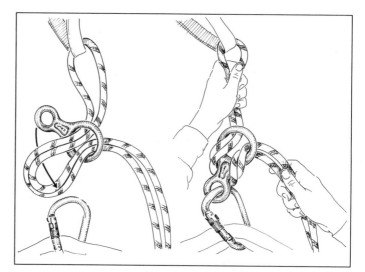

can feed the rappel rope through the smaller hole, though this often results in excessive friction. There is no hard and fast rule dictating which procedure is better. The climber's weight, whether you are on a double or single rope, and the steepness of the rappel all must be taken into account. A little experimenting under controlled circumstances should tell you which way is best for you, and when.

The advantages of the figure eight are ease of rigging and the relative fail-safe nature of the device. The disadvantages are that they put a twist in the rope which causes kinking; they're generally heavier and more bulky than other belay rappel devices; and they allow twists to pass which could get your rope stuck. The simple solution here is to clip a sling into your harness and then to one of the rappel lines above your figure eight, so no twists can pass. Figure eights do work better on icy ropes, but most rock climbers will never deal with iced ropes.

The Petzl Gri Gri has recently come into favor for belaying sport climbs and for guiding. The Gri Gri can accommodate only one strand of rope, so it's generally only useful for descending on a single line.

Carabiner Brake

Every climber should also know one or two alternative rappelling methods in case they forget or drop their rappel device, which happens. The age-old standard carabiner rappel is well-known, but it takes a bit of time to rig.

Clip either a large-diameter locking biner or two regular biners (gates opposed) into your harness. To this, clip in two more biners, gates opposed. This second group forms the "platform" for the "braking" biners. To set up the rappel, face the anchor and, straddling the ropes, pull a bight of rope up through the platform biners. Clip the braking biners – gates down – over the platform biners and under the bight of rope.

A single brake biner usually provides enough friction when rappelling on two 11-mm ropes. On vertical or overhanging rappels, you'll want two. Rappelling on two 9-mm ropes or a single 10- or 11-mm rope, you may want three brake biners. Your weight, the rock steepness, plus how much braking you do with the brake hand, will determine how many braking biners work best for various rappels. Several rappels will tell you what works best for you. Two biners as the brake is the configuration to start with.

Oval carabiners are much easier to use for both the platform and the brake. D's will work, but when the gates are opposed, the contrasting shapes reduce the space for the bight, and are usually a hassle to get clipped. The carabiner brake rappel is very basic and simple, but it can be set up incorrectly. Never use only one biner for the platform and be certain to reverse the gates. The bight must pass over the back of the brake biners, not the gates, or the system is lethal.

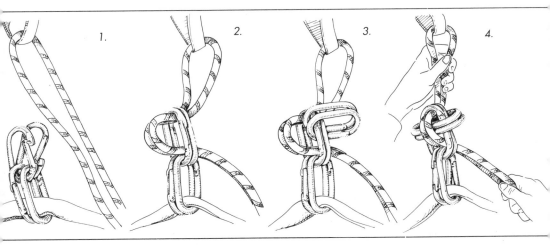

Many of the lightweight modern carabiners are not large enough to rig a carabiner rappel. If small carabiners are all you have, a separate Munter hitch on each strand of the rappel rope works, but is a major hassle. Make sure to use a locking carabiner or two carabiners with gates opposed for the Munter hitches, and extend one of the Munter hitches out from your harness with another locking carabiner or two opposed so the Munter hitches don't bind against one another. This method does put some twists in the rope because of the twisting hitches, but it serves well as a backup rappel setup for use with lightweight carabiners.

As you descend, the belay/rappel device will provide less and less friction as the weight of the rope below decreases. Sometimes even modern rappel devices don't provide as much friction as you'd like, especially if you're rappelling with a single or small-diameter rope on steep terrain, or if you're saddled with a pack or excess gear. Of course you can

CARABINER BRAKE

1. Two sets of doubled biners, gates opposed.

2. A bight of rope goes through,

3. brake biners are clipped on,

4. then clipped over to the other side, and your brake is ready to use.

1.

2.

The Dulfursitz

wrap the rope around your hip to get extra friction, but that might wear a hole in your favorite tights – or worse – your very hide. Another option is to put a carabiner, preferably locking, on your leg loop and run the rope through this and then to your brake hand. For even more friction, wrap the rope twice around the extra carabiner.

Dulfursitz, or "Body Rappel"

The body rappel is the only method that uses no devices – just the rope – and though rarely called upon, is the only viable means down a rope when other methods or gear is not available. Facing the anchors, straddle the rope. Bring the rope from behind you and across one hip, up across the chest and over the head to the opposite shoulder, over and down the back to the opposite hand, next to where the rope passes over your hip. The rope then makes an "S" and as with all rappels, the uphill hand is the "guide" hand, the downhill hand the "brake" hand. The brake hand can easily regulate speed: moving it out off the back to go faster, pulling it in around the hip to slow down. Most climbers prefer for the brake hand to clasp the rope palm up.

The body rappel is a last resort. Unless you have thick clothing under every inch of passing rope, you'll feel pain – at best. Normally, a beginning climber will make a couple of body rappels and never make another all her climbing days – but she will know how. Caught without gear and with a short, relatively low angle way below, the climber with knowledge of the body rappel has a fairly safe means down. But aside from an old-timer showing how it's done, or a novice learning how, I've never seen someone intentionally using a body rappel in over twenty years of climbing. The potential for pain and the effectiveness of other techniques have made the body rappel obsolete. Besides, by its definition, being without mechanical connection to the rope, you can fall out of the body rappel.

RIGGING THE RAPPEL

For safe rappelling, the anchors must be strong, both ends of the ropes must reach the next set of anchors or the ground, the gear must be rigged correctly, the harness must be properly fitted with the buckle double passed, and the climber must maintain absolute control during the descent.

There are times when rappelling comes at the end of a hard day, or in the face of poor weather, when your guard might be down a bit. Yet whenever you rappel you must never let your guard down. Many climbers don't consider the dangers really behind them until they're in the sack, smugly remembering their wild adventures.

Because every detail must be correct, it is critical that you double-check every aspect of the "safety chain" before leaning back to rappel. Double-check your harness buckle (and your partner's), the anchor and the rope's attachment to it, the rappel device and locking carabiner(s), and the rope connecting knot. Just remember "BARK" – buckle, anchor, rappel device and knot. Also, don't forget to inspect your gear often to be sure it's in good condition. Especially be sure that your harness, belay loop, slings and rope are in good shape. Occasionally check your carabiners and belay/rappel devices for wear or notches. Retire the gear as soon as you have any doubts about its condition.

> ## BARK
> Buckle
> Anchor
> Rappel Device
> Knot

THE RAPPEL FUNDAMENTALS

Your hands have separate jobs. The uphill or "guide" hand is used mainly for balance, and should never death-grip the rope. It can't stop you, and you're only instinctively trying to duplicate the friction that the carabiners or device are creating. The other hand, the "brake" hand, determines your speed. Most climbers keep their brake hand well below their hip, with the rope sliding over it. When they want more speed, they move the rope out and off the hip; to slow down or stop, they wrap the rope back around the hip. The prime rule of rappelling is never let go with your brake hand, lest you slide out of control down the rope. The brake hand feeds the rope through the rappel device. If you're right-handed, you'll probably want to brake with your right hand.

Once you are set up and ready to go, make certain any gear or clothing is well clear of the friction device and cannot get entangled no matter what you do. Long hair must be securely tied back. Anything loose can be drawn into the brake system, and it happens so fast that a whole shirttail or head of hair can be snatched into the brake with only one downward step. Extraction is very involved, often dangerous, and in the case of hair, always very painful. In most cases, when something has been sucked into the braking device, it becomes locked so tight that the climber is incapable of freeing himself, and a rescue with shears is necessary.

Proper rappel posture: angled back, feet spread slightly, and looking down.

Rappel on! High above an arid rampart, a climber glides into the free rappel on Ryolite Spire, Superstition Mountains, Arizona. With the legs out and the torso bent slightly up, a free rappel is a pleasurable affair, providing the system is prudently rigged.

Bill Hatcher photo

The crux of rappelling is often getting started, particularly if you must descend over a lip. Once the rope is weighted, backpedal to the brink. Keeping your feet there, let out some rope until you are leaning well back. Don't move your feet down too soon. Stability is gained by having your weight pressing straight into the wall, requiring you to maintain a near-perpendicular angle relative to the wall. Much less and your feet will skid off and you'll smack the wall – face first. After you have leaned back far enough and feel your weight driving into the wall, slowly pedal back, letting out rope and maintaining your perpendicular attitude. The moment you are established on the wall, bend your upper torso in, but keep your legs perpendicular to the cliff. Keep your feet spread apart at shoulder's width for a good foundation. To see where you're going, slightly twist your upper torso towards your brake hand so you can look down.

Don't bound down the rope Rambo style, rather "walk" down the cliff. The aim is a smooth descent, for several reasons. Heroic bounding moves or jerky action stresses the whole system unnecessarily. Too much speed heats up the friction apparatus and can singe the rope's sheath, making it brittle and stiff to the touch. Inching down is pointless. It wastes everyone's time and usually means you are over-gripping with the guide hand. Small steps, fluid action, keeping your eyes below to see your way, and always keeping your legs perpendicular to the cliff – these are the fundamentals of a safe rappel.

A beginner's first few rappels should be accompanied with a belay from above. If there is a problem, the climber is still on belay, which can give a trembling beginner enough confidence to try again. Usually just a couple of belayed rappels is sufficient to get the knack, and you can dispense with the belay.

A technique for belaying someone after you go first is the fireman's belay, where you hold onto the bottom of the rope. If the rappeller looses control, you pull the rope tight to stop their descent. This method doesn't back up their rappel device, nor does it allow you to check their rappel setup, however.

If you need to stop while rappelling to untangle the rope or take a photo, wrap the rope around your leg three times to free your brake hand. Be sure your brake hand is ready to take the weight when you unwrap the rope to continue your rappel.

Overhanging, "Free" Rappels

When the rappeller is hanging in free space with nothing for his feet, the rope should run between the legs, under one leg and up to the brake hand. The added friction of the rope running under the leg is considerable, and providing your rappel apparatus is giving adequate friction, you can easily stop by folding the rope over the leg. However, try to maintain a smooth, steady descent; if you go too slowly you'll

Should there be a need while rappelling to stop and free the hands, a couple of wraps of the rope around a leg will do the trick.

tend to twirl on the rope. Maintain the same posture you would while sitting in a chair. A little tension from your guide hand will keep your upper torso upright.

As you come back in contact with the rock, extend your legs out like antennae, and slowly ease back onto the wall. Never race down a free rappel and suddenly stop. The quick deceleration generates enormous stress on the whole system, and unnecessarily elongates the rope, which will abrade over even the smoothest lip.

Backups

If for some reason you are doubtful of controlling your rappel and are forced into making one – without a belay – you can rig a backup with either of two knots that bind on the rope when weighted but can be slid along the rope when not. The traditional knot is the prusik, but this requires rope smaller in diameter (and softer in nature) than the climbing rope, and nut slings are rarely long enough to work. In lieu of cord, ⁵⁄₁₆-inch sling material will not work effectively as a

Tying a prusik knot

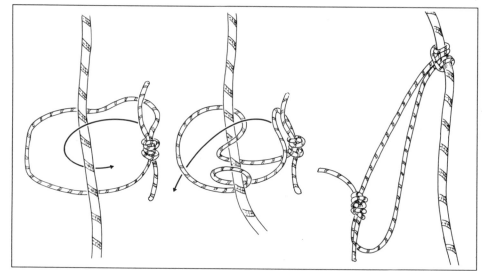

(below)
Prusik knot backup

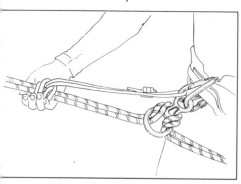

prusik, but the sling can be combined with a carabiner to form a Bachmann knot that serves the same purpose. Rig the prusik or Bachmann on the rope and attach it with a sling to a locking biner on your waist. When rappelling, cup the guide hand loosely over the knot, sliding it down as you go. Make sure the sling is not too long. If you do go out of control and the knot jams tight, it must be within reach to loosen, or you're stuck. And remember that unless the knot jams tight the moment you start sliding it will never jam, but will burn through.

A sliding knot backup (commonly referred to as a prusik backup) is rarely if ever used as a normal procedure. If you don't know how to rappel, get a belay. If you are doubtful that you can make a certain rappel, don't make that rappel. Only if you are doubtful and must rappel, and no belay is possible, should you consider the prusik backup as an option. Of the few times I've seen the prusik backup used, the prusik once got jammed so tight that the climber could not loosen it and had to be rescued. As grievous as that was, it was better than being lugged out in a black bag, however. All told, the prusik backup is a highly-contested technique. The only thing for certain is that it can be very problematic.

Retrieving the Rope

Before the last person comes down she must first double-check several things: which rope to pull; is the doubled rope crossed on itself or binding on the slings; is it clear of all notches, grooves, loose rock, and the like. As mentioned, if there is any doubt the ropes can be pulled from below, make certain they can before the last man descends. To facilitate easy retrieval, the last rappeller should separate any twists or kinks in the two ropes so they both run untangled to the ground or next anchor. You can most easily do this by keeping a finger of your guide hand between the two ropes as you descend. On the way down, note any flakes, trees, or blocks that the rope could get entangled with or perhaps pull off upon retrieval.

If you're on the ground, grab the end and walk away from the cliff with it before you start pulling. This gives you a better angle to pull from and decreases wear on the line. It also decreases the chance of dislodging any loose rock. Don't jerk the rope but pull smooth and steadily. As you draw in more line, the rope will often snake down and through the anchor on its own. Whatever the case, once the rope has been freed, always yell "rope!" The end of the pulled-through rope can lash like a bullwhip and people should be forewarned.

On multiple rappels, feed the free end through the new anchor sling as you pull the rope through the upper anchor. This avoids you having to re-tie the knot at every rappel.

Stuck Line

One of the most tense moments on a multi-rappel descent is when the rope becomes stuck. Avoiding stuck ropes is part experience and foresight, part luck. On steep, clean rock the ropes will usually pull nicely. As the angle kicks back and the rock becomes more featured, the chances of getting your rope stuck increase.

Because certain things are so important, and inevitable, let's go over them one more time. To avert stuck ropes, survey the terrain below, looking for cracks, vegetation, flakes or other features the rope can get stuck on (and sharp

The Bachmann knot, an alternative to the prusik, for use with flat webbing

edges that could cut the rope). The last person down needs to make sure the rope runs cleanly, with no twists. When using two ropes tied together, make a note which rope to pull before you go down, and tell your partner. If you pull on the wrong rope the knot won't pull through the anchors. Worse, the rope could get stuck while you're trying to pull it the wrong direction. This is fairly common.

If any doubt exists about the rope pulling, the first climber down should test-pull the rope for fifteen or so feet before the last person goes, then reset it with the middle at the anchors. If the rope won't pull, gradually tug harder to see if you can get it moving. If that fails, try: extending the anchors with webbing; pulling or flipping the rope out of a crack or other snag; running the rope through a rappel ring or carabiner rather than the nylon slings; or setting the knot below the initial lip. To set the knot below the lip, the last climber down has to downclimb or hand-over-hand down the rope to get below the knot before she can begin rappelling. In this situation, it's a good idea to give the last climber a fireman's belay while she gets started.

Make sure you get all knots and tangles out of the rope before you begin to pull it down. Once you start pulling, try to keep the rope moving so it can't lodge in a constriction. Again, if you're on the ground, walking away from the cliff reduces the bending angle of the rope on the edges above, making it easier to pull.

Sometimes the rope gets hung up regardless of the best-laid lines. As mentioned, first be certain you are pulling the correct rope; it won't work to try to pull the knot through the anchor. Next, flip the rope side to side. If that doesn't clear it, try flipping a loop up the rope straight out, giving one end a stout jerk when the ropes are away from the wall. If all else fails, get everyone to pull on the rope with all their might. That will either free it or, more likely, jam it even worse. But since the other options are pretty grievous, try it anyway.

If the rope is honest-to-God stuck fast, you have several options. If you still have both ends of the rope, tie both ends off to the new anchor and prusik up one or the other lines. If you have retrieved all or enough of one rope and the very end of the second line is mysteriously hung up (this does happen), you can re-lead the pitch on the free rope. If you only have one end and not much slack, your task is pretty hateful, but possible. You must tie off your end to the new anchor, fit a sturdy prusik on the rope, and re-lead the pitch by moving the prusik up the rope and placing protection below it. If you fall, the rope is tied off, the prusik should hold, and you are held by any protection you have placed below the prusik. It is also a good idea to tie into the rope from time to time with a figure eight or butterfly knot to back up the prusik. If you are ever forced into this position, don't worry about style. Liberally cheat, hang on every nut and place plenty of them. Do whatever is necessary to safely gain the snag.

If all else fails, yell for help. If somebody is nearby, certainly get their assistance before trying the prusik-lead. If the ropes are stuck on top of a cliff or outcrop, there are often climbers milling about, and a jammed line can be freed in seconds. A climbing team must be self-reliant, but everybody gets a rope stuck sometime and there's no shame in getting a hand if it's easily gotten and the options are dangerous.

Getting Back Up

If you rappel to a stance that has no place to anchor, you will have to ascend the rappel rope if you cannot climb back up. Rig two prusiks or Bachmann knots – one tied within arm's reach to your harness, the other to a sling into which both feet may be cinched. The procedure is: pull up legs; slide up lower knot; stand up while sliding top knot up. Repeat. Though relatively simple, you will want to practice this before you need to use it, probably in an emergency, which is a very poor situation to be learning new techniques. (As with any form of mechanically ascending a rope, the

Getting back up a rope with two prusiks or Bachmann knots is fairly simple and comfortable with a harness or leg loops. Be sure to tie into the rope from time to time, however, because prusiks can slip, and when they do, they can fail. Tie an overhand knot into a bight of rope and clip this into your harness.

biggest trick is knowing what length slings to use.) Because of the somewhat capricious nature of prusiks, it is important to tie into the rope periodically (below the prusik, obviously) during your ascent with a figure eight or butterfly knot. Be certain of your anchor before you simply prusik up the rope. In the case of a snagged line, prusik-lead the pitch as described above.

Hanging Transfers

Now that you understand the basic procedure, we can look at the most exciting/frightening of all rappel situations: rappelling down a steep wall with no ledges or even stances. This procedure is most common for climbers who are retreating from big climbs, but is also encountered by anyone who is rappelling a route with a hanging belay. The procedure is complicated and the potential for error is high, so it is essential that every precaution is taken.

Assume that the anchor is fixed, say three bolts. Because there is no ledge, you must tie a knot into the end of the rappel ropes to insure you don't rappel off the end. The first climber down prepares the anchors for the team, then clips into and hangs from the anchors, independently of the ropes. There are several methods for tying into the anchors. The most secure is to clip biners into all the anchors and secure yourself to them with a sling girth-hitched through your harness that forms a cow's tail. Only after you have done so should you unclip from the rappel rope, immediately securing the rappel rope to the anchor so it cannot get out of your reach. The next climber then comes down, clips into the anchors and pulls the rope down, while the first person feeds the rope for the next rappel. Be extra careful, double- and triple-checking everything to make sure you've got it absolutely right.

Once you have pulled the rope through the upper anchor and fed it through the new sling at your present anchor, the first rappeller rigs his rappel before he unclips from the anchor. When the last person rappels, he must remove the biners from the bolt hangers. He might find it useful to clip a sling into the rappel sling, and stand in it to get enough height to remove the biners. Then he rappels down.

CONCLUSION

Because rappelling is so easy to do, climbers sometimes race through the setup, and the annual accident report is grim evidence of their haste. Like a jet pilot, the wise climber goes through a pre-rappel check list that runs like this: Is the harness secure, knots and buckles tight? Is the anchor bombproof? Are the slings strong enough and tied correctly – particularly if you're using someone else's rappel slings? Are the ropes tied together properly? Do they reach the ground or next anchor? Is the braking system rigged correctly? Are loose clothes, gear, or hair far out of the way? Is the line of descent free of loose or rotten rock? Will the lines pull through okay? With a little experience, it only takes moments to check and double-check these things. Don't become a mother's lament; get in the habit of checking and double-checking every phase.

COILING THE ROPE

Anyone who has spent time on a sailboat knows that the scoundrel who haphazardly coils a rigging line, if found out, spends the rest of his tour bailing bilge water, polishing the toilet lid, or is simply pitched overboard. The climber who haphazardly coils the rope is twice a chump, for it's an easy task and usually takes but a few minutes to do properly. A poorly-coiled rope is a polecat to untangle and can take several climbers half an hour of steady cursing to get straight.

There are several different methods of coiling a rope. Most common is the standing coil. Leaving a tail of a couple

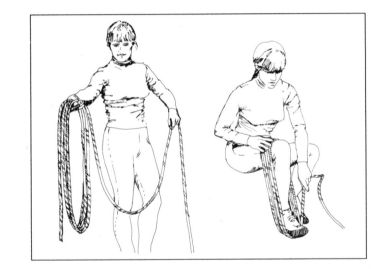

STANDING COIL
Free hand coil (left), and coiling over the knee.

After coiling the rope, secure the ends with a whip finish: lay the short end back as a loop atop the coil; wind about five or six feet of the other end around, working towards the loop and making sure that each wrap is as snug as you can make it; and finally, finish by pulling the end through the initial loop.

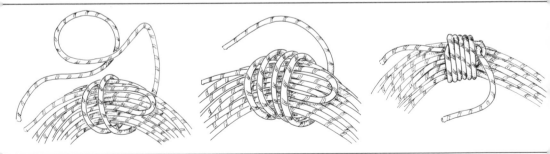

feet, form successive coils about five feet, or two arm's lengths long. The fastest, and worst, method is to coil the rope with two free arms. Next best is to sit and coil it around a foot and knee. The best method is to coil it around your neck. As you coil, shake out any kinks and twists. With a

MOUNTAINEER'S COIL

To do the mountaineer's coil:
1.Start by matching both ends of the rope, then lap the doubled rope, leaving the first fifteen feet of the ends uncoiled. 2.,3. With the free ends, wrap around the coil. 3.,4. Draw the doubled end through itself as shown. 5. Lay the separate ends over the shoulders. 6. Secure the coil by wrapping the remaining ends around the waist.

very kinky rope, another climber should help shake out the line, leaving you to coil it. If the rope is incomprehensibly twisted, you might have to walk it out and twirl it about to get it straightened. Normally this happens only to old ropes that have just been rappelled on, where the sheath has shifted around. It's best to get a new rope, though a new rope will also kink until it's broken in.

Another common way to coil the rope is the "mountaineer's coil." This is best when you don't have a pack and you need maximum arm freedom – to do some scrambling, say.

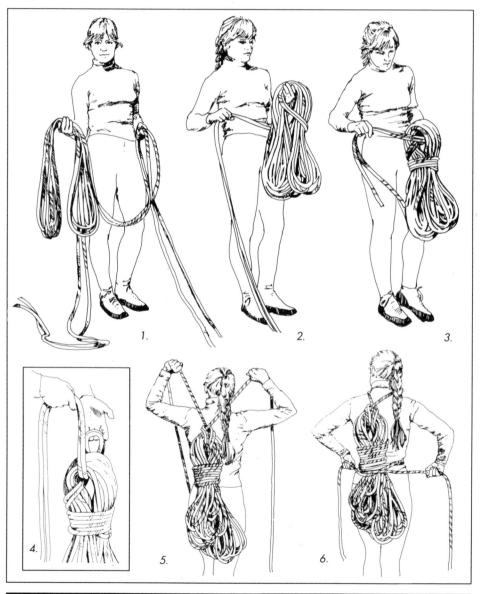

1.

2.

3.

4.

5.

6.

Sport Climbing

Sport climbing is all the rage in the 1990s. Sport climbing, by common definition, is climbing on routes protected exclusively by bolts, as opposed to traditional climbing, where the protection is provided by chocks (et cetera) placed by the leader. Of course, there is a great deal of overlap between the two types of climbing. For example, some routes have "mixed" protection, where the leader clips bolts *and* places chocks. Sport climbing has also come to include climbing competitions, indoor gym climbing, and low bouldering – basically any type of climbing that is perceived to be "completely safe."

Sport climbing removes most of the risk inherent in climbing, and allows the climber to focus solely on technical difficulty. It requires less commitment than "traditional" climbing. Generally, gear consists only of shoes, a rope, a harness and a handful of quickdraws; and if it starts raining, or the "vibes" are all wrong, you simply lower back to the ground. By engineering most of the potential risk out of the equation, sport climbing has become increasingly accessible to the masses.

While sport climbing is perceived as a safe endeavor, a casual attitude can still earn you a gravestone. Diligent attention must be paid to every detail in the safety chain. Climbers tend to place blind faith in the bolt protection found on sport routes – and for good reason. Bolts hold tens of thousands of falls each year, with very few failures. But some failures do occur, mostly with old ¼-inch diameter bolts, which can shoot from the stone like cloves from a holiday ham. Poorly placed larger bolts can, and do, fail. Sometimes the bolt is sound but the hanger is suspect. At any rate, inspect the bolt and the hanger before blindly trusting them. Since sport climbing is so reliant on bolts, it might be a good idea to go back and review the material on bolts in the anchors section.

Life at the Sport Crag

Here's a typical scene at the sport climbing crag. Two climbers arrive at the crag mid- to late morning. They stroll ten feet, or ten minutes, (rarely further) to the crag and arrive at the chosen route. Many sport climbing crags are roadside affairs, allowing the climbers to eschew hiking and "save" their energy for the actual climbing. Interface with the natural world is often a secondary notion. The emphasis is on short, gymnastic climbing in a controlled venue. If the chosen route is at a popular area, another team is probably already on it, so the arriving team either chooses another route, or drops their rope tarp at the base to reserve a place in line. They will likely scope the route (or the guidebook) to determine how many quickdraws to bring, and to plan the strategy for the route. They will scrutinize the other team on the route for any tricks or secrets about the climbing sequence, learning from the others' mistakes. They may also seek beta (a detailed description, replete with lavish body language and funky crag argot) about the moves from any milling climbers who have done or attempted the route. But if the leader is going for a "best style" ascent – the celebrated "on-sight flash" – she must climb the route with no previous information, and without falling or otherwise weighting the rope.

Now the route is freed up. With quickdraws racked on her harness and a shoulder-length sling for clipping into the belay, the leader sets off for the first bolt. Once there, she finds the most restful stance for clipping in. She clips the quickdraw in with the carabiner gates facing away from the anticipated direction of travel, then looks above to see which way the route goes and to plot a sequence. Normally, she'll clip into the bolts with a standard quickdraw, but if the climbing is especially hard above, and if the result of having the rope accidentally unclip would be disastrous, she may clip in with a locking carabiner. Higher on the pitch, with the rope clipped into several bolts, the last bolt is backed up by the bolts below, so a normal quickdraw will usually suffice.

Throughout, the leader strives to remain calm and relaxed, planning and executing moves as she comes to them. In this manner she proceeds up the pitch, always keeping good body position, using precise footwork, gripping as lightly as possible with the hands, and resting whenever possible. Her ultimate goal is to reach the anchors at the end of the pitch without weighting the rope, in the best control possible. If she reaches a difficult section and can't decipher the moves, she may climb back down to a rest or even to the ground to avoid hanging on the rope and forfeiting her on-sight flash.

Reaching the top of the pitch, she uses a sling to clip into the fixed anchors, which ideally will be two bolts (⅜-inch diameter or larger) with chains or welded cold shut hangers. After clipping a good sewn sling into both of the bolts, and then into her harness with a locking carabiner (or two carabiners with the gates opposed), she can go off belay, lean back and rest – but only after double-checking *every aspect of the anchor construct*. Even world-class climbers have failed to do so, and have paid dearly for their oversight.

Communication

One scenario: the leader calls "off belay," because he or she is finished with the lead. Oftentimes after finishing a sport climbing lead (which tend to be short – less than half a rope length), the leader will opt not to belay the second from atop the pitch, choosing instead to lower to the ground and belay there. But when the leader leans back to lower off, the belayer is nonexistent – since the leader has already called "off belay" – and the leader whistles straight into the deck. Not good.

Good communication between the climber and the belayer can always solve this problem. Also, an experienced belayer can predict dangerous situations by *questioning the climber when her suggestions or commands are confusing, misleading, or seem to point toward danger.* If there is ever any question, the belayer should keep a stout belay on *no matter what the climber says* until the situation is absolutely clear. In the aforementioned scenario, don't call "off belay" until you've been safely lowered to the ground.

LOWERING

With the advent of climbing gyms and the popularity of sport climbing routes (where a leader often cannot accomplish a lead on his or her first try and must be lowered to the ground for another go), lowering has become an integral part of the climbing game. The first rule of lowering is *never lower with the rope running through a nylon sling or cord.* This dangerous practice has given more than one climber an "E" ticket straight to the deck. It's also a sketchy practice to lower or top-rope through aluminum rappel rings, especially if your rope has any desert grit in it.

Every time you lean back to lower, first look down and make sure your belayer is still with you. Say "Lower Me" and/or give the "thumbs down" signal. Again, never say "Belay Off" at the end of a pitch if you intend to lower, because your partner needs to keep you on to lower you. A few climbers have suffered compound fractures because their belayers took them off belay when they leaned back to lower. I always hold onto the belayer's side of the rope as I begin to lower – essentially lowering myself – until the belayer has me nice and tight.

The Belayer's Role

If you're lowering someone, use two hands on the brake side of the rope to control his descent, and to prevent a kink from knocking a single brake hand from the rope. Make sure the rope is stacked to feed easily so you don't have to fight rope tangles while your partner is dangling. As soon as he gives you the command to lower, pull all the slack out of the rope, lock off your belay device and lean back so he has tension immediately. Don't make him lean back and "fall" onto your rope. Lower your partner at a nice steady pace, not too fast but not too slow, without jerking him like a puppet on a string. Slow him down as he approaches the ground, and make sure he's solidly on his feet before you feed out a bunch of slack.

The biggest fears in lowering someone are that you could drop him out of control, or let the end of the rope pass through your belay device so he falls to the ground. Both of these mistakes have often happened, and to very experienced climbers. The lowering anchors must be within a half rope length for your partner to reach the ground. If any uncertainty exists about the distance to the ground, tie into the rope or at least tie a knot in the end of the rope so it can't go whistling through your belay device if the rope is too short. Also, don't be too far from the zone your partner is being lowered into if the entire length of the rope may be needed.

A GriGri works very nicely for lowering; just squeeze the locking cam. It takes a bit of practice to lower smoothly, however. If you're having a hard time squeezing the cam, use the lever but be extremely careful not to pull back on the lever too fast or you'll drop your partner like a ton of bricks.

The Climber's Job

The most common situation for being lowered is from double or triple anchors at the top of a sport route. If you can't stand on a ledge at the top of the pitch to rig the lower, clip into one of the anchors with a sling (clip both anchors if you're a long ways above your last piece). If the hangers, chain links or other connecting hardware have a large enough opening:

1.) Pass a bight (loop) of rope through the anchors and extend the bight down to your harness.

2.) Tie a figure eight in the bight and clip this knot into a locking carabiner on your harness tie-in point or belay loop.

3.) Double-check everything, then dismantle your original tie-in knot. You're now connected to the rope through the locking carabiner and figure eight knot. Pull the end of the rope through the anchors and give the signal to lower.

This system is quick and safe because you are never untied from the rope, or off belay. If lowering requires the entire length of the rope, this trick may leave you a little short of the ground, however. Some people may complain that this technique leaves you connected to the rope with only a locking carabiner, but that's all that's holding you at the belayer's end anyway. You can certainly back up this carabiner with another if you so desire.

Another alternative, especially good if a bight of rope won't fit through the anchors, or if you need the entire length of the rope to lower, is to clip into the anchors with a sling or two, then tie a figure eight in the lead line four or so feet from the tie-in point and clip into it with a locking carabiner. This clip-off will keep you backed up by the higher pieces in the pitch, and will make it impossible for you to drop the rope, which would place you in a horribly embarrassing and potentially dangerous situation. Next, double-check everything, untie from the end of the rope, pass it through the anchors, and tie back into it. Now untie the backup knot, disconnect the slings, and lower off.

A third option that is quick but not as safe is to clip into the anchors with slings, untie the rope from your harness, pass it through the anchors, and tie back into it. The main problem here is the potential for dropping the rope and becoming stranded.

Some sport climbing areas feature open cold shuts at the top of many routes for convenience. (Cold shuts are relatively soft metal rings which can be closed with a hammer blow; "open cold shuts" have not been hammered closed, to allow a rope to be slipped through.) It is certainly handy to flip your rope through a couple of open cold shuts at the top of a pitch and lower to the ground. While the people who set cold shuts seem to have complete confidence in them, it's not a sage practice to top-rope through these because their strength is unpredictable. Remember that top-rope falls can reportedly put upwards of 1000 pounds of force on the top anchors.

The rope must pass through steel chain link, welded cold shut hangers, or carabiners to allow safe lowering. Conventional bolt hangers and aluminum rappel rings are unsuited for lowering or top-roping directly through, so the leader may have to leave a carabiner or two to lower off such anchors – or rappel rather than lower.

When climbing, lowering and top-roping, the alert climber is always on the lookout for sharp edges that may cut the rope. If the rock is especially rough, the leader may choose to rappel instead of lower, so the rope won't have to run under tension over the sharp rock.

Understand that if at some time, for whatever reason, you don't trust your belayer to lower you in a controlled manner, simply grab the side of the rope running back down to the belayer and lower yourself, hand over hand. This technique is standard on routes up to about 75 degrees. The friction of the rope running through the anchor is considerable when the line is weighted. If you're weak, or pumped (meaning that your arms are so pumped full of blood that they're swollen, weak, and useless), or the rock is steep or overhanging, wrap the rope once around your leg, grab it with both hands above the wrap, and "feed" yourself down. This method is tedious and slow, and you can get wrenched onto your side. Also, you'll probably singe your clothes and perhaps your leg; but it's a hell of a lot better than slamming into the deck. If you are extremely pumped, and the route is severely overhanging, it's best to just rest up at the anchor for a spell, then set up a rappel and get down that way. This is almost always the favored way if you have doubts or if things look dicey. I've mentioned the self-lowering methods because a belayer's inability to properly lower you is usually discovered only after you have descended a ways and can no longer return to the anchors to arrange a rappel. Climb long enough, and I guarantee you this will happen.

Cleaning the route

Typically the leader will "clean" the route (remove the quickdraws) while being lowered, so the second climber can take a top-rope ride without the onus of removing any of the gear, or so the team can move onto another climb. ("Team" may be a bit of a misnomer here. Sport climbing partners may sometimes not even climb the same routes, but rather serve as belay mules for each other on their respective projects.) If the route is exceptionally overhanging or if it has traversing sections, some key quickdraws should be left in place to provide a directional anchor so the top-roped climber won't swing too far if he falls. Sometimes the leader will leave all the quickdraws in place. When she gets to the ground the rope is pulled down and her partner also leads the climb.

Retreat

Sometimes a climber reaches an impasse, and even after many tries cannot continue up a route. When this happens, it's time to retreat. The best and most convenient way to retreat is to simply leave a carabiner on the highest bolt clipped, and lower to the ground. For safety's sake you should probably also leave a carabiner on the next lower bolt, so you'll be backed up if the high bolt fails. Before trusting your all to the top bolt, you should also thoroughly inspect it. Rather than leaving a carabiner or two (most climbers hate to leave gear), some climbers will leave a retreat sling on the high bolt and rappel from it. Unfortunately, this leaves unsightly webbing on the rock, and clogs the bolt hanger. In some cases a carabiner won't fit through such a clogged hanger, leaving the next leader in a fix when she can't clip directly into the hanger, and instead must clip into ratty old webbing. Also, rappelling from one anchor is simply a bad practice.

STYLE

More often than not, an overextended sport leader will hang on bolts to rest and work out the next moves. "Hangdogging" used to be considered poor style, but today it's a common tool used to rehearse the sequences on especially difficult routes. As soon as the leader puts tension on the rope, however, she has lost both her on-sight flash and her free ascent, so if she wants to eventually "free" the route, she'll have to try again from the ground. On a subsequent attempt she can make a "redpoint" ascent, where she places all the quickdraws on lead and never hangs on the rope; or a "pinkpoint" ascent, where the gear has been pre-placed and she merely has to clip the rope in as she goes. In sport climbing, or any type of climbing, you haven't done a route free until you've climbed it from the bottom to the top with no rests. If you've done a route in less than perfect style, be honest reporting your accomplishments. Once your integrity is compromised, it's next to impossible to get it back.

For a more thorough handling of the sport climbing game, refer to *Face Climbing,* also in the *How to Rock Climb!* series.

Training for Climbing

Few climbers, even those who take it seriously, are motivated enough to train regularly with climbing in mind. The great majority of climbers are only in it for fun, and have lives or work schedules which preclude the necessary time for specialized workouts. But as the top climbs become increasingly more physical and leading climbers recognize themselves as world-class athletes, the attitudes trickle down into the mainstream. Over the last decade, even weekend warriors have begun hitting the weight room, pull-up bar, and climbing gym hoping to increase their performance. This trend has resulted in the development and supply of training equipment specifically for climbing.

The early training apparatus had some major drawbacks. The rope ladder, popular about a dozen years ago, resulted in grievous elbow injuries from the wrenching and stress of repeated one-arm lowering. Fingertip pull-ups caused joint problems in many. Other devices, like various hand squeezers and finger-tension gadgets, were fine for recovering from injuries, but did little to increase strength or endurance. Many common work outs were geared to gain the strength to do circus feats – like one-arm pull-ups – which had surprisingly little positive effect on people's climbing. As certain exercises are being eliminated if they cause injuries and new devices are introduced almost daily, it's still not clear how to attain optimum results while staying injury-free. Likewise, it is virtually impossible to discuss various exercises and devices without taking up training philosophies. Still, there are several physiological facts that cannot be denied.

First, strong fingers are every climber's dream. And since the fingers don't have muscles, it's the sinew connections in the forearms (and the attending muscles) that must be strengthened.

Second, most every climbing exercise involves some form of pull-up – duplicating the movement on the rock – and it's the latissimus dorsi, or "lats," which are the prime mover in this action. You simply cannot strengthen the lats alone, though. You must also train the antagonistic muscles required for the pulling movement – the chest and trapezius, even the abdominals – to provide balanced muscled groups and avoid injury. Lastly, any muscle group which you train to the point of failure requires at least 48 hours to recover. These comments are not opinions, but incontrovertible facts that must be factored into any workout. They tell us certain things that have long been overlooked by the climbing world. It is fine to concentrate on the lats and forearms, but not to the exclusion of the other muscles. To do so is to invite injury. And totally blasting those muscles every third day will bring much better results than doing so every day, or every other day.

From this we can conclude that while it is probably desirable to do specialized exercises which closely ape the climbing movement – and focus on the muscle groups most involved – it is likewise important to round out the routine and physique with an equal amount of general conditioning exercises. Anything else results in an unbalanced machine, where weak antagonistic muscles are throwing the whole body out of kilter.

Of course, the best training for climbing is climbing itself. Nothing substitutes for mileage on the rocks for gaining strength, endurance and fluidity of movement. For developing sheer power, bouldering has no rival. Technique, power and endurance can also be improved in a climbing gym. If there isn't one near you, there probably will be soon. And for general conditioning, weight training is second to none.

Bouldering

Bouldering is essentially climbing on rocks small enough that a rope is unnecessary. The world's hardest climbing – in terms of individual moves and small sequences – has always been, and always will be, done on boulders. The controlled medium, the ease of trying, trying, and trying again, and the ferocious (though mostly friendly) competition that surrounds the pastime make ideal conditions for the best climbers to try the hardest sequences imaginable. The first time I saw a world-class boulderer in action I was thunderstruck. I'd been climbing about three months, clawing up easy climbs made all the harder because – in the spirit of the great mountaineers – we bore weighty packs and climbed in hiking boots. And before me was a man in shorts, varappe shoes, and a chalk bag, powering up overhanging rock like it was nothing, ever controlled, graceful, with precision and explosive strength that was mind-boggling. The experience re-oriented me in seconds. No more packs, off with the hiking boots – it was time to start bouldering.

Bouldering is such an engaging and stimulating endeavor that many climbers prefer it to roped climbing. Unquestionably, bouldering is the quickest way to gain climbing skill. A dedicated boulderer brings a lot of artillery to a roped climb. Strong fingers and good footwork, requisite for any difficult bouldering, are his in abundance. But it's the experience of having done thousands of different sequences that gives him the real edge. It's doubtful that an experienced boulderer will encounter anything on a roped climb that he hasn't already done – in some fashion or another – on the boulders. Beginning climbers can master the fundamentals in several months, intermediate climbers

(page opposite)

John Long cranks the "Pinch Overhang," a classic problem at one of the premier bouldering areas in the world – Horsetooth Reservoir, near Fort Collins, Colorado.

Michael Kennedy photo

can become experts in a year, and experts can maintain their edge with a couple of good bouldering sessions a week.

All bouldering is not low-level work, however. High bouldering, essentially free soloing, has long been a popular game of Russian roulette amongst experts. Because of their tremendous skill level, however, the chamber rarely fires on an expert soloist. For the novice and intermediate climber, you will not want to climb any higher than a point where you feel comfortable jumping off. If you must assume an upside down or awkward position, have a friend spot you. Make sure your spotter is alert and ready, with his hands up, ready to prevent your head and shoulders from hitting the ground if you fall. And remember, if you fall off, you do hit the ground. Always clear the landing zone of the problem stones or other detritus that could cause twisted or broken ankles – the most common injuries in bouldering. If there is any doubt about the seriousness of a bouldering "problem" – that it's too high – rig a top rope.

Top-Roping

TOP-ROPING
Remember to use
doubled biners
on the anchor!

Top-roping involves rigging an anchor above the desired climb. The rope runs up through the anchor and back down to the ground – one end for the climber, the other for the belayer. This way a climber can ascend with a belay from above, and a fall is no longer than the stretch in the rope, usually just inches. There are several considerations to bear in mind. The anchor must be bomber and directly above the climb. The anchor slings must extend from the anchor to just over the lip of the climb, allowing the rope to run freely through it. Even if you clip the rope off with locking carabiners, use at least two. Many times it is difficult to find an anchor at the base of boulders. If the angle of the rock is less than vertical, it is often unnecessary for the belayer to use one, though it is always desirable. The combination of stretch in the rope, friction on the top anchor, and the belayer's own bulk is often adequate if a ground anchor is unavailable. But if the angle is steep or there is a discrepancy in weights between belayer and climber, an anchor is useful, particularly for lowering climbers to the ground.

Climbing Walls

Artificial climbing walls – many of them indoors – have been springing up all over the country. Not only do they provide good exercise, they're good fun. Most are big enough that an enterprising climber can traverse up, around, and across one indefinitely, thus simulating the feel and

Jeff Smoot pumps up one of the oldest artificial climbing walls in the United States, the University of Washington Practice Rock.

Smoot collection photo

exertion of a long lead. The bigger gyms actually have lead climbing, usually on steep walls where the pump factor is high and the risk of hitting something is low. This is not cross-training, but climbing itself. Cast out of resin and sand, the holds simulate actual rock very well. In addition, the wide availability of modular holds encourages the indoor creation of home walls in basements and garages. Climbing walls are great places to hone footwork and general technique. And a little friendly competition can push a climber to exhaustion. A caution, however: since many indoor walls try to squeeze "bang for buck" by utilizing only small holds and building overhanging walls, the routes can be difficult, and it is essential injury prevention to warm up sufficiently before launching off onto the wall. If you're just getting started indoor climbing, or if you haven't done it lately, start off slow, and be sure to take rest days; finger tendons are quite delicate, and you're likely to end up on the sidelines with a strained tendon if you crank too hard too fast.

Specialized Apparatus

Hang boards, first introduced in late 1986, are wooden or molded-resin boards (usually about a foot high by 2½ feet long) that are mounted up high like a pull-up bar. The "board" features various holds resembling those on a climb, from good jugs to rounded nothings, and the usual routine involves pulling up on the holds, as well as free hanging for timed intervals. There are half a dozen commercially available, and each comes with a suggested workout. There

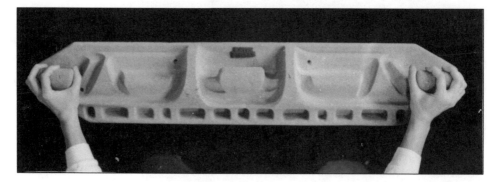

Typical hang board, this one by Entre Prises.

is no doubt that they can increase finger, hand, and forearm strength, and that the carryover value to climbing is high; but the verdict is not yet in on whether they cause more injuries than benefits. It is probably a matter of the routine. Increasing stress beyond normal climbing levels, especially free-hanging for long periods on the board's punier holds, virtually assures injuries. The primary danger is that the tendon connections at the shoulder – if you are hanging fully extended – have less strength than you can develop with your fingers. This means that as you hang to exhaustion on your fingertips, your body weight naturally sags to the tendon connectors at your shoulder; it is these connectors that risk separating. Adding weights will reduce the time spent on your fingers, and that will tend to keep you off your shoulders, or use elastics or some device to help prevent the transfer of load from muscle to unprotected joint connectors. Whatever routines you decide on, remember that if you push yourself to muscle failure, you need 48 hours to fully recover. So to optimize your results on any board, heavy workouts every third day are far superior to those every day, or every other day. And again, be sure to start off slow, and gradually increase the intensity of your workouts.

Cross-Training

The practice of training for a sport by doing exercises outside the sport itself is nothing new. Called crossover training, we see it in all professional athletics: skiers run stairs and lift weights; football players run, lift weights, and do stretching exercises to reduce the chance of injury; divers jump on a trampoline and lift weights; swimmers lift weights, jump rope, and ride a stationary bike, as do basketball players. All of these athletes count on their routines to give them a sharp conditioning edge that will cross over to their actual sport.

Weight Training

For years climbers scorned weight training, usually for the wrong reasons. Strength-to-weight ratio has long been deemed the aim of all climbing workouts, and most climbers are loath to add any size to their whippet-thin physiques – not knowing that a mere five pounds of brawn might increase their strength upwards of ten percent. (Also, many people think you can throw on five or ten pounds of muscle with a couple of workouts. A dedicated lifter is lucky to add one pound of muscle every two to three months.) Correct weight training is tough duty, certainly more toil than joy, which makes it all the more unpopular.

Other misconceptions have also kept many climbers off the iron. The first is the notion of excess bulk. As absurd as it is, people think that weights automatically make you huge. It's food, rather than iron, that increases body size. Controlling one's diet controls size, and you can't eat a dumbbell. Second is the notion of the musclebound oaf, who can't comb his hair for all the huge deltoids. If anything, correct weight training – which entails full range exercises and a lot of stretching between sets – increases flexibility. But you have to do things right.

This is not the venue to spell out specific workout routines. A comprehensive iron routine can be easily designed to focus on a climber's needs. There are hundreds of books and videos to show you what's what. The best routines take account of a person's physique and mentality and are so personal that little applies across the board. For the climber new to weights, it's best to start a normal, conservative routine and customize it as your knowledge increases. Perhaps the best thing about weight training is that it is very difficult to incur serious injuries. Soreness and tweaked muscles are part of any training, but in over fifteen years of being an "iron rat," I've never once gotten an injury lifting weights that has kept me out of the gym for more than a week.

Freehand Exercises

Essentially calisthenics, freehand exercises involve all the Jack LaLanne-type routines (save towing the boats): push-ups, pull-ups, sit-ups, dips. It's pretty hard to get a well-rounded workout doing just freehand exercises, but they require little in the way of specialized gear and are certainly better than doing nothing. Also, it is hard to injure yourself doing them.

Aerobics, jazz dancing, swimming, Nautilus machines, and untold other routines are also possible and popular. Anything that promotes overall fitness can only help your climbing.

Cardiovascular Exercises

A strong heart and good wind are vital for strenuous climbs. Any action sport, like basketball or racquetball, is good. Pure running or bicycling are also good. But the king of them all is the jump rope, which has steadily gained popularity in the climbing world, probably because it requires a lot of skill to be good. Single revolutions on a rope marks beginning level; double revolutionsbetween jumps, intermediate; triple revolutions, advanced. The person who can consistently do triple revolutions on a skip rope has the heart of a lion and lungs strong enough to fill the sails of a good-sized bark. Make sure to get a leather rope.

Stretching

With today's gymnastically difficult routes, flexibility is becoming increasingly important. Being flexible will help you with wide stems, high steps, and will help keep your hips closer to the rock on steep terrain, allowing you to get more weight onto your feet. Good flexibility will also help prevent injuries. Traditional stretching exercises are good, and a few sport-specific stretches have also been developed. Many rock gyms offer stretching classes to help improve your flexibility.

Injuries

As the technical envelope is pushed further, debilitating injuries are becoming more commonplace. Aside from the normal muscle tweaks and strains inherent in any physical endeavor, climbers are particularly prone to elbow and finger injuries, most of which involve some form of tendonitis. Having suffered these impairments on numerous occasions, I can assure you that ignoring the injury can result in pain so intense that straightening the arm or closing the fingers is virtually impossible, and climbing is out of the question. Concerning treatment for these conditions, I defer to climber/orthopedist Dr. Mark Robinson, who has conducted several studies involving climbing injuries, and is in the best position to give advice. Writes Dr. Robinson:

"Self-cure for tendonitis. 1) Decrease activity until pain is gone, and all swelling and tenderness disappear. 2) Wait two weeks more. 3) Start with easy strength exercises – putty, gum, rubber squeezers (2-3 weeks). 4) Low-angle big-hold climbing (1 month). 5) High-angle big-hold climbing (1 month). 6) Back to full bore.

"Anti-inflammatory medicines (aspirin, motrin, nuprin, etc.) can be used to control symptoms and speed the recovery process. They should not be used to suppress pain to allow even more overuse, since this will eventually lead to worse problems and a longer recovery period.

"Various mystical and pseudo-scientific remedies, such as copper bracelets, dietary modifications, herbal cataplasms, spinal manipulations, electrical machines with imposing control panels, horse liniments, ethnic balms, etc., are at best unproven. Very few, if any, of them bear any conceivable relation to what is known to be the basis of the problem."

What the doctor is telling us is that time and patience are the key ingredients to a full recovery, and that returning prematurely to high-stress climbing is as foolish as ignoring an injury in the first place. "The tissues of the musculoskeletal system are capable of remarkable feats of repair and restoration," Dr. Robinson assures us, "but these processes are slow." Furthermore, there is nothing in known medicine that can accelerate these processes, except the use of anti-inflammatory drugs, which simply eliminate the restrictions and allow the healing to proceed. All the fancy gadgets and therapy are virtually useless for tendon injuries, though any sports medicine clinic will gladly take all the spare coinage one has.

The tendency is to race back onto the cliffside and crank our brains off the second the pain is gone, but experts assure us this can only exacerbate the injury. Do as you want, but Dr. Robinson's advice is probably the sagest course to full recovery.

Injury Prevention

We know the medical experts have told us that certain exercises virtually assure injuries, and we should avoid these if we're in for the long haul. But aside from that, what can we do? Some support of critical tendons can be achieved by taping. Trouble spots: around the fingers on either side of the main (second) joint, around the wrist, and around the forearm just shy of the elbow. But professional athletes are more and more relying on two things to avoid injuries: stretching and warming up. Aerobics and yoga might not make you stronger, but they may keep you from getting injured. And a very important practice is to do a little stretching and some easy climbing before jumping onto a hard climb. Warming up is part of any sport, and is essential for climbers whose movements so stress the elbows and fingers. This is particularly true for bouldering. Get limbered up with a running sweat, then max yourself. And if you tweak something, stop before you make it worse.

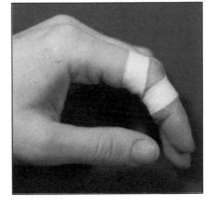

Supporting the finger tendons with tape.

Getting Started and Staying Alive

As little as fifteen years ago, finding professional instruction was a difficult task. Today, there is nearly always a guide service/climbing school operating around every popular crag, and good instruction is easy to find. For the complete neophyte, I highly advise taking at least a beginning seminar. It allows one to get a good grip on the fundamentals, and is the single most valuable investment a beginner can make. The appendix following this chapter lists sources of information on both instruction and equipment.

For an outlay of about $250, a beginner can buy a pair of rock shoes and two days of professional instruction. If you choose to carry on, you will need to purchase some climbing gear. Richard Leversee of Black Diamond Equipment has plotted the following course for the beginner looking to make climbing his or her sport.

After mastering basic techniques for safety and movement on rock, the novice should seek the company of more experienced partners to advance his skill. After buying a pair of rock shoes, his investment can be minimal, since the new climber can limit his purchases to personal rather than community necessities. The gear listed below will allow the beginner to climb with anyone with a rope and rack (and, of course, the knowledge to use them).

Sit harness or swami w/ leg loops	$65.00
Locking carabiner	$18.00
Belay/rappel device	$16.00
Four oval carabiners @ $6.00 each	$24.00
Gear sling	$12.00
Chalkbag, chalk	$18.00
Total	$153.00

Climbing with others is a crucial learning time, as a novice needs mileage before jumping out on the lead. The opportunity for adventure really opens up once a climber buys a rope and rack. There are many options available in selecting a rope, but the beginner can't go wrong buying either a 10.5-mm or 11-mm UIAA-approved fifty-meter kernmantle rope from any of the manufacturers listed in the appendix.

(page opposite)

Ron Kauk climbs "Dios Nidon (7c)," Siurana, Spain.

Beth Wald photo

A "foundation rack" should include a variety of passive (non-mechanical) nuts – tapers and hexentrics and the like – for their light weight, simplicity, security, and low price. At this stage it is important to become adept at placing passive nuts. Even spring-loaded camming devices require this knowledge for sound placements. The following foundation rack will allow the climber to set up top-ropes.

Rope	$150.00
Carabiners (8 @ $6 each)	$48.00
Locking carabiners (2 @ $18 each)	$36.00
Taper nuts (5 @ $7.50 each)	$37.50
Hexentrics (5 @ 7.50 each)	$ 37.50
Nut extraction tool with keeper sling	$10.00
Shoulder length sewn slings (6 @ $3.OO)	$18.00
Extra webbing (20' at $.30/foot)	$6.00
Local guidebook	$15.00
Total	$358.00

As the climber builds a solid base of experience, he will naturally want begin leading, so he must upgrade the foundation rack, allowing for more versatility and safety. SLCD's, three-cam units, sliding nuts, micro-nuts, and other sophisticated forms of protection will complete the rack for leading. A standard lead rack might consist of the following gear:

Rope	$150.00
Micro wedge nuts (5 @ $10 each)	$50.00
Wedge nuts (10 @ $7.50 each)	$75.00
Small passive camming devices (3 @ $15 each)	45.00
Spring-loaded camming devices from 0.5" to 3" (9 @ $60 each)	$540.00
Carabiners (36 @ $6.00 each)	$216.00
Locking carabiners (4 @ $18 each)	$ 72.00
Quickdraws (8 @ $3 each)`	$24.00
Shoulder-length slings (6 @ $3.50 each)	$21.00
Double-length sling	$5.00
Nut extraction tool with keeper sling	$10.00
Gear sling	$12.00
Total	$1220.00

Add and subtract gear as required for the chosen route, or add gear if you protect a lot. If you plan to climb only at bolt-protected sport climbing areas, you can pare this whole list down to just a rope, twelve quickdraws with carabiners, a couple of shoulder-length slings, and a couple of locking carabiners, for a total cost of less than $350.

For just over $1200 an advanced leader can have a world-class rack, which makes rock climbing the cheapest of all adventure sports. Moreover, after the initial investment, there are no additional expenses save gas to get to the cliff and minimal fees to climb inside state or national parks. Rock climbing is essentially free: no lift tickets, no referees, nothing but you, your friends, and the challenge at hand. By far the biggest cost of climbing is that once you get hooked you don't want to work anymore.

RESPONSIBILITIES

Throughout rock climbing's evolution, the simple joy of being the master of one's fate, of seeing success or failure as a result of one's efforts has – as in any great sport – remained the heart of the experience. Self-reliance and the ability to take responsibility for one's actions are among the virtues that climbing encourages.

But there are many more climbers out on the cliffs than ever before. The community of climbers – once a small, counterculture, "outcast" society – now impacts the outdoors in profoundly visible ways. Trails and trash are found at the base of "wilderness" cliffs. The responsibility for this lies with all of us, of course. Part of the allure of rock climbing is that it is more than just a physical exercise; we are intrinsically bound to features that nature has provided us. The environment is fragile, and the responsibility to maintain it is an integral part of our outdoor experience. The following suggestions address some of these issues.

Serve yourself and others by picking up trash when you find it, whether or not you brought it to the cliffs yourself. Relieve yourself away from the bottom of the route. Make a practice of carrying a small plastic bag into which to carry out all toilet paper and, mindful that uncovered feces decompose faster, keep such deposits well clear of established trails and paths. On longer routes, try to urinate away from where others must climb.

Stick to established trails whenever possible. We know ourselves competent at travelling over the roughest country in pursuit of the most direct line to our selected route; we should more often demonstrate our sensitivity to the effects of rampant erosion that are the result of zealous proliferation of access trails. Nesting birds should be respected and left as we find them. We are guests of the crags and its inhabitants.

Codes of proper cliffside etiquette are, of course, no different than those most people practice in the greater world. There are, however, situations that are unique. Usually, the first party to the base of a route gets the route first. You might offer the route to a clearly faster party, but once on a route, feel under no obligation to let a party pass if for any reason you are not comfortable with them above you. Again, if they are obviously a quicker team, it is probably a nice thing to offer, but if, for instance, loose rock is an issue, don't feel compelled to let anybody by; they made their choice at the beginning of the route.

As climbing moves into the 1990s and beyond, one of the biggest problems confronting all climbers is access to the cliffs. The loss of access to climbing or bouldering areas is an issue that affects every climber, regardless of technical ability or stylistic preference. The responsibility for solving or preventing access problems likewise rests with each and every climber. Minimizing environmental impact, being sensitive to behavior which could affect access, and taking responsibility for your own actions by not suing landowners, climbing gym owners, or belayers if you get hurt, will help prevent problems. When access problems do arise, the Access Fund can help negotiate, organize, and even litigate closures of climbing areas. In some situations they actually finance the purchase or preservation of climbing and bouldering areas. Your tax-deductible contribution to the Access Fund is a concrete way of giving something back to climbing and making a real difference in the effort to save the rich diversity of climbing resources in the United States. Send your donation (of any amount) to the Access Fund, P.O. Box 17010, Boulder, CO, 80308.

STAYING ALIVE

Rock climbing is potentially hazardous, and it is the responsibility of the individual to learn and understand the proper techniques to ensure the safest possible participation.

Though no substitute for professional instruction or experience that only years of climbing can provide, this manual has hopefully helped both the novice and the expert to a greater knowledge of rock climbing's fundamentals and nuances. In summary, I offer part of a longer essay on safety which appeared under the same name in the introduction of the 1987 Yosemite guidebook. Prepared by head rescue ranger John Dill, the essay contains wisdom distilled from nearly three decades of seeing every kind of accident in every kind of situation by every kind of climber – from rank beginner to world-class hero. To one and all, says John:

State of mind is the key to safety. It's impossible to know how many climbers were killed by haste or overconfidence. Many accident survivors will tell you that, somehow, they lost their better judgement just long enough to get hurt. It's a murky subject. Nevertheless, these mental lapses generally fall under three categories: ignorance, casualness, and distraction.

Ignorance

Even the most conscientious climber can get into trouble if he's unaware of the danger ("I thought it never rained..."). There is always something more to learn, regardless of experience. There are two basic steps to fighting ignorance.

• Continue to read, and listen to climbers who have survived. Back issues of climbing magazines are full of pertinent articles. Case histories in the American Alpine Club's *Accidents in North American Mountaineering,* a yearly compilation of accident reports, will show you how subtle factors may conspire to catch you unaware. Such accounts are the next best thing to being there.

• Practice. Reading may make you aware but not competent. Regardless of the written word, which is sometimes wrong, you must ultimately think and act for yourself. Several climbers have waited to learn how to prusik until it was dark, raining, overhanging, and they were actually in trouble. They had read about it, but they still had to be rescued despite having the gear to improvise their own escape. Book-learning alone gave them a complacency that could have proved fatal.

Casualness

"I just didn't take it seriously." It's a common lament. It's often correct, though it's more a symptom than a disease – there may be deeper reasons for underestimating your risk. Ignorance is one. Here are some more.

• Habit reinforcement occurs when nothing goes wrong. The more often you get away with risky business the more entrenched your lazier habits become. Have you unconsciously dropped items from your safety checklist since you were a beginner?

• Your attitudes and habits can be reinforced by the experiences (and states of mind) of others. The sense of awe and commitment of the 1960s is gone from the big-wall "trade routes," and young aspirants with no Grade VI's (or even V's) to their credit speak casually about them. Yet most of the accidents on El Capitan occur on "easy" pitches.

MEMORY DECAY "I'm not going up again without rain gear – I thought I would die!" A week later this climber has forgotten how scared he had been in that thunderstorm. Rain gear was now too heavy and besides, he'd rap off the next time. Many of us tend to forget the bad points. We have to be hit again.

CIVILIZATION With fixed anchors marking the way and ghetto blasters echoing behind, it may be hard to realize how high the potential danger actually is. Some say the idea of a fast rescue added to their casualness. Maybe, but who wants a broken leg, or worse, in the first place?

OVERCONFIDENCE "It'll never happen to me. I'm a safe, cautious climber." Many of those killed were described by friends as very cautious.

Distraction

It is caused by whatever takes your mind off your work: fear, thirst, sore feet, skinny-dippers below – the list is endless. Being in a hurry is one of the most common causes. Here are two ways it has happened.

• Experienced climbers have often been hurt after making "beginner errors" (their words) to get somewhere quickly. There was no emergency or panic, but their minds were elsewhere – on a cold beer, a good bivouac, or just sick of being on that route for a week (often called "summit fever"). Their mistakes were usually shortcuts in protecting easy pitches, on both walls and day climbs. As one put it, "We were climbing as though we were on top."

• Darkness has caught two day-climbers for the first time. Unprepared, upset, and off route, they rushed to get down, arguing with each other about what to do. After several errors, which they knew to avoid, one climber was killed rappelling off the end of his rope.

• Learn to recognize when you or your partner are becoming distracted. Stop, get your act together, then proceed.

Rescues

Despite the macabre sound of all ranger Dill's observations, the percentage of accident victims is minuscule compared to the hundreds of thousands of active rock climbers. But the dangers are real, and should you or a ropemate be so unfortunate as to suffer injury, Dill has put forth the following concerning rescues:

Despite the best of preparations, an accident can happen to anyone. Self-rescue is often the fastest and safest way out, but whether it's the wise course of action depends on the injury and how well prepared you are. Combining with a nearby party may often give you the margin of safety you need, but do not risk aggravating an injury or getting yourselves into a more serious predicament – ask for help if you need it. Sometimes a bit of advice, delivered through loudspeaker, is all that's required.

If you don't have formal first aid training (which is highly recommended), at least know how to keep an unconscious patient's airway open, how to protect a possible broken neck or back, and how to recognize and deal with a flail chest, external bleeding, and serious blood loss (shock). These procedures are life-saving, do not require fancy gear, and are easy to learn and perform.

• Head injury victims are apt to be irrational and very strong. Even if he's unconscious, if you have to leave him, make it impossible for him to untie himself.

THE OTHER SIDES OF THE GAME

Climbing is a broad game to which rock climbing is only a part – a fundamental, popular part, but by no means even half the game. Big walls will always provide the most awesome form of pure rock climbing,because the venues – towering monoliths like El Capitan and Mt. Watkins in Yosemite Valley – are peerless for grandeur and intimidation. Huge sixth class routes are steep, often unnerving trials that terrify and amaze twenty-year veterans. They are sometimes three-quarters of a mile high, and a hammock bivouac at that altitude is an ordeal no climber is fully prepared for – or ever gets completely accustomed to. It's always a game of "keeping the lid on" when most everything around you, as well as your own instincts, tells you that you're a raving loon. Sometimes you are. But the climber who paws over the lip of a big wall, still whole in body and soul, has memories that no other sport can hope to match.

Mountaineering, in its extreme form, is the riskiest of all the climbing games. Sudden storms, avalanches that sweep entire mountains, horrific rock falls, hidden crevasses, and physiological disorders from altitude and cold are all out of a climber's hands and have drawn the curtain on hundreds of veterans. The old method of sieging the mountain, using armies of climbers, oxygen, and countless other helpful strategies, has slowly given way to "alpine" ascents, where a handful of climbers go for broke with little or no backup, are irreversibly committed, and survive only through personal prowess, iron will, and the grace of God. Successful parties invariably return with tales fantastic and astounding; and the ill-fated, by no count the minority, have stories none the less remarkable, though often with a tragic twist.

There are a hundred different games that fall somewhere in the middle, somewhere between the ace poised on a boulder in the British Virgin Islands and the ironman who has just soloed Mt. Everest. Some make a specialty of ice climbing, clawing up overhanging icicles, or up gleaming arctic gullies. There are peakbaggers who rarely use a rope, solo climbers who rarely use a rope, sea cliff climbers, limestone climbers, desert climbers, gym climbers, snow climbers, ski mountaineers, and people who own thousands of dollars of gear and only talk a good game. Chances are that the modern climber, whatever his specialty, has mastered the fundamentals while rock climbing. It remains the basic form in acquiring the knowledge of rope management, physical movement, and the mental conditioning requisite and applicable to any mode of ascent. The competent rock climber can readily cross over into big walls or big mountains and is qualified to make the transition quickly and safely. Happy climbing.

Appendix: Sources

One of the happier consequences of a wider participation in rock climbing is easy access to good information. What follows is a listing of many of these sources.

Magazines, Books, and Video

Climbing magazines are colorful and well-produced and, besides offering accounts of climbs and cliffs, are regularly a wealth of information on the latest gear and how it's used. Current guidebooks to just about every crag in America are published every few years and can be found in most local specialty mountain equipment shops. Climbing and mountaineering has perhaps the most active literary heritage of all sports, and many books and videos, from expedition accounts to full-color documentary pictorials, are constantly being published.

Climbing Magazine
Post Office Box 339
Carbondale, CO 81623
(303) 963-9449

Rock & Ice Magazine
Post Office Box 3595
Boulder, CO 80303
(303) 499-8410

Sport Climbing Magazine
Post Office Box 82158
Las Vegas, NV 89180-2158
(702) 256-7985

Chockstone Press, Inc.
Post Office Box 3505
Evergreen CO 80439

The Mountaineers Books
1011 S.W. Klickitat Way
Seattle, WA 98134

The American Alpine Club
710 Tenth Street
Golden, CO 80401
(303) 384-0110

Chessler Books
Post Office Box 399
Kittredge, CO 80457
(303) 670-0093
(800) 654-8502

Guides and Instruction

There are many schools competent in the instruction and guiding of modern rock climbing. Most are members of the American Mountain Guides Association (reached at Post Office Box 2128, Estes Park, CO 80517; (303) 586-0571). In addition, many of the specialty outdoor shops have seasonal classes in rock climbing.

Equipment

Current issues of climbing magazines are a good source of manufacturers and distributors of climbing gear. The magazines will also give an indication of the diversity of equipment available; if your local outdoor shop only handles a few carabiners, nuts, and ropes, chances are good they are not knowledgeable about what is happening in the sport.

Glossary

The following is a compilation of some of the technical terms and jargon used throughout this book. This is a strictly American glossary; Brits, the French, or Japanese undoubtedly use somewhat different terminology.

aid: using means other than the action of hands, feet, and body English to get up a climb

anchor: a means by which climbers are secured to a cliff

arête: an outside corner of rock

armbar, armlock: a means of holding onto a wide crack

bashie: a piece of malleable metal that's been hammered into a rock seam as an anchor; used in extreme aid climbing

belay: procedure of securing a climber by the use of a rope

bight: a loop (as in a bight of rope)

biners: see carabiners

bolt: an artificial anchor placed in a hole drilled for that purpose

bomber or **bomb-proof:** absolutely fail-safe (as in a very solid anchor or combination of anchors)

bucket: a handhold large enough to fully latch onto, like the lip of a bucket

cam: to lodge in a crack by counterpressure; that which lodges

carabiners: aluminum alloy rings equipped with a spring-loaded snap gate; sometimes called biners or krabs

ceiling: an overhang of sufficient size to loom overhead

chock: a wedge or mechanical device that provides an anchor in a rock crack

chockstone: a rock lodged in a crack

clean: a description of routes that may be variously free of vegetation, loose rock, or the need to place pitons; also the act of removing nuts from a pitch

cold shut: a relatively soft metal ring that can be closed with a hammer blow; notoriously unreliable for withstanding high loads

crimper: a small but positive edge

crux: the most difficult section of a climb or pitch

dihedral: an inside corner of rock

drag: usually used in reference to the resistance of rope through carabiners

dynamic, dynamo, or **'mo:** lunge move

edge: a small rock ledge, or the the act of standing on an edge

exposure: that relative situation where a climb has particularly noticeable sheerness

free, free climb, or **free ascent:** to climb using hands and feet only; the rope is only used to safeguard against injury, not for upward progress or resting

gobis: hand abrasions

hangdog: when a leader hangs from a piece of protection to rest, then continues on without lowering back to the ground; not a free ascent

jam: wedging feet, hands, fingers or other body parts to gain purchase in a crack

jugs: like a jug handle

lead: to be first on a climb, placing protection with which to protect oneself

lieback: the climbing maneuver that entails pulling with the hands while pushing with the feet

line: the path of weakness in the rock which is the route

mantle: the climbing maneuver used to gain a single feature above one's head

move: movement; one of a series of motions necessary to gain climbing distance

nut: same as a chock: a mechanical device that, by various means, provides a secure anchor to the rock

on-sight: to climb a route without prior knowledge or experience of the moves, and without falling or otherwise weighting the rope (also **on-sight flash**)

opposition: nuts, anchors, or climbing maneuvers that are held in place by the simultaneous stress of two forces working against each other

pinkpoint: to lead (without falling) a climb that has been pre-protected with anchors rigged with carabiners

pins: pitons

pitch: the section of rock between belays

pitons: metal spikes of various shapes, hammered into the rock to provide anchors in cracks (also **pins** or **pegs)**

placement: the quality of a nut or anchor

protection, or **pro:** the anchors used to safeguard the leader

prusik: both the knot and any means by which one mechanically ascends a rope

quickdraws: short slings with carabiners that help provide drag-free rope management for the leader

rappel: to descend a rope by means of mechanical brake devices

redpoint: to lead a route, clipping protection as you go, without falling or resting on pro.

runout: the distance between two points of protection; often referring to a long stretch of climbing without protection

second: the second person on a rope team, usually also the leader's belayer

sling or **runner:** a webbing loop used for a variety of purposes to anchor to the rock

smear: to stand on the front of the foot and gain friction against the rock across the breadth of the sole to adhere to the rock

stance: a standing rest spot, often the site of the belay

stem: to bridge between two widely-spaced holds

thin: a climb or hold of relatively featureless character

top-rope: a belay from above; protects the climber from falling even a short distance

traverse: to move sideways, without altitude gain

wall or **big wall:** a long climb traditionally done over multiple days, but may take just a few hours for ace climbers